Applehood & Motherpie

handpicked recipes from Upstate New York

JLR Publications
The Junior League of Rochester, Inc.
Rochester, New York

The Junior League of Rochester, Inc is an organization of women committed to promoting voluntarism, developing the potential of women and to improving communities through the effective action and leadership of trained volunteers Its purpose is exclusively educational and charitable. Proceeds from the sale of *Applehood & Motherpie* directly support the purpose and community projects of the Junior League of Rochester, Inc

For additional copies, use the coupons at the back of the book or write:

JLR Publications
The Junior League of Rochester, Inc
110 Linden Oaks   Suite A
Rochester, New York 14625-2888
585-385-8590 (Phone)
585-385-1873 (Fax)
jlroch@frontiernet.net (E-mail)

Suggested retail price $18 95 plus shipping charges of $3 50

As we celebrate this our fourteenth printing we would like to salute the chairpersons whose foresight has gotten us here.

1979–1981	Priscilla Minster, Lucia Shaw
1981–1982	Alice Smith
1982–1983	Nancy Brown
1983–1984	Nancy Frank
1984–1985	Louise Criticos
1985–1986	Susan Bickel
1986–1987	Pat Morris
1987–1988	Jean Morely
1988–1989	Georgie Bramley
1989–1990	Lynne Phelps
1990–1991	Judy Randall
1991–1992	Colleen Altavela
1992–1993	Susan Henderson
1993–1994	Janice Reilly
1994–1995	Patrice Pallone
1995–1996	Lindy Svatek
1996–1997	Christine Petrone
1997–1998	Suzanne Laese
1998–1999	Cindy Harper
1999–2000	Amy Dharawat
2000–2001	Barb Eltinge
2001–2002	Kim Chance

With their dedication and the support of the League we have returned over $1,000,000 to the Rochester community through our projects.

introduction

The Genesee Valley yields a rich harvest of produce. Perhaps most well known is the upstate apple in its many varieties. In this book, in addition to all types of cookery, you will find many recipes which feature the apple to its fullest potential. Every recipe in this book has been tested and retested and all achieved very high ratings. They were all evaluated for efficiency of preparation as well as excellence of taste. The absolutely highest of the high show our green apple. These pleased all of the tasters all of the time and every cook knows how difficult that can be. Budding chefs need not fear, however, as all our recipes are delicious.

Our Upstate New York area is a fruit belt abounding also in cherries, peaches, and grapes. Climatic conditions here provide the ideal growing environment for many vegetables as well and we lead the nation in producing cabbage for sauerkraut. The wine industry centered around our Finger Lakes is the U.S.A.'s second largest wine producer. Locally, our population is a mélange of urban, suburban, and rural folk many of whom work for major U.S. corporations based in the Rochester area. Consequently, we are a melting pot for people who have been transferred from other parts of the country. They bring their cooking expertise to us, blend it with our local heritage and achieve some of the delectables in this book.

So, with our thanks and encouragement we ask you to turn the page, pick a recipe, and cook as we do in apple country: wholesomely and from the heart!

Original Cookbook Committee

Co-Chairmen
Priscilla Leadley Minster
Lucia Hellebush Shaw

Sustaining Advisor
Malinda Berry Fischer

Secretary
Jeanne Puder Massey

Treasurer
Elizabeth Gregory Garrett

Recipe Chairman
Alice Kapusta Smith

Editor
Tracy Kole Kessler

Marketing Co-Chairmen
Linda Williams Obourn
MaryBeth Tully Pratt

Distribution Chairman
Emily Danford Henderson

*Our sincere thanks to all the
tireless testers, tasters, and
committee members whose
efforts made this book a reality.
They are truly the apples of our
eyes.*

*One of the most important acts of our lives is eating, so it
follows that preparing food is equally vital. There are
times when this job is denounced as boring, mundane, and
repetitious. Creativity in the kitchen not only nourishes our
bodies, it nurtures our psyches too. So be proud of the job
entrusted to you, shake hands with nature's bounty, and start
cooking with style!*

appetizers & beverages

appetizers & beverages

artichokes with shrimp dip

Yield: 4 servings

An outstanding combination.

4 whole artichokes
2 tablespoons cooking oil
1 tablespoon lemon juice
1 teaspoon salt
dash pepper
1 bay leaf
1 teaspoon tarragon
½ teaspoon rosemary

1. Wash and trim artichoke leaves with scissors.
2. Cook artichokes, in boiling water to cover, with oil, lemon juice, and seasonings. Cook for 45 minutes to 1 hour or until leaves pull away easily.
3. Drain and serve immediately on individual plates with dipping sauce.

Shrimp Sauce:
⅓ cup mayonnaise
1 tablespoon Dijon mustard
½ teaspoon Worcestershire sauce
1 tablespoon minced green onion
1 4½-ounce can shrimp, drained and chopped

Shrimp Sauce:
1. Mix all ingredients together and serve as dip for artichokes.

Hint: Remove choke from cooked artichoke and fill center with sauce.

Susan S. Taylor

sandy's beef dip

Yield: 1½ cups

A tangy collage of flavors.

2 teaspoons dried minced onions
2 tablespoons dry sherry
2 tablespoons mayonnaise
1 8-ounce package cream cheese, softened
1 3-ounce package corned beef, chopped
¼ cup pimento-filled green olives, chopped
sesame seed crackers

1. Soften onions in the sherry.
2. Add mayonnaise to cream cheese and blend well.
3. Add all remaining ingredients, except crackers, and mix.
4. Refrigerate overnight to allow flavors to blend.
5. Serve with sesame seed crackers.

Must be done one day ahead.

Pamela E. Ferguson

spicy mexican dip

Yield: 8 servings

Olé!

1 pound ground beef
½ cup chopped onion
½ cup catsup
3 teaspoons chili powder
1 16-ounce can kidney
  beans

Topping
1½ cups chopped green
  olives
1 cup shredded Cheddar
  cheese
½ cup chopped onion
corn chips, to dip

1. Brown meat and onions in a
   skillet. Drain fat. Set aside.
2. Whirl catsup, chili powder, and
   kidney beans in a food
   processor or blender until
   smooth.
3. Add bean mixture to browned
   meat and onions. Simmer for 10
   minutes.
4. Put warm mixture in a bowl. Top
   with concentric circles of olives,
   cheese, and onions. Serve with
   corn chips.

Hint: Dip may be frozen or refrigerated before adding topping.
To serve, warm to room temperature, heat at 350° for 25
minutes, and add topping.

Cathie S. Meisenzahl

 hot pecan dip

Yield: 9-inch quiche dish

Lovely to look at, delicious to eat.

Pecans
½ cup chopped pecans
2 tablespoons butter,
  melted
½ teaspoon salt

Pecans
1. Mix pecans with butter and salt.
2. Bake at 350° for 15 minutes.
   Set aside.

Dip
1 8-ounce package cream
  cheese, softened
2 tablespoons milk
2½ ounces dried beef, cut
  up
¼ cup chopped green
  pepper
1 small onion, grated
¼ teaspoon pepper
½ teaspoon garlic powder
½ cup sour cream

Dip
1. Thoroughly mix all ingredients,
   except sour cream.
2. Fold in sour cream and pour
   into a baking dish.
3. Sprinkle with nut mixture and
   bake.
4. Serve hot with crackers or
   party pumpernickel bread.

Temperature: 350°
Time: 20 minutes

Lynne G. Bishop

6

hot sherry crab dip

Yield: 15 to 20 servings

A cocktail party pleaser.

3 8-ounce packages
    cream cheese
½ cup mayonnaise
2 scant teaspoons
    prepared mustard
dash of garlic salt
2 teaspoons
    confectioners sugar
1 teaspoon onion juice
½ to 1 teaspoon seasoned
    salt
⅓ to ⅔ cup sauterne wine
    or sherry
1 pound lump fresh
    crabmeat or 3 cans
    good quality crabmeat
    or 3 6-ounce packages
    frozen crabmeat

1. In top of double boiler, melt cream cheese until softened.
2. Add remaining ingredients except crab. Stir until smooth.
3. Fold in crab. Heat thoroughly.
4. Serve very hot in a chafing dish or on a hot tray with warmed crackers or melba toast.
5. If made ahead, reheat in 350° oven until hot.

Lindsay R. Garrett

canoe crab dip

Yield: 4 cups

Eye catching, easy, and so good.

2 loaves unsliced Italian
    bread
1 cup mayonnaise
1 cup grated Cheddar
    cheese
1 cup crabmeat or shrimp
1 cup chopped onions

1. Hollow out one loaf of bread. Break or cut the part you have removed and the entire second loaf into bite-size pieces.
2. Combine mayonnaise, cheese, crab, and onion in baking dish. May be done ahead to this point and refrigerated.
3. Bake until hot and pour into hollowed-out bread. Serve surrounded with bread pieces for dipping.

Temperature: 350°
Time: 20 to 30 minutes

Hint: If using canned shrimp, improve its flavor by soaking the can in ice water for 1 hour before opening.

Nancy C. Alderman

pepperoni dip

Yield: 3 cups

Men especially like this.

1 pint sour cream
½ pound pepperoni, finely
    chopped
1 round loaf of bread

1. Mix sour cream and pepperoni
   well. Store, covered, in
   refrigerator for two days before
   serving. This allows the sour
   cream to absorb the pepperoni
   flavor and the pepperoni to
   soften.
2. Serve in a hollowed-out loaf of
   bread with bread pieces for
   dunking, or with plain crackers.

Must do two days ahead.

Peggi M. Godwin

dill dip

Yield: 2 cups

It's a dilly!

⅔ cup sour cream
⅔ cup mayonnaise
3 ounces cream cheese,
    softened
1 tablespoon dill weed
1 tablespoon onion flakes
1 tablespoon parsley
1½ teaspoons Beau
    Monde seasoning
3 drops Tabasco
1 tablespoon
    Worcestershire
salt and pepper to taste

Must do ahead.

1. Mix all ingredients together
   thoroughly.
2. Refrigerate overnight.
3. Serve with raw vegetables or
   crackers.

Suzy M. Hengerer

chunky guacamole

Yield: 1½ to 2 cups

Great texture and very pretty with the pieces of red and green.

½ cup mayonnaise
½ cup sour cream
2 tablespoons lemon juice
1 large tomato, peeled,
   seeded, and chopped
½ cup minced onion
2 medium or 1 large
   avocado, peeled and
   chopped
salt, pepper, and garlic
   salt to taste

1. Mix all ingredients. Refrigerate.
2. Serve with plain tortilla chips.

Hint: Can be made ahead to allow flavors to blend. Keep avocado pit in dip to prevent browning until ready to serve. Leftover dip makes a good salad topping.

Margaret B. Hoffower

cucumber dip

Yield: 4 cups

A snap to prepare in your food processor!

2 large cucumbers
½ cup vinegar
2 teaspoons salt
2 8-ounce packages
   cream cheese
¾ cup mayonnaise
½ clove garlic, minced (or
   ½ teaspoon garlic salt)

1. Peel and grate cucumber.
2. Mix cucumber with vinegar and salt and refrigerate overnight.
3. When ready to serve, thoroughly blend cream cheese, mayonnaise, and garlic.
4. Press all liquid from the marinated cucumber. Discard the liquid and stir the cucumber into the cream cheese mixture.
5. Serve with fresh vegetables or a thin corn chip.

Must do one day ahead.

Jeanne P. Massey

hummus

Yield: 2 cups

Serve with small wedges of pita bread.

1 one-pound can chick peas, drained and rinsed
½ cup olive oil
6 tablespoons sesame seed paste (tahini)
5 tablespoons lemon juice, strained
1 medium clove garlic, mashed
½ teaspoon salt
3 tablespoons olive oil
3 tablespoons sesame seeds, lightly toasted
2 tablespoons minced fresh parsley

1. Combine first 6 ingredients in a food processor or blender.
2. Blend until smooth.
3. Transfer to a shallow serving dish.
4. Drizzle with olive oil.
5. Sprinkle with sesame seeds and parsley.

Nancy Robbins

loie's ginger dip

Yield: 2 to 3 cups

Oriental magic!

¼ cup grated onion
1 8-ounce can water chestnuts, drained and very finely chopped
2 to 2½ tablespoons crystallized ginger, very finely chopped
1 cup mayonnaise
1 cup sour cream
¼ cup chopped fresh parsley
1 tablespoon soy sauce
dash Tabasco

1. Mix all ingredients together thoroughly.
2. Refrigerate 1 or 2 days to allow all flavors to blend fully.
3. Serve with raw vegetables, crackers, or chips. Corn chips are especially good with this.

Must do one to two days ahead.

Hint: Use leftover dip as salad dressing.

Patsy M. Gilges

russian vegetable dip

Yield: 1½ cups

A distinctive, rich taste.

1 cup mayonnaise
2 tablespoons chili sauce
2 tablespoons chopped
  chives
2 tablespoons grated
  onion
2 teaspoons tarragon
  vinegar
⅛ teaspoon thyme
¼ teaspoon curry powder
¼ teaspoon salt
pepper to taste

1. Combine all ingredients until
   well blended.
2. Refrigerate until serving time.
3. Serve with raw vegetables.
   Shrimp is wonderful, too!

Suzanne H. Madison

dragon dip

Yield: 3 cups

Tart apple wedges make good dippers.

1 8-ounce package cream
  cheese
2 cups shredded Cheddar
  cheese
6 tablespoons half and
  half
1 teaspoon
  Worcestershire sauce
¼ teaspoon dry mustard
¼ teaspoon onion salt
3 drops Tabasco sauce
6 slices bacon, cooked
  and crumbled

1. Mix ingredients, except bacon,
   in top of double boiler. Cook,
   stirring continually, until
   smooth and blended. Add
   bacon.
2. Keep hot in chafing dish. Serve
   with bland crackers, apple
   wedges, or fresh vegetables.

Hint: We suggest using the leftovers for Welsh Rarebit.

Judy G. Curry

chicken liver paté

Yield: 2 to 3 cups

Suited to a man's taste.

½ cup walnuts, finely
   chopped
½ pound chicken livers
¼ cup minced onion
3 tablespoons butter
½ teaspoon curry powder
¼ teaspoon paprika
½ teaspoon salt
¼ cup dry vermouth
8 ounces cream cheese,
   softened
rye bread or crackers

1. Toast walnuts lightly in pan for
   3 to 5 minutes. Set aside.
2. Sauté livers and onions in
   butter.
3. Add curry, paprika, and salt.
   Cool slightly.
4. Using food processor or blender,
   blend liver mixture until
   smooth.
5. Add dry vermouth and cream
   cheese. Blend well.
6. Stir in walnuts and place in
   serving container.
7. Chill at least 5 to 6 hours. Serve
   with rye bread or favorite
   crackers. Can be kept in freezer
   for weeks.

Must do ahead.

Violet E. Kapusta

pineapple curry

Yield: 6 to 8 servings

Very attractive for summer entertaining.

8 ounces cream cheese,
   softened
¼ cup chutney
¼ teaspoon dry mustard
1 teaspoon curry powder
1 fresh pineapple
almonds, toasted
crackers

1. Mix cream cheese, chutney, dry
   mustard, and curry thoroughly.
2. Chill for 4 hours.
3. Halve pineapple. Do not cut off
   leaves. Hollow out and save
   pineapple chunks for a salad or
   a dessert.
4. When ready to serve, fill
   pineapple with cream cheese
   mixture and top with almonds.
   Serve with plain crackers.

Must do ahead.

Hint: Use pineapple chunks for our dessert "Pineapple
Saucery"—see index.

Lindsay R. Garrett

smoked salmon spread

Yield: 30 to 40 canapés

Great for summer—cool and crisp.

1 8-ounce package cream cheese, softened
3 ounces smoked salmon, finely chopped
2 teaspoons prepared horseradish
1 teaspoon dill weed
2 pounds zucchini, unpeeled, 2-inches in diameter
parsley for garnish

1. Combine cream cheese with salmon.
2. Add horseradish and dill weed. Set aside.
3. Score sides of zucchini with a fork (optional).
4. Cut zucchini into ¼-inch thick slices. Cook slices in boiling salted water for 5 to 7 minutes. They should remain crisp.
5. Rinse slices with cold water and dry well.
6. Spread mixture on zucchini slices. Decorate with small parsley sprigs. Serve or refrigerate. Take out of the refrigerator before serving to let cream cheese spread soften.

Hint: May use as a dip by adding ¼ cup milk or more.

Betty S. Middleton

marinated spareribs aloha

Yield: 12 to 16 servings

For a memorable luau, start with this.

Ribs
5 pounds spareribs

Ribs
1. Have butcher prepare ribs or cut ribs crosswise into thirds with meat cleaver. Then cut lengthwise to separate each one.

Marinade
¾ cup sugar
½ cup catsup
½ cup soy sauce
1 tablespoon salt
2 ounces sherry
¼ teaspoon ginger

Must do ahead.

Marinade
1. Mix all ingredients together.
2. Marinate ribs for 3 to 4 hours or overnight.
3. Bake in oven or grill over charcoal.

Temperature: 250° to 300°
Time: 1½ hours

Dorothy G. Centner

13

blue cheese paté

Yield: 2⅔ cups

People who dislike liver paté will enjoy this one.

1 8-ounce package cream cheese, softened
4¾ ounces or ⅔ cup liverwurst
2 ounces or ½ cup blue cheese
2 tablespoons dry sherry
4 ounces water chestnuts, chopped
2 slices bacon, cooked and crumbled
2 tablespoons minced onion
2 tablespoons chopped pimento-stuffed olives
leaf lettuce
1 hard-boiled egg
crackers

Must do ahead.

1. Mix cream cheese, liverwurst, blue cheese, and sherry together in blender or food processor.
2. Add the next 4 ingredients and mix well.
3. Lightly oil a 3-cup mold.
4. Place mixture in mold, cover, and chill overnight.
5. Unmold on bed of lettuce. Garnish with sieved egg.
6. Serve with crackers or vegetable slices.

Alice K. Smith

creamy cheese and bacon spread

Brighten a brunch!

½ pound sliced bacon, cooked and crumbled
8 ounces cream cheese, softened
¼ cup orange marmalade
celery
apple slices
crackers

1. Combine bacon, cream cheese, and marmalade.
2. Refrigerate mixture. Allow spread to reach room temperature at serving time.
3. Serve with celery sticks, apple slices, and crackers.

Judy G. Curry

chili caseoso

Yield: 24 to 30 pieces

Good as a main dish, too.

3 4½-ounce cans mild green chilies, seeded and chopped
1 pound Monterey Jack cheese, shredded
1 pound Cheddar cheese, shredded
4 eggs
1 5⅜-ounce can evaporated milk

Must do ahead.

1. In a greased 9 x 13-inch pan, place a layer of chilies, a layer of cheeses, repeating another layer of each.
2. Beat 4 eggs and add evaporated milk. Pour over top of cheese layers.
3. Bake. Chill. Cut into squares.
4. Warm to serve.

Temperature: 350°
Time: 1 hour

Peggi M. Godwin

cherry tomato canapé

Yield: 25 canapés

Your guests will rave!

1 cup grated Swiss cheese
⅔ cup mayonnaise
½ cup minced green onion
6 tablespoons minced green pepper
¼ teaspoon garlic salt
¼ teaspoon seasoned salt
⅛ teaspoon cayenne pepper
½ pound bacon, cooked and crumbled
1 pint cherry tomatoes, washed and sliced
1 loaf party rye or pumpernickel

1. Combine first seven ingredients. Set aside.
2. Toast bread on one side. Spread other side with additional mayonnaise.
3. Top with tomato slice and cheese mixture. Sprinkle on bacon. Bake until bubbly and brown.

Temperature: 350°
Time: 5 minutes

Lynn P. Natapow

kraut appeteaser

Yield: 4½ dozen

Very unusual—we love it!

1 medium onion, finely chopped
3 tablespoons butter or margarine, melted
1 cup finely chopped cooked ham
1 cup finely chopped corned beef
½ medium clove fresh garlic, crushed
6 tablespoons flour
1 egg, beaten
¼ teaspoon seasoned salt
¼ teaspoon Worcestershire sauce
1 tablespoon chopped parsley
2 cups well-drained sauerkraut, finely chopped
½ cup beef stock or boullion
2 cups milk
2½ cups sifted flour
2 cups fine, dry bread crumbs
oil for frying

Must do ahead.

1. Sauté onion in butter and cook over low heat for 5 minutes.
2. Stir in ham, corned beef, and garlic. Mix well. Cook 10 minutes, stirring occasionally.
3. Blend in 6 tablespoons flour and the egg.
4. Stir in seasonings, kraut, and stock. Cook over low heat, stirring occasionally, until thickened. Chill.
5. Shape into walnut-size balls.
6. Thoroughly combine milk and flour. Coat balls with this batter. Roll them in bread crumbs.
7. Fry in deep hot oil (375°) for 2 to 3 minutes, or until lightly browned. Drain on absorbent paper. Kraut balls may be refrigerated at this point and reheated in oven before serving.
8. Serve warm, using cocktail picks.

Temperature: 375°
Time: 2 to 3 minutes

Hint: To freeze, prepare Appeteasers for frying. Place in freezer container, dividing layers with foil or freezer wrap. Freeze, making sure container is well sealed. Remove from freezer and partly thaw at room temperature for one hour before serving time. Increase frying time by one minute.

Sue H. Madison

crispy chicken livers and mustard dip

Not everyone likes chicken livers, but if you do, you'll love these. The sauce is great!

8 tablespoons butter
1½ pounds chicken livers
1½ cups bacon-flavored cracker crumbs

1. Melt butter in 9 x 9-inch pan.
2. Cut chicken livers in half; roll in crumbs. Place in pan in a single layer. Sprinkle with remaining crumbs.
3. Bake. May be done a few hours ahead and reheated.

Mustard Sauce:
2-ounce can dry mustard
1 cup vinegar
2 eggs, beaten
1 cup sugar

Mustard Sauce:
1. Mix mustard and vinegar. Let stand six hours.
2. Cook mustard mixture, eggs, and sugar in double boiler until thick.
3. Serve hot, surrounded by chicken livers.

Must do part ahead.

Temperature: 350°
Time: 45 minutes

Sue B. Moscato

apple sausage jumble   Yield: 8 to 10 servings

A piquant palate pleaser.

2 pounds Kielbasa (sausage)
¾ cup brown sugar
1 35-ounce jar *chunky* applesauce
¼ cup finely chopped onion (or 1 tablespoon dried onion flakes)

1. Cut sausage into ½-inch pieces.
2. Combine sugar, applesauce, and onion in an oven-proof casserole.
3. Mix in sausage pieces; bake.
4. Transfer to a chafing dish or fondue pot at serving time.

Temperature: 325°
Time: 1½ to 2 hours

Hint: Brown sugar should always be packed down when being measured.

Ginny Y. Gray

clams la fitte

Yield: 6 servings

Easy, but with gourmet appeal.

¼ cup chopped onion
½ cup chopped celery
1 clove garlic, minced
¼ cup butter
1 tablespoon flour
½ teaspoon salt
¼ teaspoon pepper
¼ teaspoon thyme
1 tablespoon chili sauce
few drops of Tabasco
3 6½-ounce cans minced
　clams
1 beaten egg
½ cup cornflake crumbs
2 tablespoons chopped
　parsley
2 tablespoons melted
　butter
½ cup salted cracker
　crumbs
lemon wedges

1. Sauté onion, celery, and garlic in butter.
2. Blend in flour.
3. Add salt, pepper, thyme, chili sauce, Tabasco, clams, plus juice from 2 cans. Blend well.
4. Stir in beaten egg, cornflake crumbs, and parsley.
5. Spoon mixture into 6 large clam shells for first course, or smaller shells for hot hors d'oeuvres. Can freeze at this point.
6. Before serving, melt 2 tablespoons butter. Toss in cracker crumbs and put on top of clam mixture.
7. Bake. Serve with hot lemon wedges.

Temperature: 400°
Time: 25 to 30 minutes (large
　　　shells)
　　　15 to 20 minutes (small
　　　shells)

Cynthia E. Hay

mushrooms in dilled sour cream

Yield: 4 to 6 servings

A rich and interesting combination of flavors.

2 pounds mushrooms
　(caps only)
3 tablespoons butter
½ cup dry sherry
½ cup minced onion
salt and pepper to taste
1 pint sour cream
2 teaspoons dill weed (or
　more, to taste)

1. Sauté mushroom caps in butter with sherry, onion, salt, and pepper for about 10 minutes.
2. Drain off all but ½ cup of liquid. (Can be done ahead to this point and refrigerated.)
3. Heat mushrooms, the ½ cup of liquid, sour cream, and dill. Do not allow to boil.
4. Pour into warmed chafing dish and serve with toothpicks.

Jane F. Bailey

susan's mushroom croustades

Yield: 4 to 4½ dozen

You can never make enough of these bite-size appetizers!

Filling

3 tablespoons minced green onions
4 tablespoons melted butter
½ pound minced mushrooms
2 tablespoons flour
1 cup heavy cream
½ teaspoon salt
⅛ teaspoon cayenne pepper
2 teaspoons parsley
2 tablespoons chives
2 tablespoons water
2 tablespoons lemon juice

Filling

1. Sauté green onions in butter.
2. Add minced mushrooms and cook for 10 to 15 minutes, or until moisture is gone.
3. Remove from heat and add flour, stirring until well blended.
4. Add heavy cream, bring to boil, and simmer for 2 minutes.
5. Remove from heat. Add salt, cayenne pepper, parsley, chives soaked in 2 tablespoons water, and lemon juice. Mix well and cool.
6. Using a long-handled baby spoon or other small spoon, fill the baked croustade cups. (Can be frozen at this stage.)
7. Bake and serve.

Temperature: 350°
Time: 10 minutes (12 to 15 if frozen)

Croustades

1 loaf firm, square bread, sliced
¼ cup butter, melted

Croustades

1. Trim crusts from bread slices.
2. With rolling pin, flatten each bread slice and cut into 4 squares.
3. Using small size muffin tin, place ½ teaspoon melted butter into each muffin cup.
4. Gently push each bread square into muffin cups.
5. Bake croustades until browned.
6. Fill with mushroom filling.

Must do ahead.

Temperature: 350°
Time: 8 to 10 minutes

Judy U. Murray

chinese shrimp balls

Yield: About 60

Alias 'Magic Shrimp Balls' because of their fast disappearing act.

2 pounds raw shrimp, cleaned and deveined
2 5-ounce cans water chestnuts
1 teaspoon sherry
1 tablespoon cornstarch
2 teaspoons salt
½ teaspoon sesame oil*
1 egg white, beaten
2 cups peanut oil or cooking oil
½ cup light soy sauce
2 tablespoons rice vinegar (white Chinese vinegar)

1. Chop shrimp and water chestnuts very fine.
2. Add sherry, cornstarch, salt, and sesame oil to shrimp and water chestnuts and mix well.
3. Form mixture into 1-inch balls and dip into egg white.
4. Heat oil in deep fryer or wok to about 375°.
5. Drop balls, a few at a time, into hot oil and fry until golden. Balls will float when done.
6. Balls may be frozen after frying. To reheat, place frozen balls on a rack on a cookie sheet. Heat in oven at 375° for about 15 minutes or until hot.
7. Serve with lemon wedges or a small bowl of soy sauce-vinegar mixture for dipping.

Hint: *Sesame oil may be found in Chinese food stores or gourmet department of supermarket.

Lucia H. Shaw

creamy stuffed mushrooms

Yield: 20 to 24 mushrooms

Mushrooms stay crisp.

8 ounces fresh mushrooms, cleaned, stems removed
8 ounces cream cheese, softened
1 tablespoon parsley, chopped
½ teaspoon onion salt
¼ teaspoon garlic salt
½ teaspoon Worcestershire sauce
paprika for garnish

1. Combine all ingredients and mix thoroughly.
2. Spoon mixture into mushroom caps. Sprinkle with paprika. (At this point, they can be refrigerated until baking time.)
3. Place mushrooms on oven-proof platter and bake until hot.

Temperature: 400°
Time: 5 minutes

Suzy M. Hengerer

party sandwiches

Yield: 24 sandwiches

Always a hit at office parties.

1 8-ounce package cream
   cheese, softened
8 tablespoons butter,
   softened
½ teaspoon garlic salt
3 tablespoons chopped,
   fresh parsley
1 loaf thinly sliced
   sandwich bread, crusts
   removed

1. Mix cream cheese, butter, garlic
   salt, and parsley to a soft
   cream.
2. Spread mixture on one slice of
   bread. Add second slice of
   bread and spread with mixture.
   Top with third slice of bread.
3. Cut into four squares. Spread
   mixture on the sides of each
   square.
4. Place on cookie sheet, cover
   with foil, and refrigerate until 20
   minutes before serving.
5. Remove foil and bake until
   lightly brown.

Temperature: 400°
Time: 6 to 8 minutes

Caroll J. Meyers

walnut stuffed mushrooms

Yield: 8 servings

A nutty variation

16 large or 24
   medium-size
   mushrooms
2 tablespoons butter or
   margarine, melted
garlic salt
1 tablespoon finely
   minced fresh onion
2 teaspoons
   Worcestershire sauce
1 tablespoon mayonnaise
3 tablespoons grated
   Parmesan cheese
3 tablespoons finely
   chopped walnuts
fresh parsley for garnish

1. Clean mushrooms. Remove
   stems and set aside.
2. Brush mushroom caps with part
   of butter and lightly sprinkle
   them with garlic salt.
3. Chop stems and sauté with
   onion in remaining butter. Add
   other ingredients and fill caps
   with this mixture. (These can be
   done ahead to this point and
   refrigerated.)
4. Place in oven-proof dish and
   bake just until mushrooms are
   tender and tops are browned.
5. Garnish with a sprinkle of fresh
   chopped parsley or a parsley
   sprig and serve.

Temperature: 400°
Time: 10 minutes

Karin N. McNamara

rich cheese wafers

Yield: 40 to 60 cakes

These crisp wafers are delicious alone or with their Cheddary filling!

Pastry

1 cup butter, softened
2 cups grated sharp Cheddar cheese
2 cups flour
⅛ teaspoon cayenne pepper

Pastry

1. Cream butter and cheese.
2. Sift flour and pepper together and work gradually into butter mixture.
3. Wrap dough in foil. Chill 1 hour.
4. Roll dough in ¼-inch thickness. Cut into 1½-inch rounds.
5. Bake on buttered cookie sheets until golden. Cool wafers. (These can be frozen or stored in an airtight container until serving time.)

Filling

1½ cups grated sharp Cheddar cheese
½ cup butter, softened
1 tablespoon Sherry
salt and cayenne, to taste

Must do ahead.

Filling

1. Cream cheese and butter.
2. Blend in sherry and seasonings. (Can be refrigerated until 1 hour before serving. Bring to room temperature.)
3. Spread a wafer with filling at serving time and top with another wafer.

Temperature: 350°
Time: 15 minutes

Nancy S. Brown

One league husband gamely took over testing recipes when his wife broke her arm. He had never cooked before, so Nancy carefully supervised his every move. The results, though excellent, required such effort and concentration on Bill's part that he now has new respect for her homemaking abilities.

🍎 poached trout

Yield: 6 to 8 servings

Elegant but easy.

1 whole trout (about 12 inches)
½ cup red wine vinegar
½ cup water
1 bay leaf
2 teaspoons pickling spice

1. Place trout in shallow baking pan.
2. Combine other ingredients and pour over trout.
3. Bake 30 minutes. Turn fish over and bake another 30 minutes.
4. Chill thoroughly. Skin and bone fish.
5. Serve on a platter with bacon-flavored crackers and top with dill sauce.

Dill Sauce
½ cup mayonnaise
2 tablespoons fresh lemon juice
1 teaspoon dill weed

Dill Sauce
1. Mix all ingredients thoroughly and refrigerate.
2. Pour over fish at serving time.

Must do ahead.

Temperature: 250°
Time: 1 hour

Alternative serving suggestion: Arrange bite-sized chunks of fish on a bed of lettuce. Add lemon slices and parsley for garnish. Serve with toothpicks.

Suzanne W. Devereaux

prawn canapés

Yield: 36 canapés

Simple, yet impressive.

1 pound fresh shrimp, cooked, cleaned, and well drained
¾ cup mayonnaise
1 tablespoon minced onion
1 teaspoon minced celery
1 teaspoon green pepper
2 teaspoons lemon juice
½ teaspoon grated lemon rind
¼ teaspoon salt
4 to 5 drops Tabasco
dash of pepper
36 rounds of bread, about the size of half dollars
fresh parsley for garnish

1. Cut shrimp into fine pieces and drain again to prevent mixture from being too moist.
2. Mix shrimp together with all other ingredients except bread and parsley. Correct seasonings to taste.
3. Chill. May be done ahead to here.
4. To serve, mound a heaping teaspoon of shrimp mixture on each round of bread.
5. Garnish with parsley

Sue P. Larson

steak tartare

Dinner in the raw.

1 pound beef tenderloin,
  or choice sirloin
1 small onion, finely
  chopped
1 small shallot, finely
  chopped
2 anchovy fillets, mashed
1 2- to 3-ounce jar capers
2 tablespoons cognac
1 teaspoon salt
¼ teaspoon freshly
  ground pepper
2 drops Tabasco sauce
1 egg yolk, slightly beaten
1 hard-boiled egg,
  chopped
1 onion, chopped
fresh parsley
party rye bread

1. Grind meat.
2. Add onion, shallot, and
   anchovies to meat, mix
   thoroughly.
3. Mix one tablespoon drained
   capers, cognac, salt, pepper, and
   Tabasco into meat. (If using food
   processor, cube meat. Place in
   processor with quartered onion
   and shallot. Add cut anchovies,
   capers, cognac, salt, pepper, and
   Tabasco. Process on and off
   until meat is chopped but not
   smooth. Remove mixture to a
   bowl and continue.)
4. Thoroughly blend egg yolk into
   meat mixture.
5. Press into small buttered
   container. Chill.
6. To serve, unmold on serving
   plate. Press additional drained
   capers on top. Garnish with
   rings of chopped egg, onion and
   parsley around edge. Serve with
   party rye.

Must do ahead.

Sue M. Hanson

When looking through old cookbooks for recipe ideas, remember this rule: The quality of a recipe is directly proportional to the number of grease spots on the page!

zesty shrimp and artichoke hearts

Yield: 8 servings

Flavor shines through this light marinade.

1 15-ounce can artichoke
  hearts
25 medium-size shrimp,
  cooked and cleaned
1 egg yolk
¾ cup oil
¼ cup red wine vinegar
2 tablespoons Dijon
  mustard
2 tablespoons fresh,
  chopped parsley
2 tablespoons chopped
  chives
1 tablespoon minced
  shallots or green onions
salt and pepper to taste

1. Cut artichokes and shrimp into bite-size pieces.
2. Combine egg yolk, oil, vinegar, and mustard in a bowl. Beat well.
3. Gently stir in artichokes, shrimp, and remaining ingredients.
4. Marinate in refrigerator, at least 2 hours, stirring occasionally.
5. Before serving, drain off the marinade. Serve with toothpicks or melba toast rounds.

Must do ahead.

Hint: May also be served on lettuce as a salad.

Linnea O. Donahower

tuna antipasto

Yield: Approximately 6 cups

Gets better the longer it sits.

3 carrots, thinly sliced
3 large onions, chopped
3 green peppers, chopped
1 cup olive oil
1 8-ounce can tomato
  sauce
1 teaspoon vinegar
1 20-ounce bottle catsup
2 teaspoons
  Worcestershire sauce
4 sweet pickles, chopped
2 3-ounce cans
  mushroom pieces,
  drained
3 6½-ounce cans white
  tuna, drained
4 bay leaves
8 to 12 peppercorns
salt to taste

1. Cook carrots 8 to 10 minutes and drain.
2. Sauté onions and green peppers in olive oil. Add tomato sauce, vinegar, catsup, and Worcestershire sauce. Cook over low heat for 3 minutes.
3. Add pickles and mushrooms and cook 3 more minutes.
4. Add remaining ingredients including carrots and cook for 15 minutes.
5. Cool. Place in a jar or airtight container and refrigerate.
6. Can be kept in refrigerator for weeks.
7. Remove bay leaves and peppercorns. Serve chilled in a bowl, surrounded by crackers.

Must do ahead.

Patsy M. Gilges

savory steak slices

Yield: 40 slices

Whets the most discriminating appetites.

1½ pounds flank steak
⅓ cup soy sauce
⅓ cup dark rum
2 tablespoons salad oil
party rye bread, lightly
   buttered
sliced radishes and
   watercress, optional

1. Trim excess fat from steak.
2. Combine soy sauce and rum in
   large shallow dish. Marinate
   steak in mixture. Refrigerate,
   covered, for 24 hours, turning
   occasionally.
3. Remove steak from marinade.
   Brush steak with oil. Place in
   broiler pan without rack.
4. Broil steak 6 inches from heat,
   for 1 minute on each side, then
   5 minutes on each side or until
   medium rare.
5. Remove from pan and let cool.
   Refrigerate until serving time.
6. To serve, cut steak diagonally
   into thin slices. Arrange on
   platter with bread. May garnish
   with radishes and watercress.

Must do ahead.

Temperature: Broil
Time: 12 minutes

Nancy J. Cameros

pepper jelly

Yield: 6 jelly jars

Unusual—cool and hot!

¾ cup ground sweet
   pepper with juice
¼ cup ground seeded
   jalapeño peppers with
   juice
6½ cups sugar
1½ cups cider vinegar
1 6-ounce bottle fruit
   pectin
green food coloring,
   optional

1. Combine peppers, divide in half,
   and set aside.
2. Put sugar, vinegar, one-half of
   peppers, and juice in blender
   and blend thoroughly.
3. Cook mixture 10 to 15 minutes
   in a saucepan.
4. Add remaining peppers, juice,
   and pectin. Stir and cook for 4
   minutes. A few drops of food
   coloring may be added if you
   wish.
5. Pour into hot sterilized jars and
   seal.
6. Serve over cream cheese with
   crackers or as an
   accompaniment to cold meats.

Betty B. Edgerton

marinated vegetables

Yield: 8 to 10 servings

A favorite of bridge groups

Vegetables
cauliflower
artichoke hearts
pitted black olives
green olives
cherry tomatoes
red pepper
green pepper
mushrooms
carrots
zucchini
cucumber

Vegetables
1. Choose any combination of vegetables in season. Cherry tomatoes or red peppers are necessary for color.
2. Prepare vegetables in bite-size pieces.
3. Place vegetables, except for cherry tomatoes, in bowl.

Marinade
1½ cups corn oil
⅔ cup white vinegar
2¼ teaspoons salt
1 teaspoon white pepper
2 cloves garlic
½ cup sugar

Marinade
1. Mix marinade ingredients together.
2. Pour marinade over vegetables and refrigerate. Vegetables should extend above the marinade by 2 to 3 inches.
3. Stir daily for 3 days. Add tomatoes the last day.
4. Remove garlic cloves. Drain well. Serve with toothpicks.

Must do three days ahead.

Nancy M. Frank

marinated sliced mushrooms

Yield: 12 to 14 servings

Tangy taste tempter.

1½ pounds mushrooms, thinly sliced
1½ onions, finely chopped
1½ cloves garlic, crushed
⅜ cup vegetable oil
3 tablespoons tarragon vinegar
1½ teaspoons oregano
salt and pepper to taste
pumpernickel or rye bread, sliced and buttered

1. Mix all ingredients together in a wooden bowl.
2. Cover and refrigerate for 3 to 4 hours, stirring every 30 minutes with a wooden spoon.
3. To serve, spoon onto bread using a slotted spoon.

Must do ahead.

Mary Ann Whitmore

summer sausage

Yield: 4 rolls

Much less expensive than the commercial variety.

3 tablespoons boiling water
1 teaspoon mustard seed
1 teaspoon ground allspice
1 teaspoon coriander seed
2 teaspoons monosodium glutamate
½ to 1 teaspoon cayenne pepper
2 teaspoons seasoned black pepper
2½ teaspoons seasoned salt
5 teaspoons salt
5 pounds very fresh ground beef

1. Add boiling water to combined spices and cool.
2. Mix with ground beef and knead thoroughly.
3. Refrigerate 3 days, kneading daily.
4. Form meat mixture into 4 rolls.
5. Bake, turning about every 2 hours to keep shape.
6. Cool. Store in refrigerator, or freeze.
7. Serve cold or at room temperature with crackers, Cheddar cheese, and spicy mustard.

Must do three days ahead.

Temperature: 140°
Time: 8 to 10 hours

Pam M. Morgan

shrimp remoulade

Yield: 6 to 8 servings

Spicy and sophisticated.

¼ cup brown mustard
2 tablespoons paprika
1 teaspoon cayenne pepper
4 teaspoons salt
½ cup tarragon vinegar
1⅓ cups olive oil
1½ cups chopped scallions
½ cup chopped celery
½ cup chopped parsley
3 pounds medium-size cooked shrimp
1 large head iceberg lettuce, shredded

1. Combine mustard, paprika, cayenne, and salt in a deep bowl and stir with whisk until thoroughly combined.
2. Beat in vinegar.
3. Whisking constantly, pour in oil in a slow, thin stream and continue to beat until sauce is smooth and thick.
4. Add scallions, celery, and parsley and mix well.
5. Cover bowl tightly, and let sauce rest at room temperature for 4 hours.
6. When ready to serve, make a bed of shredded lettuce on a platter or individual plates. Place chilled shrimp on lettuce, and pour remoulade sauce over the shrimp.

Must do ahead.

Peggi M. Godwin

après ski gin

Yield: 6 to 8 servings

Soothing after winter activities; even clears your head when you have a cold!

1 cup sugar
1 cup lemon juice
5 cups water
1 cup gin
lemon slices

1. Mix sugar, lemon juice, and water in saucepan. Stir until sugar dissolves. Bring mixture to a boil.
2. Remove from heat. Stir in gin.
3. Serve immediately in mugs with a lemon slice floating on top.

Peggi M. Godwin

sleighride

Yield: 8 to 10 drinks

Warming and non-alcoholic.

8 cups hot coffee
½ cup sugar
4 tablespoons chocolate syrup
1 cup heavy cream
1½ teaspoons vanilla
candy canes

1. Whip cream with vanilla.
2. Mix coffee with sugar and chocolate. Pour into stemmed glasses or Irish coffee mugs.
3. Place a generous dollop of whipped cream in each mug. Garnish with a candy cane and/or a sprinkle of crushed candy. Serve. To make this alcoholic and even more warming, add a little chocolate, coffee, or mint liqueur.

Alice K. Smith

 hot buttered rum

Yield: 1 quart of batter

Cozy and warm on a wintry night.

1 pound dark brown sugar
1 cup butter, softened
1 pint vanilla ice cream
½ teaspoon cinnamon
½ teaspoon allspice
¼ teaspoon nutmeg
rum
cinnamon sticks, optional

1. Mix all ingredients, except rum, together in large bowl. Blend until smooth.
2. Store batter in freezer.
3. To prepare each drink, put one heaping tablespoon of ice cream batter and 1½ ounce of rum into each mug.
4. Fill mug with boiling water. Stir well.
5. Can be served with cinnamon stick, if desired.

Must be frozen.

Bonnie W. Hindman

glowing glogg

Yield: 32 servings

A spectacular flaming beverage.

2 quarts claret or
   burgundy wine
2 quarts port wine
1 4-inch strip orange peel
25 whole cloves
25 cardamon seeds
4 cinnamon sticks
2 6-ounce cans blanched
   almonds
1 pound seedless raisins
1 pound lump sugar
1 pint brandy

1. Combine wines in large
   saucepan.
2. Tie orange peel and spices in
   cheesecloth and add to pan
   along with almonds and raisins.
3. Simmer mixture 15 minutes.
4. Pour punch through a strainer
   into a heat proof punch bowl or
   glogg pot, reserving almonds
   and raisins.
5. Place a rack over the top of the
   bowl, one which fits fairly well
   and can hold the sugar.
6. Pour warmed brandy over sugar
   and ignite. (Be careful of flames.)
7. After sugar has burned down
   serve glogg in heat proof punch
   cups adding a few almonds and
   raisins to each cup.

R.T. French Consumer Services

apple cider wassail

Yield: 25 6-ounce servings

Wonderful accompaniment for outdoor winter activities.

6 cloves
5 allspice berries
1 gallon apple cider
1 cup brown sugar
1 6-ounce can frozen
   lemonade concentrate
1 6-ounce can frozen
   orange juice
   concentrate
1 tablespoon nutmeg
6 cinnamon sticks
1 pint light or amber rum

1. Tie cloves and allspice berries in
   a cheesecloth bag.
2. Put all ingredients, except rum,
   into a large pot with spice bag.
   Simmer 20 minutes.
3. Remove spice bag. The above
   may be done ahead. Reheat to
   serve.
4. Add rum. Serve warm.

Terry S. Butwid

finale

Yield: 4 servings

An after-dinner coffee guaranteed to please a gourmet's palate.

Liqueur Mixture
2 ounces white creme de cacao
2 ounces Amaretto
2 ounces light rum

hot, strong, black coffee
½ pint heavy cream, whipped (may be sweetened with 1 tablespoon confectioners sugar)
cinnamon or cinnamon sticks for garnish

Liqueur Mixture
1. Mix together first three ingredients. May be done far in advance and stored in a jar.

For each serving:
1. Put 1½ ounces of liqueur mixture into a stemmed glass or Irish coffee mug.
2. Add about ¾ cup of hot coffee. Stir.
3. Place a heaping tablespoon of whipped cream in each drink. Sprinkle with a bit of cinnamon or garnish with a cinnamon stick.

Lucia H. Shaw

*O*ne of Rochester's more elegant restaurants refused to divulge its recipe for its best selling drink. Lucia visited there a few times and managed to wheedle some ingredient information from the waiter. She then experimented in her own kitchen and created Finale, the delicious double of that heretofore "secret" drink!

wassail

Yield: 16 4-ounce servings

Mild, fragrant and delicious.

½ gallon apple cider
1 teaspoon whole cloves
4 pieces stick cinnamon
½ cup rum
¼ cup brandy
1 to 2 oranges (optional)

1. Heat cider with cloves and stick cinnamon just to boiling. *Do not boil.*
2. Add rum and brandy. Serve immediately.
3. If serving from a punch bowl, float 1 or 2 clove-studded whole oranges on top which have been baked in a slow oven for ½ hour.

Cecy R. Szuba

sunshine slush

Yield: 12 to 14 servings

A fruity summer cooler.

1 cup sugar
3 cups water
2 ripe bananas
2 6-ounce cans frozen, unsweetened pineapple juice concentrate, thawed
1 16-ounce can orange juice concentrate, thawed
1 6-ounce can frozen lemonade concentrate, thawed
1½ cups light rum or vodka (optional)
1 28-ounce bottle club soda, chilled
lemon or orange slices for garnish

Must be frozen.

1. Boil sugar and water for 3 minutes or until sugar dissolves. Cool.
2. Whirl bananas and one can of the pineapple juice in the blender. Pour into large container.
3. Mix second can of pineapple juice, orange juice, lemonade, cooled syrup and liquor if used with banana mixture and put into freezer.
4. To serve, let stand at room temperature until softened. Add chilled club soda.
5. Pour into glasses and garnish with a slice of orange or lemon.

Caroll J. Meyers

overnight frozen daiquiri

Yield: 6 to 8 servings

One of the best variations of a popular drink.

1 6-ounce can frozen limeade concentrate
6 ounces water
9 ounces rum
16 ounces lemon-lime carbonated beverage
green food coloring (optional)
lime slices, sprigs of mint, or cherries for garnish

Must do one day ahead.

1. Stir all ingredients together.
2. Freeze overnight in a bowl or plastic container large enough to allow room for expansion. Stir occasionally to keep ingredients well mixed. The mixture will become quite slushy but will never freeze solid because of the rum.
3. When ready to serve, ladle into glasses and garnish with a slice of lime, sprig of mint, or a cherry.

Malinda B. Fischer

fall refresher

A surprisingly different drink.

6 ounces apple cider
1½ ounces vodka
wedge of lime

1. Fill large glass with ice.
2. Pour in apple cider and vodka.
3. Squeeze lime into drink and stir.

Judy G. Curry

celebration punch

Yield: 70 4-ounce cups

Dry, light, and refreshing!

3 fifths champagne
3 fifths dry sauterne
3 28-ounce bottles club
   soda
8 ounces brandy
8 ounces orange Curaçao
maraschino cherries
   frozen in ice for garnish
1 large block of ice

1. Chill champagne, sauterne, and
   soda at least 24 hours.
2. Mix the liqueur and brandy in a
   punch bowl.
3. Add a large block of ice.
4. Pour chilled ingredients over the
   ice and blend very slightly.

Must do one day ahead.

Louise S. Criticos

tea punch

Yield: 20 servings

A dry punch. Serve with sweets at a shower.

6 cups strong tea
1 46-ounce can orange
   juice
1 46-ounce can pineapple
   juice
2 6-ounce cans frozen
   lemonade concentrate,
   undiluted
32 ounces cranberry juice
1 quart gingerale
1 quart blended whiskey
2 oranges, sliced
1 lime, sliced
1 lemon, sliced
1 ice ring

1. Combine first 5 ingredients.
2. Add gingerale and whiskey just
   before serving.
3. Float fruit slices on punch along
   with an ice ring.

Alice K. Smith

coffee punch

Yield: 60 cups

Rich enough to take the place of dessert at a luncheon.

1 gallon strong coffee
1¾ cups sugar
1 pint heavy cream
1 gallon vanilla ice cream
Homemade Coffee
   Liqueur, optional
(see index)

1. Dissolve sugar in hot coffee and chill.
2. Add heavy cream. Stir well. Return to refrigerator.
3. At serving time, pour coffee mixture into punch bowl. Add ice cream, either broken into small chunks or made into scoops.
4. Stir in coffee liqueur to taste, if desired.

Must do ahead.

Hint: Any leftover punch can be frozen and used later as a "coffee ice."

Nancy L. Brown

homemade coffee liqueur

Yield: 2 25-ounce bottles

A delicious and inexpensive substitute for commercially prepared liqueurs.

3 cups sugar
1¼ cups water
1 tablespoon vanilla
2 tablespoons instant
   coffee
1 fifth (26 ounces)
   inexpensive vodka

1. Put first 4 ingredients in a large pan. Bring to a boil and simmer 10 minutes. Be very careful because this mixture will boil over very quickly.
2. Cool. Add vodka and mix thoroughly.
3. Use as you would use any coffee liqueur.

Hint: It may be stored in bottles in a cool place indefinitely.

Paula S. Howk

 whisper

Smooth and satisfying, a real winner.

Yield: 4 servings

1 pint vanilla ice cream
1 ounce brandy
1 ounce creme de cacao
2 ounces black coffee

1. Place all of the ingredients in a blender and whirl on high speed until smooth.
2. Keep refrigerated at least 2 hours, or until ready to serve.
3. Blend quickly before pouring.

Must do ahead.

Nancy S. Milbury

eliza's golden pheasants

Yield: 8 servings

A rare and delightful experience!

6 ounces vodka
6 ounces fresh lemon juice
⅓ cup confectioners sugar
1 egg
2 quarts cream soda (a carbonated beverage)

1. Whirl first 4 ingredients in blender.
2. Put 1½ ounces of above mixture over ice cubes in an 8-ounce glass. Fill glass with cream soda.

Linnea O. Donahower

Many League husbands enjoyed the variety that tasting and testing for this book gave to their meals. Particularly appealing was the rating system where they were able to judge dishes as "outstanding," "very good," "average," "below average," or "forget it." Some of these sly spouses continue to rate their meals even though testing has long been over!

frosty fruit 'n brandy

Yield: 1 serving

A lovely drink for special summer occasions.

2 cling peach halves
1 ounce peach brandy
1½ tablespoons orange
Curaçao
3 ounces heavy cream
½ cup crushed ice
maraschino cherry and
peach slices for garnish

1. Combine all ingredients and
whirl in blender until smooth.
2. Serve in long-stemmed, 8-ounce
glass.
3. Garnish with a peach slice on
rim of glass. Spear a cherry with
a toothpick and attach to peach
slice.

Louise S. Criticos

sangria córdoba

Yield: 4 to 6 servings

Adds pizzazz to a backyard barbeque.

1 orange, sliced and
seeded
1 lemon, sliced and
seeded
1 handful strawberries
1 handful raspberries
1 peach, peeled and sliced
2 teaspoons sugar
1 ounce orange liqueur
1 ounce brandy
ice
1 bottle dry red wine (25.4
fluid ounces)

Must do ahead.

1. Put fruits in large pitcher.
2. Mix sugar with liqueur and
brandy, and pour over fruit.
3. Let soften for several hours.
Occasionally mash and stir the
fruit with wooden spoon.
4. At serving time, fill pitcher with
ice and add wine. Stir with
wooden spoon until it is very
cold.
5. Serve in chilled goblets.

Mary W. Schwertz

ashleys

Yield: 4 servings

A favorite with everyone who's tried it.

1 6-ounce can frozen
limeade concentrate
6 ounces light rum
1 12-ounce can beer
lemon or lime slices for
garnish

1. Whirl all ingredients in blender.
2. Serve over crushed ice.
3. Garnish with slice of lemon or
lime in each glass.

Kay B. Edwards

holiday eggnog

Yield: 6 servings

Creamy, rich, and nutritious.

6 egg yolks
1 cup confectioners
    sugar
1⅔ cups peach-flavored
    brandy
1 cup cold milk
1 pint heavy cream
3 egg whites
freshly ground nutmeg

1. Beat egg yolks in a large bowl
   until they are light and
   lemon-colored.
2. Gradually beat in sugar.
3. Slowly pour in brandy, while
   beating constantly.
4. Let rest 10 minutes.
5. Beat in milk. Refrigerate,
   covered, overnight.
6. Next day, whip cream until stiff.
   Beat egg whites until stiff.
7. Fold both into brandy mixture.
8. Pour into individual goblets and
   garnish with nutmeg.

Must do one day ahead.

Kathryn P. Weider

orange frost

Yield: 6 to 8 servings

The perfect brunch eye-opener! Kids love it frozen as popsicles.

1 6-ounce can frozen
    orange juice
    concentrate
1 cup milk
1 cup water
⅓ to ½ cup sugar
1¼ teaspoons vanilla
12 ice cubes
sprigs of mint for garnish

1. Mix all ingredients, except ice,
   together in blender.
2. Add a few ice cubes at a time,
   beating at high speed until all
   ice cubes have been crushed.
3. Garnish with a sprig of mint and
   serve immediately.
4. This is also delicious with the
   addition of some gin or vodka.

Serve immediately.

Sally S. Moore

There is an almost legendary orange drink we love which originated in New York's Times Square For years aficionados have tried to duplicate its taste at home, but with poor results. Our Orange Frost hits the mark so exactly that Pris's teenage daughter, Jessica, retested it 25 times after a recent trip to New York City. She finally convinced herself that we have indeed found the clone of that famous drink!

37

buccaneer vixen

Yield: 1 serving

A new version of piña colada.

crushed ice
1 ounce 151-proof light
  rum
½ ounce lemon juice
½ ounce orgeat syrup
  (non-alcoholic,
  almond-flavored syrup)
2 ounces pineapple juice
maraschino cherries for
  garnish

1. Before preparing drinks, take
   time to crush plenty of ice.
2. Put all ingredients, except
   cherries, into blender, filling no
   higher than 12-ounce mark.
   Amount of ice may be varied
   depending on strength of drink
   desired. Blend well.
3. Serve in 12-ounce brandy glass,
   topped with cherry.

Susan P. Larson

poor richard's whiskey sours

Yield: 6 drinks

Smooth and creamy—but don't substitute other whiskey for bourbon.

1 6-ounce can frozen
  lemonade concentrate
6 ounces bourbon
6 ounces beer
1 egg
8 ice cubes
maraschino cherries and
  orange slices for garnish

1. Combine all ingredients in
   blender at high speed.
2. Serve immediately with garnish.

Richard W. Minster

vitality drink

Yield: 1 serving

Tasty, filling and full of vitamins.

8 ounces skim milk
¼ cup dry milk (instant)
1 tablespoon
  molasses-grown yeast
1 tablespoon protein
  powder
6 ice cubes
1 ripe banana

1. Put all ingredients in blender
   and whip at high speed until
   well blended.
2. Serve immediately.

Hint: When you first begin drinking this, put in only 1 teaspoon of yeast. It takes a while to get used to its taste.

Emily M. Henderson

soups & sandwiches

soups & sandwiches

SOUPS

Hot

Hot or Cold Soups

Cold Soups

SANDWICHES

harvest asparagus-tomato soup

Yield: 6 to 10 servings

Unusual flavor, elegant results!

1½ cups cooked
   asparagus
5 cups chicken stock
1 medium onion, chopped
1 carrot, coarsely
   chopped
1 tablespoon chopped
   parsley
1 bay leaf
2 cups canned tomatoes
⅛ teaspoon freshly
   ground pepper
½ teaspoon thyme
1 teaspoon salt
pinch of ground cloves
½ teaspoon sugar
2 tablespoons butter,
   melted
2 tablespoons flour
½ teaspoon butter and
   fresh parsley *or* 1
   tablespoon sour cream
   and ½ teaspoon minced
   chives, for garnish

1. Combine all soup ingredients except butter and flour. Cover, and simmer for 45 minutes.
2. Whirl in food processor or blender until fairly smooth. This may need to be done in 2 to 3 batches. Return to pot over low heat.
3. Blend butter and flour together. Stir into soup.
4. Simmer 20 to 30 minutes.
5. Garnish as suggested.

Jeanne P. Massey

french mushroom soup

Yield: 10 cups

Adapted from Paris by a slim gourmet.

1 pound mushrooms,
   sliced
½ cup chopped onion
3 tablespoons butter
8 cups water
2 tablespoons instant beef
   bouillon
2 cups thinly sliced
   carrots
1 teaspoon salt
⅛ teaspoon pepper
½ cup sherry or Madeira
chopped fresh parsley

1. Sauté mushrooms and onion in butter until tender.
2. Reduce heat and simmer 10 minutes.
3. Stir in water and bouillon. Cover and simmer 45 minutes.
4. Add carrots. Cover and simmer 15 minutes.
5. Stir in seasonings and sherry. Heat to boiling.
6. Garnish with parsley.

Terry S. Butwid

cream of mushroom soup   Yield: 3 quarts

Mushrooms that are a few days old enhance the flavor of this favorite.

1 pound mushrooms, sliced
1 pound mushrooms, chopped
4 tablespoons butter or margarine
6 cups chicken stock
1½ cups chopped celery
¾ cup chopped onion
½ cup chopped parsley
1 bay leaf, crumbled
½ cup butter
½ cup flour
4 cups half and half

Optional:
½ cup dry white wine
pinch of nutmeg
pinch of Beau Monde

1. Sauté mushrooms in butter until golden. Do not overcook. They should still be firm.
2. Add chicken stock.
3. Add celery, onion, parsley and bay leaf to soup. Simmer, covered, 20 minutes.
4. Melt butter in another saucepan. Stir in flour.
5. Add half and half gradually, stirring until smooth and thick.
6. Stir sauce into mushroom mixture. Add optional ingredients. Cook and stir until smooth.

Hint: Freeze this in 1½-cup portions. Thaw and use in recipes calling for a can of mushroom soup.

"Sam" E. Lawless

busy day mushroom soup   Yield: 4 to 6 servings

Taste the distinctive difference that homemade makes!

½ pound mushrooms, sliced
2 cups chicken stock
2 cups milk
5 tablespoons butter
5 tablespoons flour
salt and pepper to taste
½ cup light cream
¼ cup white wine or 3 tablespoons sherry
fresh parsley for garnish

1. Simmer mushrooms in chicken stock and milk for 20 minutes. Set aside.
2. Melt butter in a 3-quart saucepan. Add flour, gradually, making a roux.
3. Blend in mushroom mixture. Cook and thicken, stirring constantly.
4. Season with salt and pepper.
5. Add cream and wine just before serving. Garnish with parsley.

Judy McKelvey

mushroom barley tureen

Yield: 8 servings

A hearty, nourishing soup.

½ cup diced onion
½ cup diced celery
½ cup diced carrot
½ pound fresh
  mushrooms, sliced
2 tablespoons butter
1 tablespoon flour
3 cups chicken broth
½ cup medium pearled
  barley
½ cup milk
1½ cups cooked and
  diced turkey or chicken
salt and pepper to taste

1. In large saucepan, sauté vegetables in butter for 10 minutes.
2. Stir in flour. Add the broth and heat, stirring constantly, until mixture comes to a boil.
3. Add barley. Cover and simmer soup until barley is cooked through, about 1 hour.
4. Stir in the milk, meat, salt, and pepper. Heat thoroughly and serve.

Linda G. Stenstrom

tangy-tomato-mushroom soup

Yield: 6 servings

A spicy soup that brims with mushrooms.

1 tablespoon butter
1 tablespoon olive oil
1 medium onion, diced
1 clove garlic, split
1½ pounds mushrooms,
  sliced
1 6-ounce can tomato
  paste
4 cups chicken stock
⅓ cup vermouth
½ teaspoon salt
½ teaspoon pepper
6 teaspoons grated
  Parmesan cheese
toasted croutons

1. Melt butter and stir in oil.
2. Sauté onion and garlic.
3. Remove garlic, continue to sauté onion until brown.
4. Add mushrooms and sauté 5 minutes.
5. Add tomato paste, mix well.
6. Blend in chicken stock, vermouth, salt, and pepper. Simmer 10 minutes.
7. Garnish each serving with 1 teaspoon Parmesan, and a few toasted croutons.

Jean H. Whitney

chelmsford cauliflower soup

Yield: 6 servings

Different, hearty, and a crowd pleaser.

1 medium cauliflower, washed but left as a head

2 to 3 carrots peeled and cut into ¼-inch pieces

1 to 2 celery stalks, cut into ¼-inch pieces. Reserve top leaves and chop.

¼ fresh lemon

¼ cup butter

1 medium onion, chopped

4 to 6 fresh mushrooms, sliced

2 tablespoons flour

4 cups chicken broth or 6 chicken bouillon cubes dissolved in 4 cups cooking liquid reserved from the cauliflower

¼ cup medium pearl barley

¼ teaspoon white pepper

1 teaspoon salt

½ cup heavy cream

½ cup milk

1. Add cauliflower, carrots, celery stalks, and lemon piece to a large pot of boiling water and simmer until the cauliflower is tender, about 10 minutes. Discard the lemon, drain the vegetables, and reserve one cup of cooking liquid plus 4 more if using bouillon cubes. Break cauliflower into florets.

2. In same pot, melt butter and sauté onions, mushrooms, and a few celery leaves until onions are transparent.

3. Stir in flour and, mixing constantly, cook over low heat for 1 to 2 minutes, being careful not to let flour brown. Add 1 cup of reserved cauliflower liquid and cook, stirring constantly, until mixture is thick and smooth.

4. Add additional 4 cups of chicken broth or bouillon, barley, cauliflower, celery, carrots, salt, and pepper.

5. Simmer 15 to 20 minutes after barley has softened.

6. Add cream and milk just before serving and heat through.

Ellyn Gissin

forest hills zucchini soup

Yield: 3 to 4 quarts

Also doubles as distinctive spaghetti sauce.

1 pound Italian sausage links, (mild or hot), cut in 1-inch chunks
½ pound ground chuck beef
2 cups celery, sliced ½-inch thick
2 pounds zucchini, sliced ½-inch thick
1½ cups coarsely chopped onion
2 28-ounce cans tomatoes in sauce
2 teaspoons salt
1 teaspoon Italian seasoning
1 teaspoon oregano
½ teaspoon basil
½ teaspoon garlic powder
2 green peppers, cut in ½-inch pieces
shredded Mozzarella cheese
grated Parmesan cheese

1. Brown sausage and ground beef in large Dutch oven. Drain off fat.
2. Add celery. Cook 10 minutes, stirring often.
3. Add remaining ingredients, except green pepper and cheeses. Simmer, covered, 20 minutes.
4. Add green pepper. Cover, and cook 10 minutes.
5. Ladle into soup bowls at serving time.
6. Sprinkle generously with Mozzarella and Parmesan cheese. Brown under broiler if desired.

Lucia H. Shaw

cabbage soup

Yield: 4 to 6 servings

Old world goodness from a secret recipe.

4 cups chopped cabbage
4 cups beef stock
2 slices bacon, diced
1 large onion, chopped
1 tablespoon flour
1 cup sour cream
salt and pepper
¼ cup chopped parsley

1. Boil cabbage in stock until wilted, but still crisp. Drain, reserving stock.
2. Fry bacon pieces until crisp; remove from pan.
3. Add onion to bacon drippings and cook until transparent.
4. Combine bacon, bacon drippings, and onion in a soup pot.
5. Blend in flour, then sour cream.
6. Add stock and cabbage. Simmer 5 minutes.
7. Season to taste with salt and pepper. Garnish with parsley.

Violet E. Kapusta

essence of tomato
and celery soup

Yield: 12 servings

A light and lovely soup or appetizer.

Soup
1 bunch celery
10 cups chicken stock
4 medium tomatoes,
    peeled, seeded, and
    diced
2 tablespoons butter
1 teaspoon salt
¼ teaspoon thyme
pepper to taste

Garnish
thinly sliced day old
    bread
1 cup butter, melted
celery seed

Soup
1. Trim and dice celery.
2. Bring stock and celery to a boil.
   Simmer 30 minutes and set
   aside.
3. Toss tomatoes, butter, and
   seasonings together in a skillet.
   Simmer, covered, for 10
   minutes.
4. Increase heat, uncover, and
   cook until liquid evaporates.
5. Purée tomatoes in a food
   processor or blender.
6. Place purée in a large pan.
   Strain stock into same pan.
   Discard celery.
7. Heat to boiling. Season to taste
   and garnish.

Garnish
1. Spread 12 slices of bread with
   butter.
2. Sprinkle with celery seed.
3. Bake at 275 degrees for 20
   minutes.
4. Cut slices of toast to fit bowls
   and float them on the soup.

Alice K. Smith

cream of brussels sprouts

Yield: 6 servings

You'll enjoy this even if you think you don't like Brussels sprouts.

4 cups Brussels sprouts
3 cups chicken broth
6 tablespoons butter
3 tablespoons flour
2 cups milk
pinch of nutmeg
½ cup heavy cream
2 or 3 drops Tabasco sauce
salt and pepper

1. Trim tough outer leaves of sprouts and put an X in each stem.
2. Drop sprouts in boiling chicken broth and simmer until tender (about 10 to 15 minutes)
3. Blend sprouts in a food processor or blender, reserving the cooking liquid.
4. Melt 3 tablespoons of the butter in a saucepan and stir in flour using a wire whisk. Blend well.
5. Add reserved liquid, stir rapidly with whisk, simmer 5 minutes.
6. Add puréed sprouts, milk and nutmeg. Simmer 5 minutes more. Can prepare ahead to this point.
7. Add cream and Tabasco. Salt and pepper to taste. Heat *just* to a simmer.
8. Swirl in remaining butter and serve hot.

Jeanne P. Massey

oyster stew

Yield: 4 servings

A delicate soup that's especially popular at holiday time.

4 cups milk
4 soda crackers, crushed
4 tablespoons butter
salt and pepper to taste
½ pint fresh oysters
4 teaspoons butter

1. Heat milk until almost at a boil.
2. Add crackers, 4 tablespoons butter, salt, and pepper; bring to a scalding point (*do not boil*).
3. Add oysters, and cook until edges curl (just a few minutes).
4. Ladle soup into bowls. Swirl 1 teaspoon butter into each bowl. Serve immediately.

Joan M. Hill

hearty vegetable soup
Yield: 10 servings

A fantastic soup . . . and as easy as opening a can!

3 pounds stew beef cut in bite-size pieces
1 cup chopped onions
1 teaspoon minced garlic
2 tablespoons olive oil
1 teaspoon salt
¼ teaspoon pepper
3 cans beef broth
2 cups water
1½ teaspoons Italian herb seasoning
1 one-pound can stewed tomatoes, undrained
1 14½-ounce can kidney beans, undrained
1¾ cups ripe olives, pitted and sliced in half, and 1 cup olive liquid
1½ cups thinly sliced carrots
2 small cans zucchini
1 one-pound can corn, undrained
1 cup shell macaroni
Parmesan cheese to taste

1. Brown the meat, onions and garlic in the olive oil. Season with salt and pepper.
2. Add broth, water, and Italian seasoning, and simmer for one hour.
3. Add tomatoes, beans, olives, carrots, zucchini, corn, and macaroni and simmer for an additional 45 minutes.
4. Before serving sprinkle with Parmesan cheese.

Marilyn Wehrheim

hearty beef chowder
Yield: 10 to 12 servings

Make ahead and freeze for unexpected guests.

1 pound ground beef (or ground chuck)
2 large onions, chopped
1 tablespoon oil
3 tablespoons converted rice (or brown rice)
5 potatoes, diced into ½-inch cubes
1 tablespoon sugar
1 tablespoon salt
1 28-ounce can tomatoes
2 cups diced carrots
1 zucchini, diced (optional)

1. Brown beef and onions in oil. Pour off fat.
2. Stir in remaining ingredients.
3. Add water to almost cover; bring to a boil.
4. Reduce heat to low and simmer 2 hours.
5. Stir often during last hour to avoid burning.
6. Add seasonings of your choice, and serve.

Nancy M. Frank

🍎 soupe à l'oignon

Yield: 6 to 8 servings

This rates as one of the best!

1½ pounds (5 cups) yellow onions, sliced thinly
3 tablespoons butter
1 tablespoon oil
1 teaspoon salt
¼ teaspoon sugar
3 tablespoons flour
2 quarts beef stock or canned beef bouillon
½ cup dry white wine (or dry vermouth)
salt and pepper
3 tablespoons cognac
8 rounds day old French bread, toasted
1 to 2 cups grated Swiss or Parmesan cheese

1. Cook onions slowly in butter and oil in a heavy-bottomed 4-quart covered saucepan for 15 minutes.
2. Uncover, raise heat to medium.
3. Stir in salt and sugar and cook 30 to 40 minutes, stirring frequently, until onions are a deep golden brown.
4. Sprinkle with flour, cook and stir 3 minutes. Remove onions from heat.
5. Boil stock or bouillon in another saucepan.
6. Stir boiling liquid into onions.
7. Blend in wine and season to taste.
8. Simmer, partially covered, 30 to 40 minutes. Skim occasionally.
9. Correct seasonings and set aside, uncovered, until serving time.
10. Reheat to simmer and add cognac.
11. Pour into soup tureen or soup bowls over rounds of bread. Sprinkle with cheese and broil until it melts.

Diane Heald

bay scallop chowder

Yield: 4 to 6 servings

Delightfully seasoned . . . a scallop lover's chowder.

3 medium potatoes, diced
3 small carrots, chopped
2 large celery stalks,
  chopped
1 large onion, chopped
2 cups chicken stock
½ teaspoon salt
½ teaspoon pepper
1 bay leaf
½ teaspoon thyme,
  crumbled
¾ pound fresh
  mushrooms, sliced
1½ tablespoons butter
1¼ pound bay scallops (or
  1¼ pounds sea scallops,
  cut into pieces)
½ cup white wine
1 cup heavy cream
1 egg yolk, lightly beaten
2 tablespoons chopped
  fresh parsley
dash of paprika

1. Place vegetables in a large pot. Cover with chicken stock and bring to a boil.
2. Season with salt, pepper, bay leaf and thyme.
3. Simmer, covered, until vegetables are tender. Discard bay leaf.
4. Pour stock mixture into a blender or food processor. Whirl until smooth.
5. Sauté mushrooms in butter in a large pot.
6. Add scallops and wine and cook 2 minutes.
7. Mix cream and egg yolks and blend into mushroom-scallop mixture.
8. Stir in puréed vegetables and heat thoroughly.
9. Garnish with parsley and paprika.

Kristin W. Williams

busy day vichysoisse

Yield: 8 servings

A velvety, thick, chilled soup.

1½ cups chopped onions
3 cups pared and sliced
  potatoes
3 cups water
1 teaspoon salt
4 chicken bouillon cubes
3 tablespoons butter
2½ cups milk
¼ teaspoon pepper
chopped chives for
  garnish

1. Cook onions and potatoes in boiling, salted water for 40 minutes. Do not drain.
2. Pour potato mixture into a blender and blend until smooth. (This may have to be done in two batches.)
3. Put remaining ingredients in the top of a double boiler and heat until bouillon cubes are dissolved. Combine with potato mixture.
4. Chill soup thoroughly before serving.
5. Garnish with chopped chives.

Must do ahead.

Beverly A. Gifford

pistou

Yield: 10 to 12 servings

A filling French soup that's a vegetarian's dream.

2 cups diced potatoes
2 cups diced onions
2 cups diced carrots
3 quarts water
1 tablespoon salt
2 cups cut green beans
1 10-ounce package
  frozen peas
2 cups canned navy
  beans
½ cup spaghetti, broken
  into pieces
1 slice stale white bread
⅛ teaspoon pepper
pinch saffron
4 cloves garlic, mashed
4 tablespoons tomato
  paste
1½ tablespoon basil
½ cup freshly grated
  Parmesan cheese
½ cup olive oil

1. Simmer potatoes, onions, and carrots in salted water for 45 minutes. (Can be refrigerated at this point. Reheat to boiling and continue.)
2. Add green beans, peas, navy beans, and spaghetti.
3. Crumble in bread.
4. Season with pepper and saffron. Simmer 15 minutes.
5. Meanwhile, blend garlic, tomato paste, basil, and Parmesan in a soup tureen. Beat in olive oil a drop at a time.
6. Blend 1 cup of the hot soup into paste. Pour in remaining soup and stir thoroughly.

Patsy M. Gilges

bouillabaisse

Yield: 4 to 6 servings

Serve this fish stew with fresh bread for a great meal.

1 large onion, chopped
1 cup sliced celery
2 cloves garlic, minced
¼ cup chopped parsley
2 tablespoons butter
2 16-ounce cans stewed
  tomatoes
1½ cups white wine
3 10¾-ounce cans
  chicken broth
½ teaspoon thyme
½ teaspoon chervil
2 10-ounce packages
  frozen, or fresh,
  haddock or cod filets
1 pound raw, medium-size
  shrimp
salt and pepper to taste

1. In a large pot, sauté onion, celery, garlic, and parsley in butter for 5 minutes.
2. Stir in tomatoes, wine, chicken broth, thyme, and chervil. Cover, and simmer for 15 minutes, or until vegetables are tender.
3. While fish is still frozen, cut it into 1-inch cubes.
4. Add fish and shrimp to broth mixture. Add salt and pepper to taste.
5. Cook bouillabaisse for 15 minutes and serve piping hot.

Ellyn P. Gissin

italian clam soup

Yield: 4 servings

Our favorite Sunday night company supper.

4 dozen small clams
½ cup finely chopped
    onion
4 cloves garlic, finely
    minced
⅓ cup olive oil
8 anchovies, finely
    chopped
1 teaspoon dried basil
3 tablespoons finely
    chopped, fresh parsley
1 to 2 teaspoons oregano
1 teaspoon crushed fennel
    seeds
1 6-ounce can tomato
    paste
1 cup dry white wine or
    vermouth
2 cups water
freshly ground pepper to
    taste

1. Scrub clams well under cold
   running water to remove sand.
   Set aside.
2. Sauté onion and garlic in oil
   until wilted.
3. Add anchovies, basil, parsley,
   oregano, and fennel. Cook and
   stir 3 to 5 minutes.
4. Add tomato paste, wine, and
   water. Stir, and simmer 5
   minutes.
5. Add clams, cover, and cook
   until clam shells have opened.
6. Season with pepper to taste.
7. Any leftover broth may be
   frozen.

Victoria H. Gilbert

souper shrimp creole

Yield: 10 servings

My mother's favorite Louisiana recipe.

¾ cup shortening
¾ cup flour
¾ cup chopped onion
6 cups water
2 cups tomatoes (fresh or
    canned), cut in small
    pieces
½ cup chopped green
    pepper
salt and pepper to taste
dash of Tabasco
2 pounds raw shrimp,
    shelled and deveined
cooked rice
chopped parsley

1. Make a roux in a deep heavy
   pot: melt shortening, add flour
   and cook slowly, stirring often
   until mixture is lightly browned.
2. Add onion and cook until
   tender.
3. Add water gradually, stirring to
   make a smooth, thin roux.
4. Add tomatoes and green pepper.
   Bring to a boil.
5. Season to taste with salt,
   pepper, and Tabasco.
6. Add shrimp and simmer,
   covered, 30 minutes.
7. Serve hot over a mound of rice
   in individual soup bowls. Or, you
   can freeze and reheat slowly.
8. Top with parsley.

Patsy M. Gilges

dilled potato soup

Yield: 6 servings

Serve with toasted sandwiches for a quick cool weather supper.

2 tablespoons butter
1 large onion, chopped
4 cups raw potatoes,
   diced in ¼-inch cubes
1 large carrot, chopped
4 cups chicken broth
salt and pepper
1 cup light cream
2 tablespoons chopped
   fresh dill

Optional:
1 cup grated Cheddar
   cheese
1 16-ounce can whole
   kernel corn, drained

1. Melt butter in a large sauce pan.
2. Add onion, potato, and carrot. Cover and cook over very low heat for 5 to 10 minutes.
3. Add broth and salt and pepper to taste. Simmer until the vegetables are tender.
4. Remove from heat. Purée half of mixture in blender or food processor.
5. Return purée to reserved mixture in the pan and stir in cream.
6. Add cheese and corn, if desired.
7. Garnish with dill.

Ann Richards

When Belle was a bride she tried to grow a potato plant from a whole raw potato. After four days the house smelled so bad that her husband suggested she hire someone to help her clean. Finally, the culprit spud was found and had to be discarded at arm's length. So remember, when rooting potatoes, cut a small piece with the potato's eye, immerse it in water and change the water every few days. After the roots grow, plant in a pot, using sandy soil. And if the house still smells, definitely get someone to help you clean.

cream of carrot soup

Steaming hot or refreshingly chilled . . . a versatile rich soup.

½ teaspoon sugar
½ teaspoon marjoram
½ cup water
4 cups sliced carrots
2 tablespoons chopped
  onion
2 tablespoons butter
2 tablespoons flour
2 cups milk
2 teaspoons dill weed
¼ teaspoon thyme
1 tablespoon chicken
  stock base
2 cups half and half
1 cup heavy cream
salt and white pepper, to
  taste
1 carrot, grated

1. Stir sugar and marjoram into boiling water.
2. Add carrots and onion. Steam until tender.
3. Stir in butter until melted.
4. Sprinkle with flour. Cook and stir until lightly brown.
5. Add milk gradually, stirring until smooth. Season with 1 teaspoon of the dill and the thyme.
6. Simmer 30 minutes, stirring occasionally.
7. Purée in blender or food processor and return to soup pan.
8. Add chicken stock base, half and half, cream, and season to taste.
9. Refrigerate until serving time.
10. Reheat and stir in grated carrot. Garnish with remaining dill weed.

Hint: This soup can be served chilled, but omit the grated carrot. When reheating, do not boil.

Kathryn Weider

old country borscht

Yield: 6 servings

A hearty soup for a cold winter weekend—with sour dough bread.

6 cups water
1 pound beef brisket, cut
   into 6 pieces
2 medium onions, sliced
2 stalks celery, cut in
   1-inch pieces
6 medium beets, peeled (4
   sliced and 2 grated,
   enough to equal 1 cup)
4 carrots, peeled and
   thinly sliced
1 cabbage, cut into
   wedges
1 bay leaf
1 tablespoon plus 2
   teaspoons salt
1 6-ounce can tomato
   paste
2 tablespoons vinegar
1 tablespoon sugar
½ pint sour cream

1. Place water, beef, onions, celery, sliced beets, carrots, cabbage, bay leaf and 1 tablespoon of the salt into a large kettle. Simmer, covered, about 2 hours.
2. Add grated beets, tomato paste, vinegar, sugar, and the 2 teaspoons salt. Simmer, covered, 15 to 20 minutes.
3. Cool and refrigerate.
4. Skim any fat from soup.
5. Bring soup to boil over medium heat. Reduce heat. Simmer, covered, 10 minutes.
6. Serve topped with sour cream.

Linnea O. Donahower

 vi's zucchini soup

Yield: 4 servings

A soup of infinite variety—with or without cream, hot or cold—delicious!

3 pounds zucchini, cut
   into chunks
2 cups chicken stock
2 tablespoons onion,
   minced (or 1½
   teaspoons dried onion
   flakes)
1 teaspoon garlic powder
½ teaspoon salt
1 leaf fresh herb (basil,
   bay, oregano, or mint)
¼ cup heavy cream,
   optional
½ cup grated Parmesan
   cheese

1. Cook squash in stock until tender. Pour off liquid and reserve.
2. Purée squash in a blender or food processor. Pour into saucepan.
3. Stir in stock, onion, and seasonings.
4. Heat thoroughly, stirring to prevent scorching. (May be frozen after this step.)
5. Serve either hot or cold. Stir in cream at serving time, if desired.
6. Garnish with Parmesan cheese.

Laurie W. Rosenthal

lentil soup

Yield: 6 to 8 quarts

Comforting soup for a cold winter eve.

Approximately 4 pounds
  smoked ham hocks.
  Score skins deeply.
1 pound of lean ham,
  diced
1 pound lentils
3 cups finely chopped
  celery
3½ cups sliced carrots
4 cups finely chopped
  onions
1 28-ounce can tomatoes,
  undrained
½ cup packed brown
  sugar
¼ cup cider vinegar
1 teaspoon garlic powder
2 quarts water
1 teaspoon salt
freshly ground pepper to
  taste

1. Combine all ingredients in at
   least a 10 to 12 quart pot.
2. Bring to a boil. Reduce heat and
   simmer, covered, for about 3
   hours.
3. Remove hocks, cool, cut off fat
   and pick meat off the bones.
   Return the meat to the soup.
4. Serve hot.

Cindy Bartlett

new england fish chowder

Yield: 4 servings

The catch of the day will be the hit of the evening!

3 slices bacon
1 cup chopped onion
1 cup pared, diced
  potatoes
1 cup water
1½ teaspoons salt
⅛ teaspoon cayenne
  pepper
1 bay leaf
1 pound fish filets
  (haddock, flounder, sole
  or turbot, fresh or
  frozen and defrosted)
1 10-ounce package
  frozen, mixed
  vegetables
1½ cups milk
½ cup light cream

1. Cook bacon; remove and set
   aside.
2. In bacon grease, sauté onions
   until tender but not brown.
3. Add potatoes, water, salt.
   cayenne, and bay leaf. Simmer,
   covered, 10 minutes.
4. Add fish and vegetables. Cook
   10 more minutes.
5. Add milk and cream. Heat
   through, but *do not boil.*
6. Serve with bacon crumbled on
   top.

Sheila N. Prezzano

clam chowder

Yield: 5 quarts

Best when all ingredients are finely diced!

½ pound salt pork, diced
4 medium onions, diced
4 stalks celery, diced
2 green peppers, diced
12 medium potatoes,
  diced
6 cans chopped clams (or
  1 quart frozen chopped
  clams, or 6 large fresh
  chowder clams,
  chopped)
6 cups clam juice
2-4 bay leaves, crushed
1 teaspoon thyme
1 teaspoon celery salt
pepper to taste

Sauce
6 tablespoons butter
6 tablespoons flour
2 pints half and half

1. Fry salt pork until crisp.
   Remove pork and reserve.
2. Add diced onions, celery, and
   peppers to hot fat. Cook until
   vegetables are transparent.
3. Add potatoes, clams and clam
   juice.
4. Cook over medium heat until
   potatoes are tender.
5. Season with bay leaves, thyme,
   celery salt, and pepper.

Sauce
1. Melt butter and stir in flour.
2. Add half and half gradually,
   stirring until smooth.
3. Blend sauce into chowder. Cook
   5 minutes.
4. Let stand 3 or more hours to
   blend flavors.
5. Heat thoroughly before serving.
   Garnish with reserved salt pork.

"Sam" E. Lawless

icy cucumber soup

Yield: 4 servings

Serve on a hot, sultry night.

1 chicken bouillon cube
1 cup boiling water
2½ cups coarsely
  chopped, peeled
  cucumbers
¼ cup chopped chives
¼ cup coarsely chopped
  celery leaves
3 tablespoons chopped
  fresh parsley
1 teaspoon salt
2 tablespoons flour
3 tablespoons butter,
  softened
1 cup light cream

Must do ahead.

1. Dissolve bouillon in water.
2. Place 2 cups of the cucumbers,
   chives, celery, parsley, and salt
   in a blender. Add bouillon and
   blend 20 seconds.
3. Mix flour and butter in top of
   double boiler.
4. Add cucumber mixture to
   double boiler. Heat thoroughly.
5. Remove mixture from heat. Stir
   in light cream and remaining ½
   cup cucumbers.
6. Chill well before serving.

Peggi M. Godwin

brunswick stew

Yield: 6 servings

This is a thick soup. A filling Sunday night meal.

1 2-pound chicken
3 cups water
1½ teaspoons salt
4 medium potatoes
2 onions, quartered
1 cup lima beans
1 cup corn
3 medium tomatoes,
    peeled (or 1 small can)
pinch of thyme
salt and pepper

1. Place chicken in saucepan with water and salt. Cover and simmer until tender.
2. Lift chicken from broth, set aside.
3. Add potatoes, onions, and lima beans to broth. Cover and boil gently 15 minutes.
4. Remove potatoes, mash, and return to kettle.
5. Add corn, tomatoes, and seasonings. Cover and simmer 10 minutes.
6. Remove chicken from bones, dice, return to stew, and heat thoroughly.

Hint: This can go into food processor, after cooking, to purée everything. Then put into a wide-mouth thermal container for trips.

Suzy M. Hengerer

adirondack corn chowder

Yield: 6 cups

Hits the spot after a day of skiing.

3 tablespoons chopped
    onion
½ cup chopped celery
2 tablespoons butter
1 cup pared, diced
    potatoes
2 cups water
½ teaspoon salt
½ teaspoon paprika
1 bay leaf
3 tablespoons flour
2 cups milk
1 10-ounce package
    frozen white corn in
    butter sauce
chopped parsley for
    garnish

1. In a large saucepan, sauté onion and celery in butter until transparent.
2. Add potatoes, water, and seasonings. Simmer until potatoes are tender, about 45 minutes.
3. In a separate pan, combine flour and ½ cup of the milk to make a paste. Bring paste to a boil and add to the chowder. Reduce heat.
4. Stir chowder until it thickens.
5. Heat remaining 1½ cups milk. Add corn and milk to chowder. *Do not let chowder boil.*
6. Garnish with chopped parsley at serving time.

Barbara L. Goldman

cream of macadamia nut soup

Yield: 8 servings

Rich, unusual soup makes a special first course.

2 carrots, chopped
1 leek, chopped
2 stalks celery, chopped
1 clove garlic, minced
1 cup butter
1 cup ground macadamia
   nuts
2 tablespoons flour
8 cups chicken broth
2 bay leaves
1 cup heavy cream
1 cup chopped
   macadamia nuts
salt and pepper to taste
fresh, minced parsley for
   garnish

1. In a dutch oven, sauté carrots, leek, celery, and garlic in ½ cup of the butter.
2. Add *ground* nuts and cook until the vegetables are tender.
3. Add flour and cook, stirring constantly, for 2 minutes.
4. Add broth and bay leaves. Stir, and bring mixture to a boil. Simmer broth for 1 hour.
5. Strain the soup through a colander lined with cheesecloth into a saucepan.
6. Add cream to the strained broth. Cut the remaining ½ cup butter into pieces and add to broth.
7. Add the *chopped* nuts, reserving some for garnish. Season with salt and pepper.
8. Heat soup thoroughly, but *do* not boil.
9. Garnish soup with reserved nuts and parsley.

Hint: You might want to have more than the required 2 cups of macadamia nuts on hand. It's impossible to keep from nibbling.

Caroll J. Meyers

carrot-leek soup

A delicate, summer garden soup.

Crème Fraîche
1 cup heavy cream
1 tablespoon buttermilk
   (or ½ cup sour cream)

Soup
6 carrots, chopped
2 onions, chopped
4 leeks, chopped
5 cups chicken broth
½ cup chopped parsley

Crème Fraîche
1. Blend heavy cream and
   buttermilk (or sour cream).
2. Let stand at room temperature
   for 24 hours.

Soup
1. Cook carrots, onions, and leeks
   in broth until tender.
2. Add parsley. Whirl in a blender
   or food processor until smooth.
3. Return to saucepan and heat
   through.
4. Blend in 3 tablespoons crème
   fraîche at serving time and
   serve soup warm.

Hint: Crème Fraîche keeps well for 1 to 2 weeks. Use it as you would sour cream or add sugar and serve with berries or poached fruit.

Must do part ahead

Patricia C. Norris

spinach soup

A light soup with a unique tart flavor.

1 large carrot, sliced
1 stalk celery, sliced
8 cups chicken stock
1 bag fresh spinach,
   washed and torn into
   small pieces.
3 tablespoons butter
3 tablespoons flour
3 egg yolks
juice of 1 lemon (3
   tablespoons)
2 tablespoons parsley,
   minced
1 tablespoon dill weed
salt and pepper

1. In large pot, cook carrot and
   celery in stock until tender.
2. Add spinach and simmer 15
   minutes.
3. Melt butter in a small saucepan
   and stir in flour.
4. Blend in 1 cup of the stock and
   stir until smooth.
5. Pour thickened stock back into
   pot. Simmer 15 minutes.
6. Beat egg yolks and lemon juice
   together. Add ½ cup soup and
   blend well.
7. Return egg mixture to
   simmering soup, blending
   thoroughly.
8. Bring just to boiling. Add
   parsley and dill.
9. Season with salt and pepper to
   taste.

Linda L. Clark

cream of broccoli soup   Yield: 6 to 8 servings

Good cold in summer, hot in winter.

1½ pounds broccoli
1 quart chicken stock or
  broth
¼ pound margarine
½ medium onion, chopped
1 bay leaf
¾ teaspoon salt
¾ teaspoon white pepper
¼ teaspoon onion salt
¼ teaspoon garlic salt
pinch of basil, sage and
  thyme
dash of Tabasco
2 cups milk
½ cup heavy cream
1 cup buttermilk
7 tablespoons flour
3 tablespoons sour cream
¼ pound melted butter

1. Chop broccoli in a food
   processor or by hand.
2. In a large pot, bring stock to a
   boil. Add broccoli and simmer
   until almost done.
3. Sauté onions in 2 tablespoons of
   the margarine. Add onions and
   seasonings to stock. Simmer
   until vegetables are tender.
4. Warm milk, cream, and
   buttermilk.
5. Melt remaining 6 tablespoons of
   margarine, in a large saucepan,
   over low heat. Add flour and
   whisk constantly for 1 to 2
   minutes. Add warmed liquids
   and stir until mixture is
   thickened.
6. Gradually add thickened liquids
   to stock and stir. Soup should
   be very hot, but not boiling.
   Remove bay leaf.
7. Turn off heat and stir in sour
   cream and butter. Serve or
   refrigerate overnight and serve
   cold.

Suzy M. Hengerer

turkey chowder

Yield: 4 servings

An easy answer for what to do with Thanksgiving leftovers.

2 tablespoons butter or
  margarine
1 teaspoon chopped
  onion
1 medium potato, peeled
  and cubed
½ cup diced celery
1 cup cream-style corn
1 cup hot turkey stock
1 cup cooked turkey, cut
  into pieces
¼ teaspoon salt
dash pepper
⅛ teaspoon paprika
⅛ teaspoon ginger
½ cup hot milk
1 cup hot half and half
2 teaspoons chopped
  parsley

1. Sauté onion in butter until tender, but not brown.
2. Add potato, celery, corn, stock, and turkey.
3. Cover and simmer 20 minutes, until potatoes and celery are tender.
4. Add salt, pepper, paprika, and ginger.
5. Add hot milk and half and half. Blend and heat thoroughly.
6. Garnish each serving with parsley.

Hint: This recipe doubles easily for larger families.

Ginny Y. Gray

spicy french onion soup

Yield: 4 servings

A nice change from traditional onion soup.

4 tablespoons salad oil
4 tablespoons butter
4 medium onions, sliced
1½ teaspoons salt
1 teaspoon thyme
1 teaspoon oregano
2 bay leaves
1 teaspoon accent
  (optional)
1 teaspoon black pepper
2 tablespoons flour
4 cups consomme
2 tablespoons grated
  Parmesan cheese
French bread, cut into
  1-inch slices and
  toasted
Mozzarella cheese, grated
Parmesan cheese, grated

1. Heat oil and butter in a large pan until mixture begins to smoke.
2. Add sliced onions, seasonings, and flour. Cook until brown.
3. Add consomme and the 2 tablespoons Parmesan cheese. Simmer at least 10 minutes.
4. To serve, ladle into individual casseroles. Top with French bread, turning to coat with soup. Sprinkle with grated Mozzarella and Parmesan.
5. Bake until golden.

Temperature: 375°

Linda Wells Davey

cucumber, tomato, and avocado soup

Yield: 8 servings

Good either hot or cold.

4 tablespoons butter
1 cup chopped onion
4 tablespoons flour
4 cups peeled, cubed
    fresh tomatoes
4 cups peeled, cubed
    cucumbers
salt and freshly ground
    pepper to taste
4 cups chicken broth
1 ripe avocado, finely
    cubed
1 cup heavy cream

1. Sauté onion in butter until soft.
2. Sprinkle with flour and cook over low heat for 1 minute, whisking constantly.
3. Add tomatoes, cucumbers, salt, and pepper, and blend well.
4. Add broth and whisk until soup comes to a boil. Simmer uncovered for 25 minutes.
5. Pour small quantities of soup into blender or food processor and mix until smooth. Strain into a bowl and chill thoroughly OR return to the stove and serve hot. Just before serving, add avocado cubes and heavy cream.
6. Serve *very* cold or piping hot, but do not boil.

Hint: Fresh tomatoes keep longer if stored with the stems down.

Harriet J. Toadvine

ripe olive soup

Yield: 6 to 8 servings

Even those who dislike ripe olives will never know, unless you tell.

3 cups chicken broth
1 cup pitted ripe olives
1 tablespoon grated onion
1 small clove garlic,
    crushed
2 eggs
2 cups light cream
⅓ cup sauterne wine
salt
Worcestershire sauce
lemon slices for garnish

1. Combine first four ingredients. Simmer for 15 minutes.
2. Beat eggs; add cream, and slowly combine with olive mixture. Bring almost to a boil, stirring constantly.
3. Cool slightly. Add wine, and season with salt and Worcestershire to taste.
4. Purée soup in blender. Chill thoroughly.
5. Serve in chilled mugs garnished with thin lemon slices.

Janet C. Rae

speedy gazpacho

Yield: 8 to 10 servings

Great for dieters and non-dieters alike!

32-ounce can tomato juice
1 cucumber, seeded and chopped
1 green pepper, seeded and chopped
3 stalks celery, chopped
1 teaspoon instant beef bouillon
¼ cup red wine vinegar
1 tablespoon Worcestershire
1 tablespoon chopped fresh parsley
½ teaspoon onion salt
¼ teaspoon white pepper
¼ teaspoon garlic powder

1. Whirl all ingredients in a blender or food processor. May need to do in two batches to avoid overflow.
2. Pour mixture into a large pitcher.
3. Refrigerate, or add 6 or 7 ice cubes, to hasten chilling.
4. Serve with a dollop of curried mayonnaise if desired.

Susan B. Finnegan

During the course of testing and tasting, we all noticed that the inevitable had happened: weight gain! To offset this unwelcome result, the entire steering committee became "Speedy Gazpacho" fanatics. This delicious cold soup is also dietetic and can be consumed in fairly large quantities without adding lots of calories to your daily intake. So, after a gourmandish evening, try this soup for quick slimming the next day.

grilled ham and avocado sandwich

Yield: 1 sandwich

Great for a quick dinner or lunch with a friend.

ham slices
Swiss cheese
Russian dressing
avocado
rye bread
butter

1. For each sandwich, spread Russian dressing on both slices of bread.
2. Place ham on one slice, slices of avocado and Swiss cheese on the other.
3. Place open-faced sandwiches on buttered griddle. Cover, and cook slowly until cheese melts. Be careful not to burn.
4. Put both slices together. Serve.

Susan G. Rhoda

glen haven special

Yield: 1 sandwich

What a fun way to eat bacon and eggs!

2 slices uncooked bacon, cut in half
1 egg
sharp cheese, shredded
1 slice Spanish onion
1 slice toast or a toasted English muffin
salt and pepper

1. Cook bacon until almost crisp. Drain off fat.
2. Break egg over bacon slices; allow to cook slowly.
3. When egg is set, scatter cheese over top and allow to melt.
4. Top with onion slice. Serve on toast or an English muffin. Salt and pepper to taste.

Hint: For a delightful variation, serve sandwich topped with an additional slice of toast and warm stewed tomatoes.

Elizabeth G. Paddock

crabburgers

Yield: 4 to 6 servings

Good served with chips and relish sticks.

1 6-ounce can crab meat, drained and cleaned
½ cup diced celery
2 tablespoons minced onion
½ cup shredded sharp Cheddar cheese
½ cup mayonnaise
3 English muffins, split and toasted

1. Mix first 5 ingredients together.
2. Spread on English muffins or our Sour Dough Muffins (see index).
3. Broil until bubbly and lightly browned, 1 to 2 minutes.

Hint: Tuna may be easily substituted for the crab.

Arlene A. Wright

63

sausage and peppers sandwich

Yield: 4 to 6 servings

Great to have ready for those hungry teenagers!

8 to 10 Italian sausage
  links
1 clove garlic
2 tablespoons oil
5 or 6 fresh green
  peppers, seeded and
  sliced
2 or 3 cooking onions,
  sliced
1 15-ounce can whole
  tomatoes, crushed
salt
2 tablespoons oregano
1 loaf Italian bread

1. Slice sausage into 1-inch pieces.
2. Cook with garlic in oil, over medium heat, until brown. Drain sausage. Remove garlic clove.
3. Place sausage, peppers, onions, and tomatoes in a 9 x 13-inch baking dish. Salt to taste. Mix well.
4. Sprinkle with oregano. Bake, uncovered, until brown.
5. Serve on split Italian bread sections.

Temperature: 350°
Time: 1½ to 2 hours

Hint: Serve in a chafing dish as an hors d'oeuvre.

Karen Pellett

hot ham and asparagus sandwich

Yield: 3 servings

An intimate luncheon idea.

3 slices bread
3 slices boiled ham,
  halved
1 10-ounce package
  frozen asparagus,
  cooked and drained

1. Toast, butter, and halve bread slices diagonally.
2. Place one piece of ham on each piece of toast.
3. Next, place a layer of asparagus over the ham.
4. Pour on hot cheese sauce, and serve.

Cheese Sauce
2 tablespoons butter
1 tablespoon flour
⅛ teaspoon salt
⅛ teaspoon pepper
1 cup milk
1 cup shredded American
  cheese

Cheese Sauce
1. Melt butter over low heat.
2. Slowly stir in flour, salt, and pepper.
3. When bubbly, stir in milk, and heat gradually.
4. Add cheese, and stir until it melts.

Vicki Weiskaupt

64

mexicali rolls

Yield: 4 to 6 sandwiches

A spicy, South of the Border sandwich.

2 to 3 French-style rolls
1 pound sharp Cheddar
  cheese, grated
2 4-ounce cans green
  chilies
1 15-ounce can ripe
  olives, chopped
2 small onions, chopped
1 clove garlic, crushed
1 6-ounce can tomato
  paste
¾ cup salad oil

1. Halve rolls lengthwise. Use fork
   or fingers to carefully remove
   soft centers, leaving shells
   about ¼-inch thick.
2. Combine all other ingredients
   and stuff into the bread shells.
   Wrap each roll individually in
   foil.
3. Bake until heated through.

Temperature: 350°
Time: 30 to 45 minutes

Linnea O. Donahower

hot sea-wiches

Yield: 4 servings

Temptingly out of the ordinary.

1 6½-ounce can tuna,
  drained
⅓ cup mayonnaise
¼ cup chopped green
  onion
2 teaspoons Dijon
  mustard
½ teaspoon garlic salt
1 3-ounce package cream
  cheese, softened
4 slices pumpernickel
  bread
1 cup sliced fresh
  mushrooms
4 slices tomato
1 cup shredded Swiss
  cheese

1. Combine first five ingredients;
   set aside.
2. For each sandwich: spread
   cream cheese on the bread,
   follow with a layer of
   mushrooms, tuna mixture,
   tomato, and cheese.
3. Broil sandwiches until they are
   hot and bubbly.

Kathryn P. Weider

sandwiches by thomas

Yield: 8 to 10 servings

Make a triple batch and freeze for late-night snackers.

½ cup mayonnaise
⅓ cup tomato paste
8 to 10 English muffins or
  hamburger rolls, split
2 cups diced cooked ham
½ pound Cheddar cheese,
  diced
½ cup sliced stuffed olives

1. Blend mayonnaise and tomato paste.
2. Spread mixture on bottom half of muffins.
3. Sprinkle with ham, cheese, and olives.
4. Top with other half of muffin. Wrap with foil.
5. Bake, or freeze and bake later.

Temperature: 350°
Time: 15 minutes, 30 minutes if frozen

Susan T. Nystrom

monte cristo sandwiches

Yield: 4 servings

Supper in a sandwich.

2 eggs
½ cup milk
¼ teaspoon salt
8 slices stale white bread
4 slices chicken or turkey
4 slices ham
4 slices Swiss cheese
1 tablespoon vegetable oil
2 tablespoons butter

1. Beat eggs, milk, and salt together.
2. Dip bread in egg mixture, soaking thoroughly.
3. Make sandwiches, using soaked bread. Fill each with poultry, ham, and cheese, trimmed to fit.
4. Melt butter and oil in skillet. Brown sandwiches on both sides over low heat.
5. Cut diagonally. Serve hot.

Priscilla L. Minster

breads

breads

cheese bubble loaf

Yield: 2 loaves

Serve with soup and a salad for a satisfying meal.

¾ cup milk
¾ cup water
4 tablespoons margarine
¼ cup sugar
2¼ teaspoons salt
1 package active dry
  yeast
approximately 4½ cups,
  flour
½ pound Cheddar cheese,
  grated (2 cups)
¼ cup melted butter

1. Heat milk, water, margarine, sugar, and salt until lukewarm.
2. Add heated liquids to yeast and 1 cup of the flour. Mix at medium speed for 2 minutes.
3. Add another cup of flour and mix for two minutes more.
4. Add enough flour so that dough can be kneaded. Turn out on floured board; knead for 8 to 10 minutes.
5. Add flour when necessary. Finished product should be smooth and elastic.
6. Place dough in greased bowl, turn to grease top.
7. Cover and let rise until double in bulk, about 1 hour.
8. Divide dough in half; cut each half into twenty-four small pieces.
9. Roll pieces into balls. In each of two well-greased bread pans, place twelve balls. (These will not fill bottom of pan.)
10. Brush layer lightly with melted butter.
11. Add ½ cup of grated cheese to each pan, sprinkling evenly.
12. Arrange a second layer of balls on top in each pan.
13. Brush each loaf with melted butter. Sprinkle each with ½ cup of remaining cheese.
14. Cover, and let rise in warm place for one hour or until slightly higher than edge of pan.
15. Bake in middle of oven.

Temperature: 375°
Time: 30 to 40 minutes

Nancy F. Reale

versatile sausage bread

Yield: 2 large or 4 small loaves

Freezes beautifully. Easy to wrap and transport to a party.

2 1-pound loaves unbaked
  bread or pizza dough,
  fresh or frozen
1½ pounds hot Italian
  sausage
8 ounces grated
  Mozzarella cheese
1 tablespoon fresh parsley
4 eggs
8 ounces grated Romano
  cheese
salt, pepper to taste

1. Defrost frozen bread dough, and leave out at room temperature for at least 3 to 4 hours to rise.
2. Take sausage out of casings and cook well, but *do not brown.* Drain off excess grease.
3. Add Mozzarella to sausage. Add parsley and mix well.
4. Set aside 1 egg yolk. Beat remaining eggs in separate bowl. Add Romano cheese, salt, and pepper. Blend in sausage mixture.
5. Cut each loaf of bread dough in half and roll out in long narrow strips.
6. Spread ¼ of sausage mixture down the center of each strip. Roll up, jelly-roll fashion. Seal with egg yolk. Repeat with other dough strips.
7. Brush loaves with egg yolk. Let rise until double in bulk. Bake on a cookie sheet until golden brown.
8. Slice loaves to appropriate pieces for serving. (May freeze at this point.)

Temperature: 350°
Time: 30 to 45 minutes

Susan L. Carpenter

fruited pumpkin bread

Yield: 2 loaves

Nutritious and a good snack for children.

¾ cup butter or
  margarine
1¼ cups sugar
3 eggs
¾ cup canned pumpkin
¾ cup mashed ripe
  banana
3 cups all-purpose flour,
  unsifted

1. In large bowl, beat butter and sugar together until creamy.
2. Add eggs; beat well.
3. Stir in pumpkin and banana.
4. Stir flour with soda, salt, and spices. Mix into the creamed mixture just until well blended.
5. Stir in nuts.

fruited pumpkin bread   *continued*

1½ teaspoons baking
 soda
1 teaspoon salt
1 teaspoon nutmeg
1 teaspoon cinnamon
½ to 1 cup chopped
 walnuts or pecans

6. Grease and flour two 9 x 5 x 3-
 inch loaf pans.
7. Spoon batter into pans, filling
 about ⅔ full. Bake.
8. Cool bread in pans for 5
 minutes, then turn out onto
 rack to cool completely.

Temperature: 350°
Time: 50 to 60 minutes

Mary W. Schwertz

cheese and wheat beer bread

Yield: 2 loaves

Excellent served warm, at room temperature, and toasted with butter.

12 ounces beer
⅔ cup water
½ cup oil
1½ cup whole wheat flour
4½ cups white flour
½ cup sugar
½ cup wheat germ
2 teaspoons salt
2 packages active dry
 yeast
1 egg
8 ounces Cheddar cheese,
 shredded (2 cups)

1. In a saucepan, heat beer, water,
 and oil until very warm (120° to
 130°).
2. In a large bowl, combine warm
 liquid with whole wheat flour, 1
 cup of the white flour, sugar,
 wheat germ, salt, yeast, and egg.
 Beat 2 minutes at medium
 speed.
3. By hand, stir in remaining flour.
4. Knead dough until smooth and
 elastic, about 5 minutes.
5. Place in greased bowl. Cover.
 Let rise in warm place until
 doubled in bulk (1 to 1½ hours).
6. Punch down dough and divide in
 half.
7. On a well-floured surface, work
 1 cup cheese into each half until
 evenly distributed.
8. Place dough in two 9 x 5-inch
 loaf pans which have been lined
 with foil and greased.
9. Let dough rise until doubled in
 bulk.
10. Bake.

Temperature: 350°
Time: 40 to 50 minutes

Hint: For stronger taste, try sharp Cheddar.

Peggi M. Godwin

traditional bread

Marvelous as a plain loaf, made into rolls, or shaped and decorated for fancier breads.

2 packages active dry
  yeast
2¼ cups warm water
¼ cup honey
1 tablespoon salt
2 tablespoons margarine
7 cups flour
soft butter or margarine

1. Dissolve yeast in ½ cup of the warm water.
2. Stir in remaining warm water, honey, salt, margarine, and 3½ cups of the flour. Beat until smooth.
3. Add more flour, ½ cup at a time, mixing and squeezing dough vigorously with hands. (Dough will be sticky.)
4. Continue adding flour and mixing until dough leaves the side of bowl almost clean. The dough will be rough, sticky, and lumpy.
5. Turn dough onto lightly-floured board. Knead about 10 minutes. Continue kneading until dough is elastic and blisters appear beneath the surface.
6. Place in greased bowl; turn greased side up. Cover. Let rise in warm place until double, about one hour. (Test by pressing 2 fingers into dough. It is ready if impression remains.)
7. Punch down dough. Divide in half.
8. Roll each half into rectangle 18 x 9 inches. Roll up beginning at short side. With side of hand, press each end to seal. Fold ends under loaf.
9. Press seam side down in greased loaf pans, 9 x 5 x 3. Brush loaves lightly with butter. Let rise until double, about one hour.
10. Preheat oven.
11. Place loaves on lower rack so that tops of pans are in center of oven. Bake until deep golden brown and loaves sound hollow when tapped. (If bread browns too quickly, cover loosely with aluminum foil.)

traditional bread   continued

12. Remove from pans. Cool on
    wire rack.

Temperature: 425°
Time: 20 to 25 minutes

Variation: "Hot Cross Bread"
While adding water and honey to
    Traditional Bread, also add ½
    cup chopped candied fruits and
    peels, 1 cup seedless raisins, 1
    teaspoon cinnamon, and ¼
    teaspoon nutmeg. After baking
    and cooling, frost with icing. To
    make icing, add enough milk or
    cream to 2 cups sifted
    confectioners sugar to make it
    spreadable. Add 1 teaspoon
    vanilla and a dash of salt. Mix
    well.

For Rolls:
Roll dough into rectangle as for
    bread. Cut into 16 rectangles.
    Brush butter on half of each
    tiny rectangle and fold over.
    Place folded rolls in greased 9 x
    9 x 2-inch pan. Brush butter on
    tops. Let rise until double. Bake
    15 minutes at 425°

**Hint: To help bread rise, place dough in barely warm oven with
pan of very hot water.**

Priscilla L. Minster

apple-date spread   Yield: 3 to 4 cups

This is a taste so great it cannot be described in words!

1 8-ounce package of
   cream cheese
⅓ cup milk
½ cup heavy cream
1 cup finely chopped tart
   apples
1½ cups finely chopped
   walnuts or pecans
¾ cup finely chopped
   dates

1. Soften cream cheese with milk
   and cream.
2. Stir in remaining ingredients.
3. Good served on crackers or nut
   bread.

Margaret M. Richardson

fondue bread

Yield: 12 servings

Beautiful, different, and a meal in itself.

3 teaspoons sugar
2 teaspoons salt
2 packages active dry
  yeast
4¼ cups all-purpose flour
½ cup butter
1 cup milk
2 eggs
2 pounds Muenster
  cheese, shredded
3 tablespoons sliced
  blanched almonds

1. Combine sugar, salt, yeast, and 1 cup of the flour in a bowl.
2. Over low heat, heat butter and milk until warm. Butter does not have to melt completely.
3. Using mixer, gradually beat liquid into dry ingredients for 3 minutes.
4. Beat in 1 cup of the flour and continue beating 2 minutes.
5. With spoon, stir in remaining flour to make a soft dough.
6. Turn dough onto lightly-floured surface; knead until smooth and elastic, about 10 minutes. Add a little more flour only if necessary.
7. Shape dough into a ball. Cover with bowl and let rest for 15 to 30 minutes.
8. Reserve 1 egg white. Combine remaining eggs with cheese. Set aside.
9. Grease a 9-inch round cake pan.
10. On lightly-floured surface, use a rolling pin to make dough into a rectangle about 24 x 6-inches. Lengthwise along center of dough, shape cheese mixture into a cylinder.
11. Fold sides of dough over filling, overlapping 1 inch. Pinch seam to seal and place roll with seam-side down in a pan, making a ring. Overlap ends and pinch.
12. Cover with towel and let rest 10 minutes in a warm place.
13. Brush loaf with remaining egg white. Garnish with almonds. Bake and serve, or reheat later. (Cover with foil to reheat.)

Temperature: 350°
Time: 1 hour

Kristin W. Williams

scotch oat bread

Yield: 1 loaf

Freeze this (pre-sliced) and pull out what is needed for breakfast toast.

1 cup Scotch oats
⅓ cup honey
1 tablespoon shortening
1 teaspoon salt
2 cups boiling water
1 cup whole wheat flour
3 to 4 cups white flour
1 package active dry
   yeast
¼ cup warm water

1. Combine Scotch oats, honey, shortening, and salt.
2. Pour the boiling water over this mixture.
3. Stir in the whole wheat flour and 1 cup of the white flour. Let cool.
4. While cooling, dissolve yeast in ¼ cup warm water and let stand 10 minutes.
5. Add yeast to cooled oat mixture. Work in enough of the remaining flour to be able to handle dough.
6. Turn onto floured surface; knead until elastic, about 10 minutes.
7. Place dough in bowl, cover loosely with a dish towel. Let rise until doubled in bulk. Punch down, and shape into loaf.
8. Place in a greased 9 x 5-inch loaf pan. Cover, and let rise until double in bulk.
9. Bake. Remove from pan; cool on wire rack.
10. Cover top with butter for a soft crust or leave plain for a hard crust.

Temperature: 375°
Time: 40 minutes

Patricia A. Hainen

cottage cheese dill bread

Yield: 2 loaves

Great with soups on a cold winter's day.

2 packages active dry yeast
½ cup warm water (105°–115°)
2 teaspoons sugar
2 cups creamed cottage cheese
3 tablespoons minced onion
2 tablespoons dill weed
1 teaspoon baking powder
2 teaspoons salt
2 tablespoons sugar
2 eggs
4½ cups flour

1. Sprinkle yeast on warm water. Stir until well blended.
2. Add 2 teaspoons sugar, and set aside.
3. Combine cottage cheese, onion, dill, baking powder, salt, remaining sugar, and eggs. Mix well.
4. Add yeast mixture, and mix again.
5. Add enough flour to make a stiff dough.
6. Knead on a lightly-floured surface until smooth and elastic (about 8 to 10 minutes), adding more flour if needed.
7. Place dough in a greased bowl, turning to grease all sides of dough.
8. Cover. Let rise in a warm place (80 to 85°) until double in size, about 1 to 1½ hours.
9. Punch down. Knead again on floured surface for 1 minute. Divide into 2 portions.
10. Shape each into a loaf, and place in 2 well-greased 8 x 5-inch loaf pans. Let rise until double in bulk.
11. Bake, and when loaves sound hollow, remove from oven.
12. Remove loaves from pans, and cool on rack.

Temperature: 350°
Time: 30 minutes

Nicki R. Doolittle

herb bread

Yield: 1 loaf

Great for turkey sandwiches.

1 cup lukewarm milk
2 tablespoons sugar
1 cake yeast
1½ teaspoons salt
1 egg
2 tablespoons shortening
½ teaspoon nutmeg
1 teaspoon crumbled sage
2 teaspoons caraway
   seeds
3 to 3¾ cups flour

1. Combine milk, sugar, yeast, salt, egg, and shortening.
2. Add herbs and flour.
3. Knead until smooth and elastic, about 5 to 7 minutes.
4. Place in a greased bowl, cover with a cloth. Set bowl in a warm, draft-free place and let dough rise until double, approximately 1 hour.
5. Punch down the dough. Shape into a loaf.
6. Place it in a greased 9 x 5-inch loaf pan. Let it rise 50 to 60 minutes or until it doubles in bulk.
7. Bake and serve, or freeze.

Temperature: 375°
Time: 45 to 50 minutes

Hint: Each packet of dry yeast equals ⅝ ounce of cake yeast.

Emily M. Henderson

wild winds herb butter

Yield: 1 pound

Served at Wild Winds Restaurant with homemade wheat bread.

1 pound butter, softened
1 tablespoon finely
   chopped onion
1 tablespoon freshly
   chopped parsley
1 clove garlic, pressed
1 tablespoon chopped
   fresh chives
1 tablespoon chopped
   fresh chervil, optional

1. Combine all ingredients.
2. Whip until well blended, light, and fluffy.

Hint: This is best prepared ahead to allow flavors to "marry."
Serve also on baked potatoes, fish, vegetables, or steak.

Eleanor Clapp
Wild Winds Farm

monkey bread

Yield: 1 loaf

Let your children make this recipe with you—it's such fun!

1½ yeast cakes or 2
  packages of active dry
  yeast
1 cup lukewarm milk
4 tablespoons sugar
½ teaspoon salt
½ cup butter
3½ cups flour,
  approximately
½ cup melted butter

1. Dissolve yeast in lukewarm milk. Stir in sugar, salt, and butter.
2. Add flour; beat well.
3. Knead about 7 minutes or until dough is soft and slightly sticky to the touch.
4. Place dough in a greased bowl. Turn over to grease other side. Cover, and let rise in a warm place (1½ hours) until double in bulk.
5. Flatten dough and roll out on lightly-floured board to ¼-inch thick.
6. Cut with kitchen shears in triangles about 2 inches in size.
7. Dip each piece in melted butter. Pile in bundt pan. Let rise until double in bulk.
8. Bake.
9. Invert on a plate. Let everyone pull out his own pieces. This bread is best served immediately.

Temperature: 400°
Time: 30 minutes

Nancy S. Milbury

croutons

Yield: 6 to 8 cups

Crunchy in salads or soups, or as a snack.

15 stale ends of bread
¼ pound butter
1 to 1½ teaspoons garlic
  powder
¼ cup grated Parmesan
  cheese

1. Cut bread into cubes.
2. Melt butter in a large frying pan. Add garlic powder, and stir.
3. Mix in the bread cubes. Brown 5 to 10 minutes, stirring frequently.
4. Remove from heat. Add cheese and toss well.
5. Spread croutons on a cookie sheet lined with paper towels or brown paper. Bake until crisp.

Temperature: 250°
Time: 1 hour, 30 minutes

76

Susie P. Larson

swedish kardemummakrans

Yield: 2 loaves

A spicy, holiday bread.

2½ cups milk
1 package active dry
  yeast
¼ cup warm water (115°)

¾ cup butter, melted and
  cooled
1 egg, beaten
½ teaspoon salt
1 cup sugar
1½ teaspoons ground
  cardamon
7 cups flour
red candied cherries and
  pecans for garnish

1. Scald milk, then cool.
2. Dissolve yeast in water; let
   stand 5 minutes.
3. Combine milk, yeast, butter, egg,
   salt, sugar, and cardamon. Stir
   in flour.
4. Turn dough onto floured board.
   Add more flour if needed, but
   try to keep dough as sticky as
   possible for the best texture.
5. Knead dough 10 to 15 minutes.
6. Place in greased bowl, turn over,
   and cover with plastic wrap. Let
   rise 1½ to 2 hours in a warm
   place. (In an oven with pan of
   hot water on bottom.)
7. Punch down when dough has
   doubled in bulk.
8. Divide into six equal portions.
   Form 6 24-inch ropes. Pinch 3
   together at top, and braid. Form
   braid into a ring, pinching ends
   together. Make second braid,
   repeating this procedure.
9. Cover. Let rise 40 minutes.
10. Bake.

Glaze
1⅓ cup confectioners
  sugar
¼ cup lemon juice
1 teaspoon vanilla

Glaze
1. Mix sugar, lemon juice, and
   vanilla. Drizzle over cooled
   bread.
2. Decorate with red cherry halves
   and pecans.

Temperature: 350°
Time: 35 to 40 minutes

Sue B. Moscato

cheddar pepper bread

Yield: 2 loaves

This is a delicious no-kneading, no-shaping, one-rise yeast bread.

1 package active dry
  yeast
¼ cup warm water
2⅓ cups flour
2 tablespooons sugar
1 teaspoon salt
¼ teaspoon baking soda
1 cup sour cream
1 egg
1 cup grated sharp
  Cheddar cheese
¾ teaspoon freshly
  ground black pepper

1. In large mixing bowl, dissolve yeast in warm water (110°).
2. Add 1⅓ cups of the flour, sugar, salt, soda, sour cream, and egg.
3. Blend ½ minute on low speed, scraping bowl frequently.
4. Beat 2 minutes on high speed.
5. Stir in remaining flour, cheese, and pepper. Mix thoroughly.
6. Divide batter between two well-greased 1-pound coffee cans.
7. Let rise approximately one hour, or until double in bulk.
8. Bake.
9. Remove immediately from cans and cool slightly before slicing.

Temperature: 350°
Time: 40 minutes

Hint: If a bread or cake browns too quickly before it is done, reduce heat, and place a pan of warm water on the rack above it.

Nicole R. Doolittle

fat pretzels

Yield: 2 dozen

These soft pretzels are fun to make.

1 package active dry
  yeast
1½ cups warm water
1 teaspoon salt
1 tablespoon sugar
4 cups flour
1 large egg, beaten
coarse salt

1. Dissolve yeast in warm water.
2. Add salt and sugar.
3. Blend in the flour. Knead dough until smooth.
4. Cut into small pieces and roll into ropes. Twist ropes into pretzel shapes and place on foil-lined cookie sheets.
5. Brush with egg and sprinkle with salt.
6. Bake until brown.

Temperature: 425°
Time: 12 to 15 minutes

Hint: Can also be made into thin 3- to 4-inch sticks to be used with dips or as breadsticks.

Linnea O. Donahower

 **roman bread**　　　　　　　　　　　Yield: 2 loaves

Excellent texture, taste, and good for you.

2 packages active dry
　　yeast
⅓ cup plus ½ teaspoon
　　sugar
3 cups warm water
1 teaspoon salt
¼ cup butter, softened
¼ cup instant dry milk
2½ cups whole wheat
　　flour
1½ cups rye flour
3 to 4 cups unbleached
　　white flour

1. Dissolve yeast and ½ teaspoon
　 sugar in ½ cup of the warm
　 water.
2. In large bowl, combine yeast
　 mixture, 2½ cups of the warm
　 water, salt, ⅓ cup sugar, butter,
　 dry milk, whole wheat flour, rye
　 flour, white flour.
3. Mix well, and knead in
　 additional white flour until
　 dough is smooth and elastic (10
　 to 15 minutes).
4. Place in buttered bowl; let rise
　 until doubled in bulk.
5. Punch down. Divide in half.
　 Shape into loaves and place in 2
　 greased 9 x 5-inch loaf pans.
6. Let rise until doubled in bulk.
7. Place in preheated 425° oven.
　 Lower heat immediately to 350°
　 and bake.
8. Remove from pans to cool.

**Temperature: 425° — lower to
　　　　　　　　 350°
　　　　　　 Time: 45 to 60
　　　　　　 minutes**

Maryann Fitzpatrick

iroquois raisin bread　　Yield: 5 small loaves

An old, old, family recipe.

1⅓ cups seedless raisins
1½ cups water
3 tablespoons butter
1 cup sugar
1 egg
2½ cups flour
1 teaspoon baking soda
¼ teaspoon salt
1 teaspoon vanilla

1. Cook raisins in boiling water for
　 5 minutes. Set aside to cool.
2. Cream butter with sugar. Add
　 the egg, and blend thoroughly.
3. Sift flour, soda, salt. Add to
　 creamed mixture along with
　 vanilla, raisins, and their liquid.
4. Pour mixture into five greased
　 10½-ounce soup cans until ⅔
　 full.
5. Bake. Cool 10 minutes before
　 removing from cans. Finish
　 cooling on wire rack.

**Temperature: 350°
Time: 50 to 60 minutes**

Marge H. Nelson

grandma ada's orange rolls

Yield: 24 rolls

How the conversation and the flour would fly when Gram baked!

Dough

1 package active dry yeast
¼ cup very warm water (115°)
1 cup sugar
1 teaspoon salt
2 eggs
½ cup sour cream
½ cup melted butter
3¼ cups flour
3 tablespoons grated orange rind

Dough

1. Dissolve yeast in warm water.
2. Using electric mixer, add ¼ cup of the sugar, salt, eggs, sour cream, and 6 tablespoons of the melted butter to the yeast mixture.
3. Gradually add 1½ cups of the flour. Beat until smooth.
4. Knead in rest of flour.
5. Rise until doubled, 2 to 3 hours.
6. Knead 1 minute. Divide dough in two pieces.
7. Roll ½ of dough into a 12-inch in diameter circle.
8. Combine the remaining ¾ cup of sugar and orange rind.
9. Brush dough with 1 tablespoon of the remaining melted butter and sprinkle with ½ of the sugar mixture.
10. Cut 12 equal pie-shaped pieces. Roll each piece from wide end to point, like a crescent roll.
11. Repeat the entire procedure with other half of dough.
12. Place point-side down in rows in a large rectangular pan.
13. Cover and let rise 1 hour. Bake until lightly browned.
14. Pour warm topping over immediately.

Topping

⅔ cup sugar
½ cup sour cream
2 tablespoons orange juice
½ cup butter

Topping

1. Combine topping ingredients and boil 4 minutes, stirring constantly.

Temperature: 350°
Time: 20 minutes

Linda W. Obourn

crescent rolls

These freeze beautifully.

1 package dry active
   yeast
1 cup plus 1 tablespoon
   warm water
¾ cup evaporated milk
1½ teaspoons salt
⅓ cup sugar
2 eggs
5 cups unsifted flour
¼ cup melted butter
1 cup chilled butter, cut
   into small pieces

1. Dissolve yeast in 1 cup water
   and allow to sit for 2 to 3
   minutes.
2. Mix milk, salt, sugar, 1 egg, and
   1 cup flour. Beat until smooth.
   Add yeast mixture, then melted
   butter.
3. To the remaining 4 cups of flour,
   cut in chilled butter until it is
   the size of small peas.
4. Pour yeast mixture from step 2
   over top of flour and butter; mix
   until flour is moistened.
5. Cover. Refrigerate from 1 to 4
   days.
6. Knead 6 times.
7. Divide into 4 equal parts,
   refrigerate parts not being used.
   One by one, roll and shape each
   part into a 17-inch circle. Cut
   into 8 pie-shaped wedges.
8. Roll each wedge, starting with
   wide outside edge and bend into
   a crescent. Place each on an
   ungreased baking sheet with
   point down. Cover, and let rise
   until double in size, about 1
   hour.
9. Brush with mixture of egg and
   water. Bake.

Must do ahead.

Temperature: 325°
Time: 20 to 30 minutes

Patricia A. Hainen

french toast— santa fe railroad

Yield: 4 servings

My husband loved it so much, he did the dishes!

4 ¾-inch thick slices dry
   bread from unsliced loaf
2 eggs, beaten
½ cup cream
pinch of salt
dash of nutmeg
cooking oil for browning
confectioners sugar

1. Trim crusts. Cut bread diagonally to form 8 triangles.
2. Beat eggs, cream, salt, and nutmeg together. Soak bread in egg mixture, two triangles at a time, for 10 seconds.
3. Sauté in oil in skillet until golden brown. Drain on paper towels.
4. Bake on cookie sheet 3 to 5 minutes or until puffed.
5. Sprinkle with confectioners sugar. Serve with maple syrup.

Temperature: 400°
Time: 3 to 5 minutes

Victoria P. Gilbert

date-nut bread

Yield: 1 large loaf or 2 small loaves

Slightly crunchy outside, moist inside.

1 cup boiling water
1 cup cut-up dates
1 tablespoon butter
1 egg
1 cup granulated sugar
1 teaspoon baking soda
½ cup walnuts, chopped
1½ cups flour
pinch of salt
1 teaspoon vanilla

1. Mix boiling water and dates. Whole dates and water can be put in food processor and chopped. Set aside to cool slightly.
2. In a separate bowl, beat butter, egg, and sugar.
3. Add soda to cooled water-date mixture. Combine both mixtures.
4. Gradually add nuts, flour, salt, and vanilla; mix, but *do not beat.*
5. Bake in large loaf pan lined with wax paper or greased brown paper. (When using 2 small loaf pans, bake 30 to 35 minutes.)

Temperature: 350°
Time: 1 hour

Hint: Cut up dates with buttered kitchen scissors.

Linda W. Davies

old-fashioned apple butter

Yield: 4 to 5 cups

A favorite from Pennsylvania Dutch Country.

4 pounds tart apples
2 cups cider
3 to 4 cups sugar
2 teaspoons cinnamon
1 teaspoon ground cloves
½ teaspoon ground
   allspice

1. Cut apples into quarters, but do not peel or seed them.
2. Combine apples with cider in an enameled pot. Bring to a boil, reduce heat to its lowest point, and cover the pot.
3. Simmer the apples, stirring occasionally, for about 25 minutes, or until soft.
4. Remove from heat, and with back of wooden spoon, mash apples through a sieve.
5. Measure pulp and put into a 6-quart pan. Add ⅓ cup sugar for every cup of pulp. Add cinnamon and spices.
6. Cook on low heat, stirring occasionally, until a tablespoon of the butter will stick to a saucer when turned upside down (about 4 hours).
7. Put into freezer containers. Freeze. Refrigerate after opening.

Must do ahead.

Linnea O. Donnahower

poppy seed bread

Yield: 10-inch Bundt

A delicious cake-like quick bread.

1 cup sugar
½ cup oil
2 eggs
1 teaspoon vanilla
1 cup evaporated milk
2 cups flour
1 teaspoon baking powder
¼ cup poppy seeds

1. Mix all ingredients together until smooth.
2. Pour mixture into a greased 10-inch Bundt or tube pan.
3. Bake, adjusting oven temperature after 15 minutes.

Temperature: 450°
Time: 15 minutes, then

Temperature: 350°
Time: 20 minutes

Nancy L. Brown

seneca griddle cakes

Yield: 12 to 16 medium pancakes

Serve with warm maple syrup and butter.

1 cup yellow stone ground
  cornmeal
1 cup flour
½ teaspoon salt
1 teaspoon baking powder
½ teaspoon baking soda
2 eggs, separated
2 tablespoons melted
  butter
2 cups buttermilk
bacon grease

1. Sift dry ingredients together.
2. Combine slightly beaten egg
   yolks, butter, and buttermilk.
   Blend together with dry
   ingredients.
3. Beat egg whites until stiff. Fold
   egg whites gently into batter so
   it remains fluffy.
4. Cook pancakes immediately, in
   bacon grease on hot griddle, to
   a rich brown color.

**Hint: Cornmeal requires a longer frying time than wheaten
cakes.**

Pamela W. Cheek

sourdough english muffins

Yield: 15 muffins

Delicious and fun to make.

1 package active dry
  yeast
2 tablespoons sugar
1 cup very warm milk
  (115°)
4 tablespoons butter
1 teaspoon salt
2 cups mild sour dough
  starter
4 cups unsifted flour
white corn meal

1. Dissolve yeast and sugar in
   milk.* Add butter; stir until
   melted. Add salt; mix well.
2. Stir in starter.
3. Add flour, one cup at a time,
   mixing thoroughly after each
   cup. Dough will be light and
   somewhat sticky.
4. Turn dough onto a floured
   board. Roll ½-inch thick. Cut
   out muffins with 3-inch round
   cutter.
5. Sprinkle a cookie sheet with
   corn meal. Turn each muffin in
   corn meal. Let rise 30 minutes
   on cookie sheet.
6. Place muffins in lightly greased
   electric skillet; cover, then set
   temperature to 300°. Bake on
   first side for 10 to 15 minutes or
   until browned. Turn. Bake 20 to
   25 minutes on second side.

7. Remove, and cool. Split, and
   toast. (Unused muffins can be
   frozen and toasted as needed.)

Temperature: slightly under 300°
Time: 30 to 40 minutes

Hint: *Use no metal with sourdough.

Susan P. Larson

strawberry bread
Yield: 2 loaves

Unique bread to make when strawberry season arrives.

3 cups mashed
   strawberries
3 cups flour
1 teaspoon baking soda
1 teaspoon cinnamon
2 cups sugar
1 teaspoon salt
1¼ cups oil
4 well-beaten eggs

1. Drain ½ cup strawberry juice
   from mashed strawberries and
   save for topping.
2. Mix all dry ingredients together.
3. Make a hole in center of
   mixture. Add strawberries and
   remaining juice, oil, and eggs.
4. Mix by hand until thoroughly
   combined.
5. Pour into 2 greased 9 x 5-inch
   loaf pans.
6. Bake. Cool thoroughly on a wire
   rack.

Topping
8 ounces cream cheese,
   softened

Topping
1. Mix together reserved
   strawberry juice and softened
   cream cheese.
2. Blend until smooth. Drizzle over
   top of bread.

Temperature: 350°
Time: 50 to 60 minutes

Nancy A. Koris

*The strawberry bread was inadvertently tested with the
topping ingredients within the bread itself. The submittor
was aghast when she found out about this. Her immediate
question was, "Didn't the bread look peculiar?". We told her
that it was a bit odd in texture and appearance, but the flavor
was terrific.*

pepperoni bread

Yield: 1 loaf

Hearty bread that's very easy to prepare.

1 loaf frozen bread dough
1 egg
1 teaspoon snipped
  parsley
1 teaspoon oregano
1 teaspoon salt
¼ teaspoon pepper
1 8- to 10-inch stick of
  pepperoni
1 cup grated Mozzarella
  cheese
1 cup cooked or canned
  mushrooms, drained
  (optional)
sesame seeds

1. Thaw loaf of frozen bread according to package directions.
2. Spread thawed bread dough into large rectangle on greased cookie sheet. (Cookie sheet should have rim on sides.)
3. Make an egg wash by mixing egg and seasonings. Spread half of egg wash on dough almost to edges.
4. Skin, and thinly slice the pepperoni. Layer slices, 3 or 4 to a row, down center third of bread.
5. Sprinkle with cheese and optional mushrooms.
6. Fold bread dough over filling one-third over then last third over. Flip dough over so seam side is underneath.
7. Spread loaf with remaining egg wash. Sprinkle with sesame seeds. Let rise until double in bulk.
8. Bake until golden brown.

Temperature: 375°
Time: 25 minutes

Katherine R. Wojick

apple flaps

Yield: 15 pancakes

You are in for a real treat with these pancakes!

1½ cups flour
2 tablespoons sugar
1 tablespoon baking
  powder
¼ teaspoon salt
⅛ teaspoon nutmeg
2 eggs, beaten
¾ cup milk
2 tablespoons butter,
  melted
1 cup applesauce

1. Mix first five ingredients together.
2. Combine the eggs, milk, butter, and applesauce and stir into the flour mixture just until moistened.
3. Cook on hot griddle as with any pancake.

Susan S. Yesawich

🍎 zucchini-nut bread

Yield: 2 loaves

The best you'll ever taste!

2 cups sifted flour
2 teaspoons baking soda
1 teaspoon salt
¼ teaspoon baking
   powder
3½ teaspoons cinnamon

3 eggs
1 cup vegetable oil
1½ cups sugar
2 cups grated zucchini
2 teaspoons vanilla
1 teaspoon lemon extract
1 cup raisins
1 cup chopped walnuts or
   sunflower seeds

1. Sift flour, baking soda, salt, baking powder, and cinnamon into a bowl.
2. Combine eggs, oil, sugar, zucchini, vanilla, and lemon extract in another bowl; beat thoroughly.
3. Stir flour mixture into egg mixture until smooth.
4. Add raisins and nuts or seeds. Stir to combine.
5. Pour entire mixture into greased, 9 x 5-inch loaf pans or muffin tins. (Fill muffin tins ⅔ full.)
6. Bake 40 minutes if loaves, 20 minutes if muffins. They are done if center springs back when they are lightly touched.

Temperature: 350°
Time: 40 minutes if loaves, 20 minutes if muffins

Hint: Uneven baking is caused by using old dark pans, too much dough in pans, crowding in the oven, or baking at too high a temperature.

Lucia H. Shaw

whole wheat apple bread

Yield: 2 loaves

Healthful and tasty—can even be used as cake.

1 cup oil
2 cups sugar
3 eggs, well beaten
3 cups whole wheat flour
1 teaspoon salt
1 teaspoon baking soda
2 cups chopped apples
1 cup pecans or black
   walnuts
2 teaspoons vanilla

1. Combine oil, sugar, and eggs. Set aside.
2. Combine flour, salt, and soda. Add dry ingredients to oil mixture. Mix well.
3. Add apples, nuts, and vanilla. Pour into 2 greased 9 x 5-inch bread pans. Bake.
4. Turn out of pans before cooling completely. (Can be iced with mixture of confectioners sugar and lemon juice.)

Temperature: 350°
Time: 1 hour and 30 minutes

Emily M. Henderson

apple bread

Yield: 1 loaf

Good as a coffee cake for teas or brunches.

Bread

½ cup margarine, softened
1 cup sugar
2 eggs, beaten
2 cups flour
½ teaspoon salt
1 teaspoon baking soda
2 tablespoons buttermilk or sour cream
1 teaspoon vanilla
2 cups peeled, diced apples

Bread

1. Cream margarine and sugar until light and fluffy. Add eggs, blending well.
2. Stir in flour and salt.
3. Dissolve baking soda in buttermilk; add to batter, mixing well.
4. Stir in vanilla and apples.
5. Spoon batter into a well-greased and floured 9 x 5-inch loaf pan.
6. Sprinkle with topping. Bake.
7. Cool slightly before removing from pan. Cool on wire rack.

Topping

2 tablespoons margarine, softened
2 tablespoons sugar
2 tablespoons flour
1 teaspoon cinnamon
2 tablespoons chopped walnuts

Topping

1. Cream margarine and sugar.
2. Add flour, cinnamon, and nuts. Mixture should resemble coarse crumbs.
3. Sprinkle on top of batter before baking.

Temperature: 325°
Time: 1 hour

Patricia A. Hainen

lime bread

Yield: 1 loaf

A very unusual bread with a good 'nip' to it.

6 tablespoons unsalted butter, softened
1 cup sugar
grated rind of 2 large limes (1½ tablespoons)
2 eggs
1½ cups flour
1½ teaspoons baking powder
¼ teaspoon salt
⅔ cup half and half
⅔ cup chopped walnuts

1. Cream butter and sugar.
2. Add lime rind and eggs and beat well.
3. Sift dry ingredients together. Add to butter mixture alternately with cream; begin and end with flour.
4. Fold in nuts.
5. Turn into greased 9 x 5-inch pan.
6. Bake.
7. Cool in pan on wire rack.

Temperature: 350°
Time: 45 to 55 minutes

Hint: Add juice of one-half lime for additional lime flavor.

Dorothy Lowe

cheese stuffed french bread

Yield: 8 to 10 servings

Good with a meal or as a lunch or snack.

1 large loaf crusty French
 bread
1 cup (¼ pound) freshly
 grated Swiss or
 Cheddar cheese
¼ cup chopped green
 onions, including tops
1 clove garlic, finely
 minced
3 tablespoons oil
1 tablespoon vinegar
¼ teaspoon dried oregano

1. Cut a lengthwise slice from top
 of the bread. Remove top; set
 aside. Press down on insides of
 loaf, forming a shallow pocket
 for filling.
2. Combine remaining ingredients.
 Fill pocket. Do not over-fill.
3. Replace top. Wrap in aluminum
 foil. Bake until well heated.
4. Cool slightly. Cut into slices.

Temperature: 350°
Time: 20 minutes

Lynn P. Natapow

"best-for-you" banana bread

Yield: 1 loaf

Moist and hearty, ideal for winter meals.

½ cup butter
1 cup honey
2 eggs
3 bananas
2 cups sifted stone
 ground whole wheat
 bread flour. After sifting,
 add the chaff (bran or
 wheat germ)
½ teaspoon salt
1¼ teaspoons baking
 soda

1. Mix butter, honey, and eggs in
 food processor or blender.
2. Blend in bananas.
3. Add flour, salt, and soda.
4. Bake in well-greased 9 x 5-inch
 loaf pan until center springs
 back when touched.

Temperature: 350°
Time: 1 hour

Hint: To prevent a hump in the center of a quick bread, cut
vertically down the center of batter when it starts to rise during
baking.

Joanne K. Gianniny

89

apple muffins with sauce

Yield: 12 to 14 muffins

Delicious, sweet, and nutty.

Muffins
1 tablespoon butter
1 cup brown sugar
1 egg
1 cup flour
⅛ teaspoon salt
2 tablespoons boiling
  water
1 teaspoon baking soda
1 teaspoon vanilla
1 cup peeled and diced
  tart apples
½ cup chopped walnuts
  or pecans

Sauce
1 cup brown sugar
2 tablespoons flour
½ cup boiling water
4 tablespoons butter
1 teaspoon vanilla

Muffins
1. Combine all ingredients in order given.
2. Fill greased muffin tins ⅔ full. Bake.

Sauce
1. Mix brown sugar and flour together in small saucepan.
2. Add water, butter, and vanilla.
3. Cook over medium-low heat until thickened.
4. Serve hot sauce over muffins.

Temperature: 350°
Time: 20 to 25 minutes

Phyllis Connelly
Schutt's Cider Mill

herb toast

Yield: 6 servings

Great served with salads, soups, luncheons, or as appetizers.

½ cup butter
¼ teaspoon thyme
¼ teaspoon oregano
¼ teaspoon freshly
  ground black pepper
¼ teaspoon minced garlic
½ teaspoon salt
½ teaspoon minced
  shallots
1 teaspoon chopped fresh
  parsley
6 slices thinly sliced
  sandwich bread, day old

1. Put all ingredients, except bread, in skillet. Mix over low heat.
2. Trim crusts from bread. Cut in fingers.
3. Dip in herb butter, place on baking sheet.
4. Bake until brown, turning once.
5. Serve hot, warm, or at room temperature.

Temperature: 350°
Time: 20 minutes

Caroll A. Meyers

pumpkin pecan bread

Yield: 3 loaves

A very moist bread that keeps for a long time.

3⅓ cups sifted flour
2 teaspoons baking soda
1½ teaspoons salt
1 teaspoon cinnamon
1 teaspoon nutmeg
1 cup chopped pecans
3 cups sugar
1 cup oil
4 eggs
⅔ cup water
2 cups canned pumpkin

1. Mix dry ingredients together.
2. Add remaining ingredients.
3. Mix until smooth.
4. Grease three 9 x 5-inch loaf pans. Fill each ⅓ full.
5. Bake.

Temperature: 350°
Time: 1 hour

Hint: To slice thinly, refrigerate.

Sally Foster

best baked doughnuts ever

Yield: 36 doughnuts

Lighter than regular donuts; will disappear before your eyes.

1 cup butter or
    margarine, softened
1½ cups sugar
2 eggs
3 cups flour
4½ teaspoons baking
    powder
½ teaspoon salt
½ teaspoon nutmeg
1 cup milk
½ teaspoon cinnamon

1. Blend ½ cup plus 2 tablespoons butter with 1 cup of the sugar. Add the eggs and mix well.
2. Sift together flour, baking powder, salt, and nutmeg. Add to the butter and sugar mixture.
3. Blend in the milk and mix together thoroughly.
4. Fill greased muffin tins ⅔ full. Bake until doughnuts are golden brown. (May use tiny muffin tins.)
5. Combine remaining ½ cup of the sugar with the cinnamon.
6. Melt remaining 6 tablespoons of the butter.
7. While doughnuts are still warm, roll them in melted butter, then in cinnamon sugar.

Temperature: 350°
Time: 15 to 20 minutes

Linda G. Stenstrom

grandma's old fashioned boston brown bread

Yield: 2 loaves

A great way to use up sour milk!

3 cups whole wheat flour
½ cup granulated white sugar
¾ cup light molasses
2 cups sour milk
2 teaspoons baking soda
1 teaspoon salt
1 cup dark raisins
¾ cup coarsely chopped walnuts

1. In large mixing bowl, combine all ingredients in order listed.
2. Turn mixture into two greased 9 x 5-inch loaf pans. Bake.

Temperature: 325°
Time: 35 to 45 minutes

Hint: To sour sweet milk, have milk at 70°. Place 1 tablespoon lemon juice or white vinegar in bottom of glass measuring cup. Fill cup with milk. Stir and let mixture stand 10 minutes.

Sally A. Ward

carrot bread

Yield: 1 loaf

Nutritious and surprisingly light.

3 eggs
1½ cups sugar
¾ cup cooking oil
2¼ cups sifted all-purpose flour
1¾ teaspoons baking powder
1 teaspoon baking soda
¼ teaspoon salt
1½ teaspoons cinnamon
1½ cups finely shredded carrots
½ cup raisins
3 tablespoons wheat germ
½ cup shredded coconut

1. Beat eggs, sugar, and oil in large mixing bowl until blended. Set aside.
2. Sift together flour, baking powder, baking soda, salt, and cinnamon. Blend into egg mixture.
3. Stir in carrots, raisins, wheat germ, and coconut.
4. Grease a 9 x 5-inch loaf pan; line bottom with wax paper.
5. Pour batter into pan. Bake until toothpick inserted in center comes out clean.
6. After baking, cool 10 minutes before peeling off wax paper.

Temperature: 325°
Time: 1 hour, 20 minutes

Susan N. Woehr

salads &
dressings

salads & dressings

SALADS

Fruit
Double Pear Salad, p 94
Fresh Pineapple Salad with Sauce, p 93
Golden Apple Salad, p 93
Honey Fruit Compote, p 95
Raspberry Razzle, p 96
Strawberry and Onion Salad with Poppyseed Dressing, p 95
Strawberry Nut Salad, p 94

Vegetable
Calico Slaw, p 96
Creamy Cauliflower Broccoli Salad, p 97
Cucumber Salad, p 97
Kidney Bean Relish, p 101
Mushroom Salad, p 98
Pea Pod Salad, p 100
Peas Pizzicato, p 99
Potato Salad, p 100
Sauerkraut Salad, p 99
Swedish Vegetables, p 98

Molded
Creamy Cucumber Mold, p 102
Fruited Cheese Mold, p 103
Gazpacho Aspic, p 101
Molded Cranberry-Apple Salad, p 103
Molded Spinach Salad, p 102

Main Dish Salads
Bonny's Rooftop Salad, p 106
Cold Rice-Tuna Salad, p 111
Crabmeat Salad, p 109
Eastern Rice Salad, p 104
Fruited Chicken Salad, p 108
Ham and Cheese Salad with Mustard Dressing, p 105
Korean Salad, p 111
Mexican Chefs' Salad, p 110
Shrimp and Mushroom Supper Salad, p 109
Tabouleh, p 105
Tangy Chicken Salad, p 108
Village Chicken Salad, p 107

DRESSINGS
Green Goddess Salad Dressing, p 114
Mayonnaise, p 107
Poppy Seed Dressing, p 112
Romaine Salad Dressing, p 113
Roquefort Dressing, p 114
Tangy French Dressing, p 113
Teton Blue Cheese Dressing, p 113

Condiments
Beet Relish, p 115
Chili Sauce, p 118
Easier Pickles, p 117
Easiest Pickles, p 117
Easy Pickles, p 116
Grandma Newell's Chili Sauce, p 118
Green Tomato Relish, p 116
Zucchini Relish, p 115

Side Dishes
Cinnamon Candy Apples, p 110
Escalloped Pineapple, p 104
Oriental Fruit Compote, p 112

fresh pineapple salad with sauce

Yield: 6 servings

Good choice for a ladies' luncheon as a salad or dessert.

1 6-ounce can frozen
  pineapple concentrate
1 cup heavy cream,
  whipped
2 tablespoons lemon juice
6 slices fresh pineapple
honey
mint leaves for garnish

1. Fold pineapple concentrate into whipped cream. Add lemon juice.
2. Pour mixture into refrigerator tray. Freeze until mushy.
3. Arrange pineapple slices in shallow dish. Top with a drizzling of honey.
4. Before serving, beat the frozen cream mixture. Spoon over pineapple. Serve on a bed of lettuce. Garnish with mint leaves.
5. To use as a dessert, chop the pineapple; add it to the frozen mixture just before serving.

Peggi M. Godwin

golden apple salad

Yield: 4 to 6 servings

Tangy and different.

2 medium-size Golden
  Delicious apples
1 13-ounce can pineapple
  tidbits
2 medium-size carrots,
  shredded
1 3-ounce package cream
  cheese, softened
1½ teaspoons grated
  lemon peel
2 tablespoons lemon juice
2 teaspoons sugar
¼ teaspoon ground
  nutmeg
¼ teaspoon salt
crisp salad greens
salted nuts, such as
  cashews or peanuts

1. Core, but do not peel, apples. Cut into ½ inch cubes.
2. Drain the pineapple, reserving 1 tablespoon of the syrup.
3. Combine apples, carrots, and pineapple.
4. Blend the cream cheese with the 1 tablespoon pineapple syrup, lemon peel, lemon juice, sugar, nutmeg, and salt. Gently mix into apple mixture.
5. To serve, mound apple mixture on crisp greens in salad bowl. Sprinkle nuts on top.

Hint: A variation can be made by adding 1 cup chicken cubes and fresh pineapple. Serve this in hollowed out pineapple halves.

Mary W. Schwertz

double pear salad

Yield: 4 servings

An elegant salad.

1 large bunch watercress
3 ripe pears
1 avocado pear

1. Wash watercress. Remove tough stems. Peel, and thinly slice, pears and avocado.
2. Arrange watercress, pears, and avocado on a platter.
3. Pour dressing over salad. Add some freshly ground black pepper, if desired.
4. This must be served immediately, because the fruit will discolor quickly.

Dressing
½ cup salad oil
3 tablespoons vinegar
2 teaspoons sugar
¼ teaspoon salt
1 tablespoon tomato paste

Dressing
1. Whip salad dressing ingredients together with wire whip.

Hint: To prevent discoloration of pears, place peeled pears in cold salted water for a short time. Rinse thoroughly before using.

Ann B. Irwin

strawberry nut salad

Yield: 10 to 12 servings

Great for a crowd.

1 6-ounce package strawberry gelatin
1 cup boiling water
2 10-ounce packages frozen sliced strawberries, partially thawed
one 1-pound, 4-ounce can crushed pineapple, drained
1 cup coarsely chopped walnuts
3 medium bananas, mashed (1 cup)
1 pint sour cream

1. Dissolve gelatin in boiling water. Add strawberries, pineapple, walnuts, and bananas.
2. Put half of strawberry mixture into 9 x 13-inch pan. Refrigerate until firm, about 45 minutes.
3. Spread sour cream on firm strawberry mixture in pan. Gently spoon on rest of strawberry mixture. Cover and allow to set several hours or overnight.
4. To serve, cut into squares, and place on top of lettuce leaf. Garnish with additional strawberries, if desired.

Must do ahead.

Patsy M. Gilges

strawberry and onion salad with poppyseed dressing

Yield: 8 servings

Try different fruits to fit the season, or your color scheme.

1 head romaine lettuce
1 pint fresh strawberries
  or 1 package whole
  frozen strawberries
1 Bermuda onion, sliced

1. Wash romaine lettuce. Pat dry. Refrigerate until serving time.
2. Place greens on individual salad plates, or in large salad bowl.
3. Slice strawberries. If using frozen strawberries, let partially thaw before slicing.
4. Put berries and onions on top of greens.
5. Drizzle poppyseed dressing over salad. Toss, if using large salad bowl.

Dressing
½ cup mayonnaise
2 tablespoons vinegar
⅓ cup sugar
¼ cup whole milk
2 tablespoons poppyseeds

Dressing
1. Place all ingredients in a jar.
2. Cover and shake until blended.
3. Dressing keeps several days in refrigerator.

Ginny Y. Gray

honey fruit compote

Yield: 4 to 6 servings

Does well on its own or over ice cream.

1 20-ounce can pineapple chunks, juice pack
2 11-ounce cans mandarin orange sections, drained
1½ cups seedless green grapes or red grapes, seeded and halved
3 kiwis, peeled, halved lengthwise, and sliced
½ cup freshly-squeezed orange juice
¼ cup honey
1 tablespoon lemon juice

1. Drain pineapple, reserving juice.
2. In a large bowl, combine pineapple chunks, mandarin oranges, grapes, and kiwi slices.
3. Measure reserved pineapple juice, and add water if necessary, to make 1 cup of liquid.
4. Combine pineapple liquid, orange juice, honey, and lemon juice. Pour over fruit.
5. Cover. Chill until ready to serve.

Patsy M. Gilges

raspberry razzle

Yield: 6 servings

A luscious salad or a simple dessert.

1 3-ounce package
   raspberry gelatin
1 10-ounce package
   frozen raspberries,
   thawed
1 cup sour cream
¾ cup water

1. Combine all ingredients in saucepan, using a wire whisk to dissolve lumps in sour cream.
2. Bring just to boiling over medium heat, uncovered. Stir to prevent burning.
3. Remove from heat. Pour into a 1-quart mold or serving dish.
4. Chill several hours or overnight.
5. Garnish with fresh raspberries, if available.

Must do ahead.

Carolyn H. Saum

calico slaw

Yield: 6 to 8 servings

Crunchy, colorful slaw. Lots of vitamins and fiber; low in calories.

Salad
5 cups finely shredded
   green cabbage
2 cups finely shredded red
   cabbage
2 cups tiny broccoli
   flowerettes
1 carrot, coarsely grated
2 tablespoons minced
   onion
2 tablespoons sliced
   pimiento or sweet red
   pepper

Dressing
⅔ cup salad oil
⅓ cup cider vinegar
2 teaspoons Dijon
   mustard
1 teaspoon sugar
½ teaspoon salt

1. Combine vegetables in a medium-size bowl.
2. Combine dressing ingredients by shaking in a covered jar.
3. Pour dressing over vegetables; toss. Chill until serving time.

Karin N. McNamara

creamy cauliflower broccoli salad

Yield: 10 servings

This salad is very attractive.

Salad
1 large bunch of broccoli
1 large head cauliflower
1 large red onion
1 pint cherry tomatoes
  (reserve a few for
  garnish)

Dressing
½ cup mayonnaise
½ cup sour cream
1 teaspoon garlic powder
salt and pepper to taste

1. Wash and break broccoli and cauliflower into bite-size pieces. Cut tender portion of stalks into thin slices.
2. Slice onion into thin rings.
3. Combine dressing ingredients.
4. One hour before serving, toss salad ingredients with dressing. Garnish with reserved cherry tomatoes.

Hint: Leftover salad will keep 2 to 3 days in refrigerator.

Alice K. Smith

cucumber salad

Yield: 8 to 10 servings

This one is a little bit different.

4 cucumbers
1 sweet Spanish onion,
  sliced
1 cup sugar
1 cup water
½ cup vinegar
½ cup oil
celery seed

1. Pare cucumbers. Score lengthwise with tines of fork, all around cucumber.
2. Slice cucumbers thinly. Put in salted ice water. Add sliced onion. Let stand 1 to 2 hours.
3. Cook sugar and water over low heat until sugar is dissolved. Cool.
4. Add vinegar and oil to cooled sugar syrup, and mix well.
5. Drain and rinse cucumber and onion slices. Pour vinegar and oil mixture over them to cover.
6. Sprinkle with celery seed. Refrigerate overnight.

Must do one day ahead.

Peggi M. Godwin

swedish vegetables

Yield: 12 servings

A real change from cole slaw for a summer salad.

Salad

3 10-ounce packages frozen mixed vegetables

½ medium onion, finely chopped

½ cup Italian dressing

Salad

1. Cook vegetables according to package directions. Include chopped onion. Drain.
2. Marinate in Italian dressing. Chill overnight. (This can be made a day ahead up to this point.)
3. Next day drain again.

Dressing

¾ cup mayonnaise

¼ cup chili sauce

2 tablespoons dill weed

½ tablespoon salt

1 tablespoon lemon juice

1 head lettuce

Dressing

1. Combine mayonnaise, chili sauce, dill weed, salt, and lemon juice.
2. Pour over vegetables. Mix well.
3. Serve cold on lettuce.

Must do one day ahead.

Ellen W. Cooper

mushroom salad

Yield: 8 servings

Great for a patio party; serve with a grilled steak.

1 pound mushrooms

½ cup chopped radishes

½ cup chopped celery

4½ tablespoons Dijon mustard

4½ tablespoons red wine vinegar

½ teaspoon salt

½ teaspoon oregano

½ teaspoon tarragon

¼ teaspoon pepper

¾ cup olive oil

chopped fresh parsley

1. Clean and slice mushrooms. Combine, in a bowl, with radishes and celery.
2. In a separate bowl, combine mustard, vinegar, and seasonings. Beat in olive oil.
3. Pour dressing over mushroom mixture. Toss lightly. Sprinkle with chopped parsley.

Hint: If this is to be used as an appetizer, cut vegetables into larger pieces so they may be eaten with toothpicks.

Peggi M. Godwin

peas pizzicato

Yield: 4 to 6 servings

So simple and great for summer—no cooking.

2 10-ounce packages
frozen peas
1 cup sour cream
2 scallions, sliced
diagonally
6 slices bacon, cooked
and crumbled
salt and pepper to taste
lettuce

1. Thaw frozen peas. Drain off
   excess water. Do not cook peas.
2. Combine sour cream, scallions,
   bacon, salt, and pepper. Add
   peas.
3. Chill, or serve at room
   temperature on individual
   lettuce cups.

Nicole R. Doolittle

sauerkraut salad

Yield: 6 servings

Even non-sauerkraut eaters enjoy this.

1 quart sauerkraut,
drained
1 cup sliced celery
½ cup chopped peppers
(use a combination of
red and green peppers;
if red peppers are not
available, add a 2-ounce
jar of pimiento for color)
½ cup chopped onions
1 cup sugar
¼ cup white vinegar
¼ cup oil
¼ teaspoon salt

1. Combine sauerkraut, celery,
   peppers, and onion. Mix well.
2. Combine sugar, white vinegar,
   oil, and salt. Pour over
   sauerkraut mixture; toss well.
3. Refrigerate salad at least 24
   hours ahead of serving time.
   Keeps forever!

Must do one day ahead.

Helen Williams

*L*inda's dad, Ken Williams, like many others in the Finger
Lakes area, spends hours in the garage each fall making
sauerkraut. Sauerkraut lovers for miles around Canandaigua
Lake stand impatiently in the yard with fork in hand waiting
for the first taste. Non-lovers, however, threaten all sorts of
retaliation for the wafting odors permeating the area.

potato salad

Yield: 6 to 8 servings

The curry makes a nice addition.

6 cups cooked, and diced, potatoes
¼ cup chopped green onion
½ teaspoon celery seed
½ teaspoon dill weed
2 tablespoons lemon juice
2 tablespoons parsley
4 eggs, hard-boiled
salt and pepper
1 cup sour cream
½ cup mayonnaise
1 teaspoon curry powder
2 teaspoons lemon juice

Must do ahead.

1. Combine potatoes, green onion, celery seed, dill weed, lemon juice, parsley, chopped *whites* of eggs, salt, and pepper. Chill, covered, overnight. This is the secret to the recipe.
2. Just before serving, mix sour cream, mayonnaise, curry, lemon juice, and chopped egg yolks.
3. Toss potatoes with dressing and serve.

Alice K. Smith

pea pod salad

Yield: serves 6

Something different for a luncheon!

2 6-ounce packages frozen pea pods
1 cup halved cherry tomatoes
1 5-ounce can water chestnuts, sliced
¼ cup chopped green onion

Dressing
⅓ cup oil
1 tablespoon lemon juice
1 tablespoon vinegar
dash of garlic powder
½ teaspoon salt
1 tablespoon sugar

1. Cook pea pods for only one minute according to package directions. Drain.
2. Add tomatoes, water chestnuts, and green onion. Set aside.
3. Combine all dressing ingredients in a large bowl.
4. Pour pod mixture into dressing. Toss gently.
5. Chill before serving.

Suzanne H. Barbee

kidney bean relish

Yield: 6 servings

This is most refreshing and unusual when served as a summer salad.

1 small onion
3 stalks celery
1 or 2 hard-boiled eggs
2 cups kidney beans, drained
1 tablespoon mayonnaise
2 teaspoons mustard relish
¼ teaspoon white pepper
1 teaspoon curry powder
½ teaspoon salt

1. Chop the onion, celery, and eggs into small pieces. Mix together with the beans.
2. Add remaining ingredients.
3. Refrigerate. Serve when cool.

Celia G. Riley

gazpacho aspic

Yield: 3-quart mold

Rosy favorite—with a twist!

4 large tomatoes
½ green pepper
1 onion
1 cucumber (average size)
juice of 1½ lemons
⅓ cup sugar
dash of salt
6 envelopes unflavored gelatin
1 48-ounce can tomato-based vegetable, or tomato juice

1. Quarter tomatoes, pepper, onion, and cucumber. Blend in food processor or blender. Pare only the onion.
2. Add lemon juice, sugar, and salt.
3. Soften gelatin in 1½ cups of the juice. Heat the rest of the juice.
4. Combine all ingredients. Pour into an oiled 3-quart ring mold. Refrigerate until set.
5. To serve, unmold salad on romaine lettuce. Place a bowl of Vinaigrette dressing in the center of the ring. As an alternative, fill the center of the ring with cottage cheese, cucumber salad, or chicken salad.

Must do ahead.

Hint: Soaking whole lemon in hot water for 30 minutes will yield more juice.

Joanne K. Gianniny

creamy cucumber mold

Yield: 6 servings

Pretty and refreshing!

1 3-ounce package lime
   gelatin
¾ cup boiling water
2 3-ounce packages
   cream cheese, softened
1 cup mayonnaise
¼ teaspoon salt
pinch of cayenne pepper
1 teaspoon horseradish
2 tablespoons lemon juice
¾ cup finely chopped
   cucumber
⅛ to ¼ cup chopped
   onion
watercress and cherry
   tomatoes for garnish

Must do ahead.

1. Dissolve gelatin in boiling water.
2. Add cream cheese, mayonnaise, salt, cayenne, and horseradish. Blend until smooth.
3. Add lemon juice.
4. Chill until slightly thickened. Fold in cucumber and onion.
5. Turn into a 3-cup mold. Chill until set.
6. Unmold. Serve garnished with watercress and cherry tomatoes.

Susan S. Taylor

molded spinach salad

Yield: 4 to 6 servings

A tangy compliment to meats and fish.

1 3-ounce package lemon
   gelatin
1 cup boiling water
½ cup mayonnaise
2 tablespoons lemon juice
½ teaspoon salt
1 cup chopped raw
   spinach
2 tablespoons finely
   chopped onion
½ cup finely chopped
   celery
1 cup creamed small curd
   cottage cheese

Must do ahead.

1. Dissolve gelatin in boiling water.
2. Stir in mayonnaise, lemon juice, and salt. Refrigerate until slightly jelled.
3. Fold vegetables and cottage cheese into gelatin.
4. Pour into a lightly oiled 1-quart mold. Refrigerate until firm.
5. Unmold on a bed of spinach leaves.

Susan B. Finnegan

molded cranberry-apple salad

Yield: 6 to 8 servings

A treat to serve when fresh cranberries are in season.

2 cups fresh cranberries
1 teaspoon grated orange
  rind
1 cup sugar
1 3-ounce package lemon
  gelatin
1 cup boiling water
½ cup cold water
½ cup diced celery
2 apples, diced
lettuce leaves
mayonnaise, optional

1. Combine cranberries, ground or finely chopped, with orange rind and sugar. Let stand 30 minutes.
2. Dissolve gelatin in boiling water, then add cold water. Refrigerate until slightly thickened.
3. Add cranberries, celery, and apples. Pour into 2-quart ring mold. Refrigerate at least several hours until set.
4. Unmold on lettuce leaves. Serve with mayonnaise, if desired.

Must do ahead.

Monica M. McConville

fruited cheese mold

Yield: 8 servings

Good served with rolled slices of baked ham and bunches of grapes.

1 3-ounce package lemon
  gelatin
½ cup boiling water
1 16-ounce can crushed
  pineapple (2 cups)
1 tablespoon lemon juice
1 cup shredded Cheddar
  cheese
1 cup heavy cream,
  whipped
lettuce

1. Dissolve gelatin in boiling water. Stir in undrained crushed pineapple and lemon juice.
2. Chill until slightly thickened.
3. Fold in cheese and whipped cream.
4. Pour into lightly oiled 4½-cup ring mold. Chill until firm.
5. Unmold on bed of lettuce. Garnish with carrot curls, if desired.

Pat Reed

eastern rice salad

Yield: 8 to 10 servings

You may have to hunt for a few of the ingredients in the gourmet section of your store, but it's well worth the effort.

Salad

3 to 4 cups cooked rice (white, brown, or mixed)

½ 10-ounce package frozen peas, uncooked

4 scallions, sliced, with tops

1 8-ounce can sliced water chestnuts

½ pound cooked shrimp, small or medium (fresh, frozen, or canned)

Chinese cabbage leaves

Salad

1. Mix all salad ingredients in large bowl.
2. Pour dressing over salad. Toss well.
3. Cover. Refrigerate overnight.
4. Serve in a decorative glass bowl lined with Chinese cabbage leaves.

Dressing

5 tablespoons rice vinegar

3 tablespoons soy sauce

1½ tablespoons sesame oil

5 tablespoons salad oil

1 tablespoon dry mustard, dissolved in a little water to make paste

Dressing

1. Mix all ingredients in a jar.
2. Shake well.

Must do ahead.

Hint: If you wish to add chopped celery and more shrimp, this makes a great one-dish meal.

Lucia H. Shaw

escalloped pineapple

Yield: 6 to 8 servings

Unusual side dish from a New England hotel chef.

2½ cups crushed pineapple, undrained

4 cups soft bread crumbs

1 cup sugar

1 teaspoon vanilla

1 cup half and half or light cream

4 tablespoons margarine, melted

1. Mix all ingredients together.
2. Place in well-greased, 2-quart casserole.
3. Bake, or refrigerate and bake later that day.
4. Good served with baked ham for a buffet meal.

Temperature: 350°

Time: 50 to 60 minutes

Mary Kay C. Taber

ham and cheese salad with mustard dressing

Yield: 4 servings

A quick summer supper.

Dressing
5 tablespoons Dijon
   mustard
¼ cup lemon juice
1 cup olive oil
salt and pepper to taste

Salad
4 cups julienned ham
2 cups julienned Gruyère
   cheese
2 cups broken iceberg
   lettuce

Dressing
1. Combine mustard and lemon
   juice.
2. Add olive oil in a stream,
   whisking constantly.
3. Add salt and pepper. Blend well.

Salad
1. Combine all ingredients.
2. Toss with dressing and serve.

Peggi M. Godwin

tabouleh

Yield: 4 servings

Something unusual to serve for lunch.

¾ cup bulgar wheat
water
¾ cup finely chopped
   fresh parsley
2 to 3 tablespoons
   chopped fresh mint
3 tomatoes, finely
   chopped
1 medium onion, minced
¼ cup olive oil
¼ cup lemon juice
1 teaspoon salt
pinch of pepper
pinch of allspice
pinch of crushed red
   pepper

Must do ahead

1. Soak bulgar wheat covered with
   water 3 to 4 hours or overnight.
   Drain.
2. Stir in parsley, mint, tomatoes,
   and onion.
3. Mix olive oil, lemon juice, salt,
   pepper, allspice, and red pepper.
   Add to above mixture and stir
   well.
4. Serve chilled on lettuce or in
   pita bread.

Jean H. Whitney

Jean's sister Honey is a health food enthusiast. Jean had never been too impressed. But when Honey served her "Tabouleh," tucked in pita bread, at a lakeside family picnic, she won over a whole family of instant converts.

bonny's rooftop salad

Yield: 4 servings

A refreshing summer dinner salad.

1 pound fresh green beans

1. Parboil beans 7 minutes. Drain.

Vinaigrette
¾ cup olive oil
¼ cup tarragon vinegar
salt and pepper to taste
¼ teaspoon summer
  savory

Vinaigrette
1. Mix together all ingredients.
2. Pour over beans; marinate 2
   hours.
3. Drain beans. Reserve marinade
   for another use.

Mayonnaise
1 egg
1 tablespoon lemon juice
  or vinegar
1 cup oil
1 teaspoon salt
¼ teaspoon pepper
½ teaspoon garlic salt
½ to 1 teaspoon curry

1 pound red potatoes,
  boiled, peeled, and
  cubed (3 to 4 cups)
½ pound prepared shrimp
¼ pound alfalfa sprouts
½ teaspoon lemon balm

Mayonnaise
1. Mix egg and lemon juice until
   blended.
2. Add oil slowly. Beat constantly
   with a wire whisk. (Can use a
   blender.)
3. Add seasonings, and blend
   quickly.
4. Add ¾ of the mayonnaise to the
   warm potatoes. Chill thoroughly.
5. Add remaining mayonnaise. Mix
   well. Assemble salad.

To assemble
1. Mound potato salad in center
   of a platter.
2. Circle with marinated beans.
3. Arrange shrimp on beans.
4. Garnish with alfalfa sprouts.
5. Sprinkle with lemon balm.

Jacqueline Myers Webber

village chicken salad

Yield: 6 to 8 servings

Very attractive, unusual, and delicious.

4 whole chicken breasts
  or 8 halves
½ cup soy sauce
½ cup sherry
2 stalks celery with leaves
1½ teaspoons sugar
2 cloves garlic, mashed
¾ cup mayonnaise
1 teaspoon sugar
1 teaspoon lemon juice
½ teaspoon soy sauce
1 large bunch broccoli,
  broken into flowerettes
  (not stalks)
½ cup chopped celery
½ cup chopped scallions
½ cup unsalted cashews

1. Remove skin from chicken.
2. Combine soy sauce, sherry, celery stalks, sugar, and garlic in a large frying pan.
3. Add chicken breasts. Simmer until tender.
4. Cool chicken just enough to handle. Bone and cube. Return chicken to cooking liquid until completely cool.
5. Steam broccoli flowerettes just until bright green, but still crispy. Cool.
6. Mix together mayonnaise, sugar, 2 tablespoons of the cooking liquid, lemon juice, and soy sauce.
7. Drain chicken. Add to the mayonnaise dressing.
8. Toss all ingredients together. Refrigerate several hours or overnight.
9. Serve with fresh pineapple or Oriental Fruit Compote. (See index.)

Must do ahead.

Hint: For crushed garlic, put cloves between waxed paper and hit with hammer—no mess to clean up.

Terry S. Butwid

mayonnaise

Yield: 2 cups

Fast, easy, and homemade!

3 egg yolks
1 teaspoon salt
¾ teaspoon dry mustard
½ teaspoon paprika
generous shake of white
  pepper
2 tablespons vinegar
2 cups oil
2 tablespoons water

1. Place first 6 ingredients in food processor. Using metal blade, mix thoroughly with several short pulses of power, scraping down sides of bowl between pulses.
2. With full power on, slowly add half of the oil. When very thick, add water.
3. Continue to process, and slowly add remaining oil.
4. Refrigerate before serving.

Jane K. Stevens

tangy chicken salad

Yield: 4 servings

Just the salad to serve when melons are in season.

2 cups chicken, cooked
  and cubed
½ cantaloupe, seeded,
  pared and cut into
  cubes (about 1 cup)
½ honeydew melon,
  seeded, pared and cut
  into cubes (about 1 cup)
½ cup diced celery
½ cup cashew nuts
¼ cup sliced scallions
lettuce leaves—romaine
  or iceberg
mint and paprika for
  garnish

1. In medium bowl, combine all
   ingredients, except lettuce,
   paprika, and mint. Reserve a
   few melon balls for garnish.
2. Add just enough dressing to
   coat ingredients. Cover. Chill
   one hour. Serve on romaine or
   iceberg lettuce leaves.
3. Garnish with melon balls
   blushed with paprika and
   topped with a small sprig of
   mint.

Yogurt Dressing
½ cup plain yogurt
6 tablespoons
  mayonnaise
3 tablespoons fresh lemon
  juice
1½ teaspoons ground
  coriander
1 scant teaspoon salt
dash of pepper

Dressing
Combine all ingredients.
Mix well. Save extra dressing for
  fruit salads.
Keep covered in refrigerator.

Susan S. Taylor

fruited chicken salad

Yield: 4 to 6 servings

Wonderful on a hot summer day.

2 pounds chicken breasts,
  cooked, boned, and
  chopped
1 cup mayonnaise
½ teaspoon curry powder
¾ teaspoon soy sauce
1 cup cantaloupe balls
1 cup seedless green
  grapes
¼ cup pitted black olives
¼ cup almonds, slivered
salt to taste

Must do ahead.

1. Marinate cooked and chopped
   chicken in mayonnaise, curry,
   and soy sauce until very cold
   (overnight, if possible).
2. About 1 hour before serving,
   add cantaloupe, grapes, olives,
   almonds, and salt. Toss
   together.
3. Serve in lettuce-lined bowls with
   a healthy whole-grain bread.

Suzy M. Hengerer

crabmeat salad

Yield: 4 servings

Delightful summer luncheon dish.

1 pound crabmeat, well
  drained
juice of ¼ lemon
2 celery stalks, chopped,
  including leaves
½ teaspoon salt
¼ teaspoon pepper
pinch cayenne pepper
2 tablespoons chopped
  chives
1½ tablespoons drained
  capers, chopped
2 hard-boiled eggs
1 cup mayonnaise
2 teaspoons Cognac
1 teaspoon steak sauce
2 drops pepper sauce
pinch of celery salt
1 canteloupe
lettuce

1. Toss crabmeat with lemon juice.
2. Add celery, salt, pepper,
   cayenne, chives, and capers.
3. Split hard-boiled eggs
   lengthwise. Sieve yolks and
   reserve. Cut whites into julienne
   strips; add to salad.
4. Mix mayonnaise with Cognac,
   steak sauce, pepper sauce, and
   celery salt.
5. Toss crabmeat mixture with
   mayonnaise mixture. Chill.
6. Slice canteloupe into rings.
   Remove seeds. Place rings on
   beds of lettuce and fill each with
   salad. Garnish with sieved egg
   yolk.

**Hint: It is helpful if you slash the fruit of the canteloupe (not the
rind) at bite-sized intervals for easier removal by your diners.**

Susan LaForte

shrimp and mushroom
supper salad

Yield: 4 servings

What a great way to diet!

2 cups shrimp, cooked,
  shelled, and chilled
4 cups shredded lettuce
½ pound fresh
  mushrooms, thinly
  sliced
½ cucumber, thinly sliced
8 cherry tomatoes, halved
¼ cup sliced scallions
  (optional)
6 tablespoons Italian
  salad dressing
salt and pepper to taste
¼ teaspoon dried oregano
pinch of garlic powder
  (optional)

1. Slice shrimp in half, or dice, if
   large.
2. Combine all ingredients. Toss
   gently.
3. Serve immediately.

Catherine Wiedemer

mexican chefs' salad

Yield: 6 to 8 servings

A meal in itself.

¾ medium onion
4 tomatoes
1 head lettuce
1 can ripe, pitted olives,
  drained
1 pound lean ground beef
1 15-ounce can kidney
  beans, drained
8 ounces salad dressing:
  French, Vinaigrette, or
  Thousand Island
dash of Tabasco
4 to 6 ounces Cheddar
  cheese, grated
1 8-ounce bag of tortilla
  chips, crushed (reserve
  few for garnish)
1 avocado, sliced

1. Chop onion, tomatoes, lettuce, and olives. Combine and set aside.
2. Brown ground beef; drain. Add kidney beans. Simmer 10 minutes. Cool.
3. Add Tabasco to salad dressing.
4. When ready to serve, combine salad, meat mixture, cheese, and tortilla chips. Add dressing; toss.
5. Garnish with sliced avocado and reserved tortilla chips. Great served with Margueritas.

Hint: All parts can be done ahead, kept separate, and tossed together at the last minute.

Emily M. Henderson

cinnamon candy apples

Yield: 1 to 1½ quarts

This recipe is from an apple grower. I first used it with some Girl Scouts to help them earn their cooking badge. Each girl proudly took home her own jar of apples.

½ cup sugar
1 cup water
½ cup red cinnamon
  heart candies
6 baking apples

1. In a large pan, cook sugar, water, and candies together for 5 minutes to make syrup.
2. Peel apples. Cut into wedges, removing core.
3. Place apple wedges in syrup; cover pan, and cook slowly until tender. Spoon syrup over apples frequently.
4. When tender, remove slices from pan and place in sterilized quart jar. Add syrup and cover.
5. When cooled, refrigerate.

Hint: These apples can be a side dish, condiment, or light dessert. They are excellent cooked about 5 minutes and canned in their syrup while still crisp.

Priscilla L. Minster

korean salad

Yield: 8 to 10 servings

A salad with a variety of tastes and textures.

2 large bunches of fresh
   spinach
4 hard-boiled eggs, sliced
1 small package fresh
   bean sprouts or canned
   sprouts, drained
1 8-ounce can water
   chestnuts, sliced thin
8 slices crisp, cooked
   bacon, crumbled
cherry tomato halves,
   optional

1. Wash spinach carefully. Tear
   into bite-size pieces.
2. Add remaining salad
   ingredients.
3. Add desired amount of dressing
   just before serving; toss.

Dressing
¼ cup sugar
⅓ cup catsup
¼ cup vinegar
2 teaspoons
   Worcestershire sauce
1 medium onion, grated
salt to taste
1 cup salad oil

Dressing
1. Combine dressing ingredients,
   adding oil last. Shake well.

Marilyn S. Kessler

cold rice-tuna salad

Yield: 16 servings

Super warm weather dish for a crowd.

4 cups cooked, converted
   rice
3 6-ounce cans white
   tuna in water, drained
1 onion chopped
4 small candied dill
   pickles, chopped
1 10-ounce package
   frozen peas, cooked
1 cup chopped celery
1 tablespoon dill
4 hard-boiled eggs,
   chopped
2 8-ounce cans water
   chestnuts, chopped
salad dressing

1. Combine ingredients. Add
   enough salad dressing to bind
   ingredients.
2. Chill until ready to serve.
   Garnish with tomato wedges if
   desired.
3. This recipe may be halved for a
   smaller amount.

Caroll J. Meyers

111

oriental fruit compote

Yield: 6 servings

Marvelous with any meat.

1 29-ounce can pear halves
1 29-ounce can peach halves
1 20-ounce can or 2 small cans mandarin oranges
1 20-ounce can pineapple chunks
¾ cup brown sugar
½ cup melted butter
1½ tablespoons cornstarch
1 teaspoon curry powder

1. Drain fruit well. Arrange in an 8 x 12-inch baking dish.
2. Blend remaining ingredients and pour over fruit.
3. Bake.

Temperature: 350°
Time: 1 hour

Hint: Use leftover fruit on ice cream or pound cake.

Betty S. Middleton

poppy seed dressing

Yield: 1½ cups

The perfect dressing for romaine, avocado, and grapefruit salad.

⅓ cup honey
1 teaspoon salt
2 tablespoons vinegar
1 tablespoon prepared mustard
¾ cup salad oil
1 tablespoon minced onion
2 tablespoons poppy seeds

1. Combine all ingredients, except poppy seeds, in a screw-top jar.
2. Shake well.
3. Add poppy seeds, shake again, and serve.

Martha H. Cook

tangy french dressing

Yield: 1½ cups

Zippy and delicious—would perk up any salad!

¼ cup sugar
1 teaspoon celery seed
1 teaspoon dry mustard
1 teaspoon paprika
1 teaspoon salt
1 teaspoon grated or
  minced onion
1 cup salad oil
4 tablespoons wine
  vinegar
1 clove garlic, peeled

1. Combine first six ingredients in a deep bowl.
2. Using a beater, alternately add oil and vinegar, beating until thick.
3. Add the garlic clove. Allow to stand in dressing for about one hour. Remove garlic.
4. Refrigerate if not to be used immediately. If dressing should separate, just shake before using.

Jean W. Heuer

romaine salad dressing

Yield: 1½ cups

You probably have most of the ingredients on hand.

¼ cup salad oil
¾ cup sour cream
½ teaspoon salt
⅛ teaspoon garlic powder
⅛ teaspoon onion salt
1 teaspoon vinegar
1 teaspoon lemon juice
½ cup grated Parmesan
  cheese

1. Mix all the ingredients together except the Parmesan cheese. It should be added shortly before serving.
2. Toss with freshly prepared romaine or your favorite greens.

Suzanne H. Barbee

teton blue cheese dressing

Yield: 1 quart

So good, and so easy.

4 ounces blue cheese
3 tablespoons lemon juice
1 teaspoon celery salt
1 clove garlic, minced
1 teaspoon grated onion
1 pint sour cream
1 pint mayonnaise

1. Mix first 5 ingredients, leaving some large chunks of cheese.
2. Fold sour cream and mayonnaise into mixture.
3. Divide among small jars. Refrigerate and use as needed.

Linda W. Davey

green goddess salad dressing

Yield: 1½ cups

Perfect for a green salad.

1 cup mayonnaise
½ cup sour cream
1 tablespoon lemon juice
1 tablespoon tarragon
   vinegar
¼ cup minced parsley
¼ cup chopped green
   onion
½ teaspoon salt
½ teaspoon fresh pepper
3 anchovies, chopped fine
1 small clove garlic,
   minced

1. Combine all ingredients in a
   bowl. Use a whisk to mix well.
2. Chill before serving.

Hint: The quickest way to mince parsley is to snip with scissors.

Polly C. Parker

roquefort dressing

Yield: 1¼ cups

Not creamy; more like oil and vinegar, but better!

1 tablespoon sugar
1 teaspoon salt
1 teaspoon paprika
¾ cup olive oil
¼ teaspoon pepper
¼ cup white vinegar
1 teaspoon mustard
garlic clove, crushed
8 tablespoons crumbled
   Roquefort cheese
¼ teaspoon
   Worcestershire sauce

1. Put all ingredients, except the
   Roquefort cheese and the
   Worcestershire sauce, in a glass
   jar. Shake to blend.
2. Blend Roquefort and
   Worcestershire together. Add to
   jar. Combine thoroughly.

Frances M. Wilder

beet relish

Yield: 2 quarts

A colorful accompaniment to roast beef.

1 quart beets, cooked
1 medium cabbage
1 cup grated fresh
   horseradish or prepared
   horseradish
2 cups sugar
2 tablespoons salt
2 teaspoons mustard seed
2 teaspoons celery seed
1 pint cider vinegar

Must do ahead.

1. Put beets and cabbage through a food chopper or processor.
2. Add remaining ingredients. Mix well.
3. Refrigerate, covered, for at least 24 hours. This will keep indefinitely.

Violet E. Kapusta

 zucchini relish

Yield: 5 to 6 pints

A real winner for your garden zucchini harvest.

5 tablespoons salt
10 cups finely chopped
   zucchini
4 medium onions,
   chopped
2¾ cups vinegar
2¾ cups sugar
1 teaspoon nutmeg
1 teaspoon dry mustard
2 teaspoons celery seed
½ teaspoon pepper
1 teaspoon turmeric
1 red pepper, chopped
1 green pepper, chopped

1. Sprinkle salt over squash and onions. Let stand overnight.
2. The next day, thoroughly rinse squash and onions with cold water. Drain well.
3. Bring squash, onions, vinegar, sugar, nutmeg, mustard, celery seed, pepper, turmeric, and peppers to a boil. Cook for 20 minutes.
4. Fill clean, hot jars to within ½ inch from the top of the jar. Put lids on, twist on top.
5. Cover jars with 1 inch of water. Bring water to a boil. Boil 5 minutes.
6. Remove jars and set upright to cool on a wire rack. Check jars to be sure they have sealed before storing in cool, dry place.

Must do ahead.

Mary M. McConnell

green tomato relish

Yield: 8 quarts

A great way to use end-of-season green tomatoes.

¾ pound green tomatoes
6 large onions
12 to 18 peppers
2 tablespoons pickling spice
2 tablespoons cloves
3½ cups vinegar
6 cups sugar
1 tablespoon cinnamon
2 tablespoons mustard seed
1 tablespoon celery seed

1. Grind tomatoes, onions, and peppers. Drain.
2. Boil mixture for 15 minutes.
3. Place pickling spice and cloves in cloth bag. Add spice bag and all other ingredients to relish. Boil 15 minutes more.
4. Cool. Remove spice bag.
5. Bottle relish in sterilized canning jars. Store in a cool place. Refrigerate after opening.

Susan G. Rhoda

easy pickles

Yield: 1 gallon

No canning process required.

3 quarts thinly sliced cucumbers
4 large onions, sliced thin
4 cups vinegar
4 cups sugar
⅓ cup salt
¼ teaspoon celery seed
1¼ teaspoon mustard seed
1¼ teaspoon turmeric
¼ teaspoon powdered alum

1. Mix cucumbers and onions together in gallon container.
2. Mix remaining ingredients together. Pour over cucumber mixture.
3. Put lid on container and refrigerate.
4. Shake container every day for about 3 minutes. Store jar upright the first day and upside down the second day. Continue reversing the jar daily.
5. Ready to serve in 5 days.
6. These will last a year when kept refrigerated.

Must do ahead.

Susan K. Lepkowski

easier pickles

Yield: 1 quart

Especially easy when you use store-bought dill slices.

1 quart dill pickles
2 cups sugar
2 tablespoons white
   vinegar
1½ tablespoons pickling
   spice

1. Cut pickles into ¼-inch slices. Discard dill juice.
2. Add remaining ingredients.
3. Let stand in bowl at room temperature for several hours, stirring occasionally, until it makes a syrup.
4. Put pickles and syrup into jar. Refrigerate. Turn jar every day for about a week.

Must do ahead.

Nancy C. Alderman

easiest pickles

Yield: 48-ounce jar

An interesting food gift.

1 48-ounce jar of whole,
   old-fashioned dill
   pickles, commercially
   prepared
½ cup white vinegar
½ cup water
2 cups sugar
1 tablespoon pickling
   spice
1 tablespoon dill weed

1. Drain the dill pickles, and remove them from the jar. Rinse the jar and the lid with boiling water.
2. In a saucepan, bring remaining ingredients to a boil. Boil slowly for 7 minutes, stirring gently to blend spices.
3. While liquid is cooking, take pickles and carefully quarter them into spears: cut in half lengthwise, then half again, so that each pickle gives four *long* spears.
4. Place spears into the clean jar. Place a table knife in the jar to prevent the jar from overheating; then pour sweet and sour syrup over all. When jar is at room temperature, remove the knife, replace lid, and refrigerate at least 3 days.

Must do ahead.

Kaci Peer

 # chili sauce

Yield: 10 to 13 pints

A legacy from my husband's grandmother.

1 peck tomatoes
15 medium onions, finely
　chopped
1 bunch celery, finely
　chopped
4 red peppers, finely
　chopped
5 green peppers, finely
　chopped
seeds of one pepper
8 cups sugar
1 pint vinegar
1 1¼-ounce box pickling
　spice tied in a bag
½ cup salt

1. Peel and quarter tomatoes, and start cooking in a 12-quart kettle.
2. Add onions, celery, red and green peppers, and seeds of one pepper. Stir well.
3. Add sugar, vinegar, spices, and salt.
4. Bring to a boil, then reduce to simmer and cook at least 3 hours. Stir occasionally to prevent scorching. (Can also be cooked in roaster pan in oven at 350° for 3 to 4 hours.)
5. When cooked to ½ original volume, chili sauce is ready to can. Remove spice bag.
6. Pour boiling sauce into hot, sterile jars. Seal.

Susan C. Roberts

Jean's dad, a retired executive, was so enamored with Sue's "Chili Sauce" that he bought a bushel of tomatoes and learned to make the delicious sauce himself. The venture was a huge success, and the next year he bought a food processor to facilitate his autumn labor of love.

grandma newell's chili sauce

Yield: 4 cups

As good as great-grandmother's but without the fuss!

3½ cups undrained,
　canned tomatoes, cut
　up or diced
½ cup diced onions
½ cup diced green pepper
¼ cup diced celery
¾ cup sugar
¼ cup vinegar
¼ teaspoon salt
¼ teaspoon red pepper
　flakes (or to taste)

1. Combine all ingredients in saucepan.
2. Boil uncovered for 35 minutes.
3. Cool and store in refrigerator.
4. Serve cold with meats or as a relish.

Bonnie W. Hindman

eggs, cheese, & pasta

eggs, cheese & pasta

swedish egg strata

Yield: 6 servings

Similar to a soufflé but easier.

2 cups plain croutons
4 eggs, slightly beaten
2 cups milk
1 cup (4 ounces) grated
Cheddar cheese
½ teaspoon salt
½ teaspoon prepared
mustard
¼ cup minced green
pepper
2 tablespoons chopped
scallions
4 slices bacon, fried crisp
and crumbled

1. Sprinkle croutons on bottom of a greased 9 x 13-inch baking dish.
2. Mix eggs, milk, cheese, salt, and mustard. Pour over croutons.
3. Sprinkle top with green pepper, scallions, and bacon. Bake.

Temperature: 350°
Time: 55 to 60 minutes

Hint: Unlike the usual strata recipes, **this one** *does not* require overnight refrigeration.

Linnea O. Donahower

cheese-sausage soufflé

Yield: 8 servings

Nice and easy; no last-minute fuss.

6 eggs, well beaten
2 cups milk
½ teaspoon dry mustard
½ teaspoon salt
½ teaspoon horseradish
6 slices white bread,
crusts removed and
cubed
1 pound link sausage,
diced, cooked, and
drained
1 cup grated Cheddar
cheese

1. Mix first five ingredients, and set aside.
2. Butter a 9 x 13-inch baking dish.
3. Combine egg and milk mixture with bread cubes and sausage. Pour into baking dish.
4. Top with grated cheese, and refrigerate 12 hours or overnight. Bake.

Must do ahead.

Temperature: 350°
Time: 45 minutes

Katy K. Jacobson

baked egg in tomato

Yield: 1 serving

Good for brunch; garnish with watercress.

1 firm, ripe tomato
salt
pepper
1 teaspoon finely chopped
  onion
¼ teaspoon chopped
  parsley
2 teaspoons finely
  chopped ham
1 slice white bread, crusts
  removed
½ tablespoon butter
1 egg
1 tablespoon grated Swiss
  or Cheddar cheese

1. Cut a thin slice from stem end of tomato and scoop out seeds.
2. Salt and pepper inside of tomato. Mix onion, parsley, and ham and spoon into tomato.
3. Toast and butter bread. Place tomato on toast in small oven-proof dish.
4. Break egg into tomato and sprinkle with cheese.
5. Bake in preheated oven until egg is set and cheese is melted and brown.

Temperature: 400°
Time: 12 minutes

Sue M. Hanson

rolled broccoli soufflé

Yield: 8 to 12 servings

Easier than it sounds, an unusual treat for brunch.

Soufflé
⅓ cup butter
6 tablespoons flour
⅓ teaspoon salt
¼ teaspoon cayenne
  pepper or to taste
1¼ cups milk
½ cup freshly grated
  Parmesan cheese
½ cup grated sharp
  Cheddar cheese
7 egg yolks at room
  temperature
7 egg whites at room
  temperature
¼ teaspoon cream of
  tartar

Soufflé

1. Melt butter in saucepan. Whisk in flour, salt, and cayenne pepper. Cook over low heat, stirring constantly, for 1 to 2 minutes. Add milk and bring to a boil, stirring constantly, over low heat.
2. Beat in Parmesan and Cheddar cheeses. Stir until cheese melts.
3. Lightly beat egg yolks. Stir 1 to 2 tablespoons of hot cheese mixture into egg yolks, then beat warmed yolks into cheese mixture. Set aside.
4. Beat egg whites with cream of tartar until they hold stiff peaks. Fold egg whites into cheese mixture.
5. Line a greased jelly roll pan with waxed paper, then grease paper.

120

Spread soufflé evenly in pan and bake at 350° for 15 to 17 minutes, or until firm and lightly browned. Allow to remain in pan while making broccoli filling.

Broccoli Filling

½ cup minced onion
2 tablespoons butter
1 bunch broccoli, steamed for 10 minutes, and finely chopped
⅛ teaspoon salt
½ cup sour cream
¼ cup shredded sharp Cheddar cheese plus ¼ pound sliced Cheddar cheese

Broccoli Filling

1. Sauté onions in butter until soft. Add broccoli, salt, sour cream, and the shredded Cheddar cheese and mix well.
2. Invert the jelly roll soufflé on waxed paper that has been lightly sprinkled with Parmesan cheese. Carefully peel paper from back of the baked roll.
3. Spread broccoli mixture evenly over surface and roll up the soufflé. Place seam side down on a greased cookie sheet and lay sliced Cheddar cheese over top.
4. Broil until cheese melts. Slice and serve.

Temperature: 350°
Time: 15 to 17 minutes, then broil until browned

Nancy S. Milbury

puffy cheese wedges

Yield: 9-inch pie

A mouth melting meal.

2 eggs, beaten
1 cup flour
¾ teaspoon salt
⅛ teaspoon pepper
¾ teaspoon oregano
1½ cups milk
6 ounces Muenster cheese, grated
¾ cup sliced or chopped salami, pepperoni, or dried beef

1. Mix eggs, flour, salt, pepper, oregano, and milk.
2. Set aside ¼ cup cheese for topping. Add the rest of cheese and salami or pepperoni to egg and milk mixture.
3. Pour into a well greased pie plate and bake. Do not overbake.
4. Sprinkle with remaining cheese and bake 2 more minutes. Cut into wedges and serve.

Serve immediately

Temperature: 425°
Time: 30 minutes

Paula S. Howk

egg and chipped beef bake

Yield: 10 servings

Ideal for brunch, late-night suppers, and after skiing.

Sauce

4 slices bacon, diced
½ pound chipped beef, coarsely shredded
¼ cup butter
8-ounce can sliced mushrooms*, drained
½ cup flour
1 quart milk
pepper to taste

Scrambled Eggs

16 eggs
¼ teaspoon salt
1 cup evaporated milk
¼ cup butter
* reserved mushrooms

Sauce

1. Sauté bacon until crisp. Remove pan from heat.
2. Add chipped beef, butter, and ¾ of the mushrooms. Mix well. Reserve remaining mushrooms for garnish.
3. Sprinkle flour over the chipped beef mixture. Return pan to heat.
4. Gradually add milk, stirring constantly, until thickened. Add pepper. Set aside.

Scrambled Eggs

1. Combine eggs with salt and milk.
2. Melt butter in a large skillet. Add egg mixture and scramble.
3. To assemble, put half of the eggs in a 2-quart, oven-proof, covered casserole. Top with half of the chipped beef sauce. Repeat layers.
4. Garnish with reserved mushrooms. Cover and bake; or refrigerate, and bake the next day.

Temperature: 275°
Time: 1 hour

Susan L. Carpenter

jack cheese omelette
Yield: 4 to 6 servings

Great family Sunday night supper.

8 slices bacon
4 green onions, chopped
8 eggs
1 cup milk
½ teaspoon salt
2½ cups grated Jack
   cheese

1. Fry bacon until crisp. Drain on paper towels. Crumble. Reserve 1 tablespoon drippings.
2. Sauté green onions in reserved bacon drippings.
3. Beat eggs, milk, and salt together. Stir in bacon, onions, and 2 cups of the cheese.
4. Pour into a greased 1½-quart baking dish. Bake, uncovered, until set and light brown. When almost done, sprinkle with remaining cheese. Return to oven until cheese is melted.

Temperature: 350°
Time: 35 to 40 minutes

Elizabeth T. Williams

fresh vegetable soufflé
Yield: 2 to 4 servings

Good for luncheon or side dish.

½ cup mayonnaise
¼ cup flour
¼ teaspoon salt
dash pepper
¼ cup milk
½ cup finely chopped carrots
¼ cup finely chopped onion
¼ cup finely chopped green pepper (or any combination of fresh vegetables to equal 1 cup)
4 egg whites

Serve immediately

1. In large bowl, mix mayonnaise, flour, salt and pepper.
2. Slowly add milk. Stir in chopped vegetables.
3. In small bowl, beat egg whites until stiff but not dry. Fold into mayonnaise-vegetable mixture.
4. Pour into greased 1½-quart souffle dish and bake until knife inserted in center comes out clean.

Temperature: 325°
Time: 40 minutes

Nancy L. Ralston

eggs federico

Yield: 12 servings

A nice treat for Sunday brunch.

Filling
12 eggs, hard boiled
1½ teaspoons salt
dash of pepper
1 tablespoon
   Worcestershire sauce
4 tablespoons
   mayonnaise
½ pound ricotta cheese

1½ pounds cappicola ham
   slices (lean)
4 cups medium white
   sauce
dash of nutmeg
1 cup shredded Cheddar
   cheese

Filling
1. Shred eggs. Add salt, pepper, Worchestershire sauce, mayonnaise, and ricotta cheese. Stir mixture well. (This mixture can be refrigerated overnight.)

To Assemble
1. Place large tablespoon of filling on ham slice and roll up.
2. Add nutmeg and Cheddar cheese to white sauce, stirring over low heat until cheese melts.
3. Grease large oven-proof platter or 9 x 13-inch baking dish; cover the bottom with half of sauce.
4. Place ham rolls on sauce and cover with remaining sauce.
5. Cover dish with foil and heat in pre-heated oven until rolls are heated through.

Temperature: 325°
Time: 30 minutes

Anne W. Odenbach

green chilies n'cheese

Yield: 8 to 10 servings

Good and spicy.

3 4-ounce cans whole
   green chilies
½ pound Monterey Jack
   cheese
½ pound sharp Cheddar
   cheese
1 cup half and half
2 eggs
⅓ cup flour
1 8-ounce can tomato
   sauce

1. Carefully split open chilies, rinse out seeds, and drain on paper towels.
2. Grate cheeses and mix together. Reserve ½ cup for topping.
3. Beat half and half with eggs and flour until smooth.
4. In a greased 1½-quart casserole, alternate layers of cheese, chilies, and egg mixture. Pour tomato sauce over last layer and sprinkle with reserved cheese.
5. Bake uncovered.

Temperature: 350°
Time: 1¼ to 1½ hours

Carol K. MacDonald

lo-cal vegetable quiche

Yield: 4 servings

As good as the fattening version.

1 pound zucchini squash, grated
1½ teaspoons salt
2 cups grated Monterey Jack cheese
4 eggs, well beaten
1 teaspoon dill
½ cup Parmesan cheese
tomatoes for garnish

1. Sprinkle grated squash with ½ teaspoon of the salt. Let stand 10 minutes to draw out excess liquid. Drain off liquid.
2. In a large bowl, combine cheese, eggs, dill, and remaining teaspoon of salt; beat well.
3. Stir in zucchini. Pour into a greased, 10-inch quiche pan.
4. Sprinkle top with grated cheese. Bake until quiche is set in the center.
5. Garnish, and serve.

Temperature: 350°
Time: 35 minutes

Hint: Serve this with our Speedy Gazpacho (see index) and thumb your nose at calories!

Judy Anibal

tomato quiche

Yield: 9-inch pie

Mild, different, great way to use summer tomatoes.

9-inch pie crust, partially baked
2 tablespoons butter
1 cup finely chopped onion
1 cup peeled, chopped tomatoes
pinch of thyme
dash of salt
3 eggs, beaten
1 cup milk
½ teaspoon salt
½ cup grated Parmesan cheese
1 cup grated Swiss cheese
2 large tomatoes, sliced

1. Partially bake crust at 400° for 5 minutes.
2. Melt butter and sauté onion.
3. Add chopped tomatoes, thyme, and salt.
4. Cover and cook mixture 5 minutes.
5. Uncover pan and mash tomatoes.
6. Cook, uncovered, until mixture is dry. Cool.
7. Beat eggs, milk, and ½ teaspoon salt together; stir in cheeses and cooled tomato mixture. Pour into crust.
8. Sliced tomatoes can be used either as lining of pie crust or as garnish of cooked quiche.
9. Bake until a knife inserted into center comes out clean.
10. Remove from oven. Allow to cool 15 minutes before serving.

Temperature: 350°
Time: 30 to 45 minutes

Mary E. Krell

broccoli and cheese quiche

Yield: 10-inch pie

Serve Sunday morning with champagne.

Crust

3 ounces cream cheese at room temperature
¼ pound butter at room temperature
1 cup flour

Filling

1 chopped shallot or ¼ cup chopped green onion
½ cup sliced fresh mushrooms
3 tablespoons butter
5 eggs
1 cup half and half
½ cup milk
1 teaspoon salt
dash fresh ground pepper
4 ounces Swiss cheese, grated
1 10-ounce package frozen, chopped broccoli, cooked and drained
½ cup diced tomatoes (optional)

Crust

1. Cream cheese and butter together. Add flour and mix.
2. Press into greased pie plate.

Filling

1. Sauté shallot or onions and mushrooms in butter until soft.
2. In blender, combine eggs, half and half, milk, salt, and pepper.
3. To assemble, place mushrooms and shallot in bottom of pie crust. Sprinkle with cheese. Add broccoli and tomatoes.
4. Pour egg and milk mixture over all and bake.
5. Let set 5 minutes before serving.

Temperature: 350°
Time: 1 hour

Lynn P. Natapow

126

quiche lorraine verte

Yield: Four 8 or 9-inch pies

This quiche is green; well suited for Christmas or St. Patrick's Day.

1 pound sliced bacon cut into fourths
4 unbaked pie crusts
1½ pounds Swiss cheese slices cut into ½-inch x 2-inch strips

Filling
Triple the following ingredients to fill the 4 pies:
4 eggs
1 tablespoon flour
¾ teaspoon salt
dash of ground pepper
⅛ teaspoon nutmeg
1 pint half and half
1 tablespoon soft butter
4 green onions, including tops, chopped
whole pimientos as garnish

1. Fry bacon until cooked but not too crisp. Place in bottom of crusts.
2. Place cheese strips in a criss-cross pattern on top of the bacon.
3. Set pies aside and prepare filling.

Filling
1. Combine filling ingredients 3 times in blender. Green onion tops will give this a green color. Mixture will be foamy.
2. Divide the filling among the pies and bake.
3. Garnish with pimientos cut into shapes.

Temperature: 375°
Time: 40 minutes

Hint: These may be baked for 25 to 30 minutes, then frozen. Thaw completely and bake at 375° for 10 to 15 minutes.

Nancy R. Murphy

 cranberry pilaf

Yield: 4 to 6 servings

An excellent accompaniment for poultry and pork.

2 tablespoons butter
½ cup minced onion
2 tablespoons chopped fresh parsley
2 chicken bouillon cubes
2 cups boiling water
1 cup raw rice
½ cup chopped cranberries

1. Melt butter in a covered saucepan. Sauté onion until transparent. Add parsley.
2. Combine bouillon cubes and boiling water. Add to onion and parsley.
3. Stir in rice. Bring mixture to a boil.
4. Add cranberries. Simmer, covered, for 25 minutes, or until liquid is absorbed.

Nancy M. Ralston

rochester's italian quiche

Terrific!

4 Italian sausage links,
casings removed
1 onion, sliced
4 medium tomatoes,
peeled, seeded, and
chopped
pinch each of thyme,
basil, and parsley
2 tablespoons quick
mixing flour
2 cups cubed Swiss
cheese
1 tablespoon grated
Parmesan cheese
pinch of salt and pepper
10-inch deep-dish,
unbaked pie crust
1 cup cream
½ cup milk
4 eggs, slightly beaten

1. Crumble sausage. Brown 3 to 5
minutes.
2. Add onion. Continue cooking
until onion is transparent.
3. Add tomatoes. Sauté 5 minutes.
4. Blend in spices and flour.
5. Place sausage-tomato mixture,
cheeses, salt, and pepper into
pie crust.
6. Combine cream, milk, and eggs.
Pour over ingredients in pie
crust.
7. Bake at 450° for 15 minutes.
Reduce oven heat to 375°. Bake
for 25 minutes, or until knife
inserted in center comes out
clean.

Temperature: 450°
Time: 15 minutes

Temperature: 375°
Time: 25 minutes

Susan G. Rhoda

sourdough soufflé

Yield: 8 servings

Serve at brunch, lunch, or as an hors d'oeuvre.

1 large loaf sourdough or
  French bread
butter
½ pound extra sharp
  Cheddar (grated)
2½ cups milk
3 to 4 eggs
1 teaspoon salt
1 teaspoon dry mustard

1. Slice bread. Remove crusts. Butter both sides.
2. Line a 9-x-13-inch baking dish with half of the bread. Top with half of the cheese. Repeat layers.
3. Mix together milk, eggs, salt, and mustard. Pour over bread and cheese.
4. Bake uncovered. Serve or freeze.
5. To serve after freezing, take out the night before and reheat.

Temperature: 350°
Time: 1 hour

Polly C. Parker

gruyère cheese soufflé

Yield: 6 servings

A delicious, strong cheese-flavored entrée.

1 leek
¼ cup unsalted butter
2 tablespoons all-purpose
  flour
1 cup hot milk
8 ounces Gruyère cheese,
  shredded
1 teaspoon Dijon mustard
½ teaspoon salt
⅛ teaspoon grated
  nutmeg
4 egg yolks, beaten
4 sprigs parsley
1 teaspoon chervil
4 egg whites
pinch of salt (less than ¼
  teaspoon)

1. Clean and chop leek using white part only.
2. Sauté leek in butter. Stir in flour and milk. Whisk for 5 to 7 minutes, until mixture thickens.
3. Add cheese. Stir for 3 to 4 minutes until cheese has melted.
4. Add mustard, salt, and nutmeg.
5. Combine ¼ cup of cheese mixture with beaten egg yolks. Stir this into remaining cheese mixture.
6. Pour this batter into food processor along with parsley and chervil. Purée.
7. Beat egg whites in another bowl. Add salt. Continue beating until they are stiff.
8. Fold cheese mixture into egg whites.
9. Spoon entire mixture into a buttered 8-cup soufflé dish. Bake.

Temperature: 400°
Time: 35 to 40 minutes

Nancy S. Milbury

129

barley pilaf

Yield: 8 servings

My children's favorite side dish. There's never a bit left over!

1½ pounds fresh
   mushrooms, sliced
2 medium onions,
   chopped
8 tablespoons butter
1¾ cups uncooked
   medium pearled barley
4 cups chicken broth

1. Sauté mushrooms and onions in 4 tablespoons of the butter. Place in a 2-quart casserole.
2. In same pan, sauté barley in remaining 4 tablespoons butter over low heat. Cook and stir until barley is almond-colored. This will take 10 to 15 minutes. Add to mushrooms.
3. Pour broth over all. Salt and pepper to taste. Bake. Cover casserole only during first half of cooking. Add water if barley becomes dry.

Temperature: 350°
Time: 1 to 1½ hours

Margo C. Shaw

brunch casserole

Yield: 6 servings

Popular dish for luncheon or light supper.

8 slices white bread
¾ cup melted butter
2 cups cubed, cooked
   ham
2 cups chopped, cooked
   broccoli
2 cups (½ pound)
   shredded sharp Cheddar
   cheese
4 eggs
2 cups milk
1 teaspoon salt
½ teaspoon pepper

1. Cube bread. Add melted butter and toss well.
2. In buttered 9 x 13-inch casserole layer the ingredients in the following order: half of the bread cubes, half of the shredded cheese, half of the broccoli, all of the ham, then remaining broccoli, remaining cheese, and remaining bread cubes.
3. Beat eggs and milk thoroughly with seasonings.
4. Pour over all layers.
5. Refrigerate overnight or at least 2 hours.
6. Bake until puffy and nicely brown.

Must be done ahead

Temperature: 350°
Time: 1 hour

Hint: A great way to use leftover holiday ham.

Violet E. Kapusta

swiss fondue

Authentic recipe for a delightful dish.

1 loaf French bread
1 garlic clove
1 pound Gruyère cheese
1 pound Emmenthal or
  Appenzell cheese
1 750-milliliter bottle dry
  white wine minus 1 cup
2 teaspoons arrowroot
¼ teaspoon nutmeg
freshly ground pepper
  (about 4 twists of the
  pepper mill)
¼ cup Kirsch (cherry
  flavored liqueur)

1. Cube French bread; allow cubes to sit out to get slightly dry.
2. Rub pan (cast iron is best) with garlic clove.
3. Grate the cheeses.
4. Combine cheeses with wine in prepared pan over medium-low heat. Heat until all cheese is melted, stirring with a wooden spoon. Enjoy remaining cup of wine while proceeding.
5. Slowly add arrowroot to thicken a bit. Add nutmeg and pepper. Cook over low heat until desired thickness.
6. Put mixture in a warmed fondue pot and stir in Kirsch.
7. Dip bread cubes into fondue and enjoy.

Must serve immediately

Hint: Arrowroot is usually stocked near thickeners such as cornstarch at your grocery store.

Jane F. Bailey

Jane learned to make authentic Swiss fondue while living in Mexico City! Her landlord, Guido Meister, often felt homesick for his beloved Switzerland. To recapture the tastes and smells of his Alpine homeland, he would often cook fondue, the traditional after ski repast.

sausage and pepper strata

Yield: 4 to 6 servings

Zippy change from plain strata.

1 pound bulk pork
  sausage
5 slices whole wheat
  bread, crust removed
soft butter (approximately
  ½ cup)
3 cups (¾ pound)
  shredded, sharp
  Cheddar cheese
4 eggs, beaten slightly
2 cups milk
½ teaspoon dry mustard
¼ cup chopped
  pepperoncini (*or* ¼ cup
  chopped hot banana
  peppers), drained,
  rinsed, and seeded

1. Brown sausage. Drain and set aside.
2. Butter one side of each slice of bread; cut bread into 1-inch cubes.
3. In buttered 2-quart casserole place half of bread cubes. Sprinkle with half of the cheese. Cover with sausage. Place remaining bread cubes on sausage and top with remaining cheese.
4. Combine eggs, milk, and seasonings. Pour over layers.
5. Cover and refrigerate several hours or overnight.
6. Before baking, sprinkle with peppers.
7. Bake, uncovered, until golden brown and set.

Must do ahead

Temperature: 350°
Time: 1 hour

Cynthia L. Bartlett

barley casserole

Yield: 6 servings

A good replacement for rice or potatoes.

¾ cup pearled barley
3 cups water
3 tablespoons bacon
  drippings
2 carrots, sliced
2 to 3 tomatoes, chopped
1 green pepper, diced
2 stalks celery, thinly
  sliced
1 tablespoon salt
½ teaspoon pepper

1. Combine all ingredients, and place in a 2-quart casserole. This can be done anytime the day you will be serving the barley.
2. Bake in casserole, covered, then uncovered.

Temperature: 350°
Time: 40 minutes covered then 20 minutes uncovered

Hint: Can substitute other fresh vegetables or use leftovers.

Violet E. Kapusta

mexican lasagne

Yield: 5 servings

The perfect combination of Mexican flavors—but not too spicy.

¾ pound ground beef
1 teaspoon chopped
  onion
½ teaspoon garlic salt
1 package taco seasoning
  (1¼-ounce size)
2 8-ounce cans tomato
  sauce
1 cup cottage cheese
  (small curd)
1 cup sour cream
1 4-ounce can chopped
  green chilies
1 7-ounce package tortilla
  chips
8 ounces sharp Cheddar
  cheese, shredded

1. Sauté ground beef, drain excess fat.
2. Add the onions, garlic salt, taco seasoning, and tomato sauce to the beef. Simmer for 5 minutes. Set aside.
3. In a large bowl, mix cottage cheese, sour cream, and chilies. Set aside.
4. In a deep 2-quart casserole, layer a third of the tortilla chips, half the meat sauce, half the Cheddar cheese, and half the cottage cheese mixture. Repeat layers. Cover with remaining third of the tortilla chips. Bake.

Temperature: 350°
Time: 35 to 40 minutes

Susan L. Carpenter

rice mushroom casserole

Yield: 6 servings

Easy to make and cooks right along with most any main dish.

½ cup butter or
  margarine
1 medium onion, diced
6 to 8 ounces fresh
  mushrooms, quartered
2½ cups beef or chicken
  bouillon (or 2 10-ounce
  cans consommé)
1 cup uncooked
  converted rice
¼ teaspoon salt
garlic
oregano

1. In butter or margarine, sauté onions and mushrooms until tender.
2. In a medium-size casserole, combine onions, mushrooms, bouillon, and rice. Season with salt, garlic, and oregano to taste.
3. Bake, covered. (This is very soupy but will absorb liquid as it bakes.)

Temperature: 325°
Time: 1 hour

Susan P. Larson

rice and chili pepper casserole

Yield: 8 servings

This is just spicy enough.

¼ cup butter
1 cup chopped onion
4 cups hot, cooked, converted rice
2 cups sour cream
1 cup cream-style cottage cheese
1 large bay leaf, crumbled
½ teaspoon salt
⅛ teaspoon pepper
3 4-ounce cans green chili peppers, drained and halved lengthwise, with seeds left in
2 cups grated sharp Cheddar cheese

1. Melt butter in a large skillet. Sauté onion for 5 minutes.
2. Stir in hot rice, sour cream, cottage cheese, bay leaf, salt, and pepper.
3. Put half of the rice mixture in a buttered 2-quart casserole. Top with half of the chilis and half of the cheese. Repeat layers.
4. Bake, uncovered, until hot and bubbly; or refrigerate, and bake later.

Temperature: 375°
Time: 25 minutes

Caroll J. Meyers

blue cheese rice

Yield: 4 to 6 servings

Terrific with grilled meat or poultry.

1 cup cooked rice, brown or white
2 tablespoons melted butter
2 tablespoons fresh lemon juice
½ teaspoon dry mustard
¼ cup sliced scallions
½ cup sliced black olives
2 hard boiled eggs, chopped
¾ cup sour cream
½ teaspoon salt
¼ teaspoon freshly ground pepper
4 ounces firm blue cheese, crumbled

1. Combine rice, butter, lemon juice, and mustard.
2. Add scallions, olives, eggs, sour cream, salt, and pepper. Mix well.
3. Stir in blue cheese.
4. Place in greased 1-quart casserole and bake, covered, or refrigerate until ready to bake.

Temperature: 350°
Time: 30 minutes

Nicki R. Doolittle

stuffed shells

Serve with pride and a green salad.

Sauce

2 onions, chopped
1 green pepper, chopped
3 cloves garlic, minced
2 tablespoons oil
½ pound mushrooms, chopped
2 29-ounce cans tomato purée
1 6-ounce can tomato paste
1 cup water
1½ teaspoons basil
2 teaspoons oregano
1 pound hot Italian sausage
1 box large shells

Filling

12 ounces Mozzarella cheese, diced
2 15-ounce containers ricotta cheese
4 eggs
6 tablespoons Parmesan cheese
2 tablespoons parsley
2 tablespoons chives
onion salt or salt to taste
pepper to taste
Romano cheese, grated

Must do part ahead.

Sauce

1. Sauté onions, pepper, and garlic in oil for 5 minutes.
2. Add mushrooms, and sauté 5 minutes more.
3. Stir in tomato purée, paste, water, and spices.
4. Cook and crumble sausage in a separate pan. Drain off fat.
5. Add to sauce, and simmer about 3 hours. Add more water if sauce gets too thick.
6. Shortly before assemblage, cook shells according to directions; drain.

Filling and Assembly

1. Combine all ingredients except Romano cheese. Spoon into shells. If mixture is too thin, add more Parmesan.
2. Spoon some sauce into bottom of a 9 x 13-inch pan. Lay stuffed shells in pan.
3. Pour on additional sauce. Sprinkle with Romano. Bake.

Temperature: 325°
Time: 25 to 30 minutes

Linda H. Henderson

kugel

Yield: 10 to 12 servings

This traditional Jewish dish goes beautifully with a dairy or fish meal.

¼ pound margarine, melted

6 eggs

½ cup sugar

2 teaspoons vanilla

1 8-ounce container whipped cream cheese

1 pint sour cream

1 16-ounce box egg noodles, cooked according to package directions

1. Combine margarine, eggs, sugar, vanilla, and cream cheese in a blender or food processor until well mixed. Add sour cream. Blend.
2. Mix noodles with sour cream mixture. Pour into a 2-quart oven-proof casserole.

Topping

1½ cups crushed corn flakes

¼ pound margarine, melted

½ cup sugar

Must freeze before baking.

Topping

1. Combine topping ingredients. Sprinkle over noodles.
2. Cover. Freeze kugel. Bake while frozen, covered.
3. Serve hot, cut into squares.

Temperature: 400°
Time: 2 hours

Belle Kessler

oriental rice casserole

Yield: 8 servings

A delightful blend of flavors.

⅔ cup fresh mushrooms sautéed

1 cup chopped onion

1 cup chopped celery

4 tablespoons butter

¾ cup wild rice

¾ cup long grained rice

¼ cup soy sauce

1 5-ounce can water chestnuts, drained and sliced

⅓ cup slivered almonds, toasted

3½ cups chicken broth

1. Sauté mushrooms, onion, and celery in butter.
2. Combine with all other ingredients, cover and bake in a lightly greased 2-quart casserole until all liquid is absorbed.

Temperature: 350°
Time: About 1 hour

Emily M. Henderson

salsa italiano

Yield: 4 to 6 servings

A thick, meaty, pasta sauce.

1 pound hot Italian sausage links, cut into ½-inch pieces

2 tablespoons vegetable oil

1 pound mushrooms, sliced

2 cloves garlic, minced

1 large onion (or 2 medium onions), coarsely chopped

1 pound ground beef (round or chuck)

2 teaspoons salt

¼ teaspoon pepper

½ teaspoon rosemary or basil

1 tablespoon chopped parsley

2 6-ounce cans tomato paste

1½ cups hot water

1. Brown sausage in oil. Remove from pan. Drain on paper towels. Pour off all but 2 tablespoons fat.
2. Sauté mushrooms in the fat. Remove with slotted spoon. Set aside.
3. Cook garlic and onions, in same pan, until onions are soft.
4. Add ground beef. Cook until well browned. Pour off excess fat.
5. Stir in seasonings, tomato paste, and water.
6. Add mushrooms and sausage. Simmer 30 minutes, stirring often. Correct seasonings.

Hint: If you prefer a **thinner consistency**, add canned or homemade tomato sauce.

Lucia H. Shaw

Every pasta lover knows that the only palatable way to eat spaghetti is "al dente" which, in translation, means "to the tooth," and in general usage means "firmly cooked." There is a point at which, in the boiling of spaghetti, that the hard, starchy pasta softens so that the solid center just disappears. It is at this moment that the spaghetti must be drained, and a small amount of cold water must be added so that overcooking cannot occur. Tracy's father absolutely refuses to eat anything but perfect pasta. He has sent the spaghetti back in many restaurants. Once he threw out a whole batch Tracy's mother-in-law had cooked, then cooked a new potful before her astonished gaze. She was quietly appalled at his high-handed manner, but has never cooked soggy spaghetti since.

spaghetti pie

Yield: 6 servings

Attractive and novel way to serve spaghetti.

Crust

6 ounces spaghetti
2 tablespoons margarine
½ cup grated Parmesan cheese
2 eggs, beaten

Sauce

1 pound ground beef *or* ½ pound ground beef and ½ pound ground sausage
½ cup chopped onion
¼ cup chopped green pepper
1 8-ounce can cut-up tomatoes
1 6-ounce can tomato paste
1 teaspoon sugar
1 teaspoon oregano
½ teaspoon garlic salt
1 to 1½ cups ricotta or cottage cheese
1 cup grated or sliced Mozzarella cheese

Crust

1. Cook and drain spaghetti.
2. Add margarine, eggs, and Parmesan cheese to spaghetti.
3. Form mixture into crust in 10-inch buttered pie plate.

Sauce

1. Sauté meat, onion, and green pepper, drain off excess fat.
2. Stir in undrained tomatoes, tomato paste, sugar, oregano, and garlic salt.
3. Heat through.

To Assemble Pie

1. Spread ricotta over crust.
2. Top with meat mixture.
3. Bake, uncovered, for 25 minutes.
4. Sprinkle with Mozzarella and bake 5 more minutes.

Temperature: 350°
Time: 30 minutes

Ginny Y. Gray

fettucini alfredo

Yield: 6 servings

A rich and attractive company dish.

½ cup sweet butter, softened
1 cup heavy cream
1 cup (4 ounces) freshly grated Parmesan cheese
⅓ cup chopped pimiento
1 9-ounce package frozen artichoke hearts, thawed and halved
1 pound plus 3 ounces fettucini
salt
pepper

1. Combine butter, cream, cheese, pimiento, and artichokes in a skillet. Heat thoroughly.
2. Cook the fettucini. Drain. Pour the sauce over the hot pasta. Toss lightly until noodles are coated. Add salt and pepper to taste.
3. Serve immediately.

Ann E. Prince

seafood lasagne

Yield: 12 servings

The fruits of the sea add surprise to a favorite dish!

12 lasagne noodles
1 cup chopped onions
2 tablespoons butter or
   margarine
1 8-ounce package cream
   cheese, softened
1½ cups cream-style
   cottage cheese
1 egg, beaten
2 teaspoons crushed basil
½ teaspoon salt
⅛ teaspoon pepper
2 cups medium white
   sauce:
      ¼ cup flour
      ¼ cup butter, melted
      2 cups milk
⅔ cup dry white wine
1 pound cooked shrimp,
   shelled and cut in half
   lengthwise
1 7½-ounce can
   crabmeat, drained and
   flaked
¼ cup grated Parmesan
   cheese
½ cup shredded sharp
   processed American
   cheese
fresh parsley
extra shrimp for garnish

1. Cook noodles according to package directions; drain.
2. Put two layers of three noodles each on bottom of a greased 9 x 13-inch baking dish.
3. Sauté onion in melted butter until tender. Blend in cream cheese, then add cottage cheese, egg, basil, salt, and pepper. Mix thoroughly. Spread half on top of noodles.
4. Make a white sauce. Blend flour into butter. Gradually add milk. Cook, stirring. constantly, until thickened.
5. Combine white sauce and wine. Stir in shrimp and crabmeat; spread half over cottage cheese layer.
6. Repeat layers starting with remaining noodles, then cottage cheese mixture, then seafood mixture.
7. Sprinkle with Parmesan cheese. Bake uncovered. Top with American cheese, and bake 2 to 3 minutes until the cheese is melted.
8. Let stand 15 minutes before serving. Garnish with parsley and shrimp, as desired.

Temperature: 350°
Time: 45 minutes

Nancy R. Garlick

tortellini with prosciutto and peas

Yield: 8 servings

This marvelous recipe evolved from a trip to Italy.

Pasta

3 cups unsifted flour
1 teaspoon salt
4 eggs
2 tablespoons olive oil
few drops of water
pasta machine

Pasta

1. Place flour and salt in a food processor. In a separate bowl, mix 2 of the eggs, oil, and water. Turn processor on and pour egg mixture through the feed tube. Add remaining eggs slowly until a ball of dough forms on the blades. Remove dough; knead lightly.
2. Beginning with the widest setting on a pasta machine, process ¼ of the dough to the lowest setting. (Keep dough covered throughout recipe with a damp towel or plastic wrap when it is not being handled.) If not using a pasta machine, knead the dough until smooth and elastic, and roll until paper thin. Cut dough in 2-inch rounds with a glass or biscuit cutter. Repeat this procedure with remaining dough.

Filling and Assembly

2¼ cups finely chopped, cooked chicken (3 whole breasts, skinned and boned)
½ cup freshly grated Parmesan cheese
2 egg yolks, beaten
⅛ teaspoon grated lemon peel
⅛ teaspoon ground nutmeg
salt to taste
freshly ground black pepper

Filling and Assembly

1. Mix all filling ingredients in food processor until well combined.
2. Place ¼ to ½ teaspoon filling in the center of each pasta round. Moisten edges, fold circle in half, and press edges to seal.
3. Shape into rings by stretching the tips lightly and wrapping filled half circle around your finger. Press tips together. Keep covered with plastic wrap or dampened towel.
4. Cook tortellini in a large amount of boiling salted water, stirring frequently. Remove, using a slotted spoon, when just tender, about 8 minutes. Drain carefully on paper towels.

tortellini   *continued*

Sauce
¾ cup butter
1 cup heavy cream
5 thin slices prosciutto
  ham, julienned
½ cup peas, briefly
  cooked
1 cup freshly grated
  Parmesan cheese
freshly ground pepper
freshly grated Parmesan
  cheese to taste

Must use food processor.

Sauce
1. Melt butter in a large, heavy
   skillet over medium heat. Add
   tortellini. Stir gently until well
   coated with butter.
2. Add cream and ham. Cook until
   mixture thickens slightly.
3. Add peas, cheese, and pepper to
   taste. Cook until cheese melts.
4. Serve with additional Parmesan
   cheese.

**Hint: The entire dish may be frozen. To serve, bring to room
temperature. Heat, covered, at 350° about 25 minutes or until
bubbly. Tortellini, cooked or uncooked, may be frozen on cookie
sheets, then wrapped tightly for later use.**

Cathie Meisenzahl

clam sauce poseidon   Yield: 2 servings

Serve in soup bowls over spaghetti and enjoy!

¼ cup olive oil
1 clove garlic, minced
¼ cup water
½ teaspoon salt
½ teaspoon oregano
¼ cup chopped parsley
¼ teaspoon ground
  pepper
1 6½-ounce can minced
  clams with juice

Optional:
grated Parmesan cheese
crushed red pepper

1. Heat oil in a saucepan. Sauté
   garlic in oil until lightly
   browned. Remove from heat and
   cool slightly.
2. Add water slowly.
3. Add remaining ingredients; heat
   through. Can refrigerate and
   reheat slowly at serving time.
4. Serve over al dente (firmly
   cooked) spaghetti and pass
   grated Parmesan cheese and red
   pepper.

**Hint: If recipe is doubled, do not add the juice from the second
can of clams.**

Patricia S. Driscoll

🍎 cannelloni   Yield: 24 cannellonis (6 to 8 servings)

Very light, special—worth any effort.

Tomato Sauce

4 tablespoons olive oil
1 cup finely chopped
  onion
4 cups Italian tomatoes,
  chopped
4 tablespoons tomato
  paste
2 tablespoons fresh basil
  or 2 teaspoons dried
  basil
2 teaspoons sugar
1 teaspoon salt
freshly ground pepper

Pasta

1½ cups unsifted flour
1 teaspoon salt
2 eggs
1 tablespoon olive oil
few drops of water

Tomato Sauce

1. Cook onions in olive oil until
   tender.
2. Add remaining ingredients and
   simmer, partly covered, 40
   minutes. Stir frequently.
3. Strain sauce.·

Pasta

1. Place flour and salt in food
   processor.
2. Mix together 1 egg, oil, and
   water.
3. Turn on food processor and
   pour egg mixture through feed
   tube. If ball of dough has not
   formed on blades, start adding
   remaining egg until a ball forms.
   Stop!
4. If using pasta machine: Knead
   dough for two minutes by hand.
   Sprinkle machine with flour.
   Beginning with the thickest
   setting on the machine, take
   half of the dough and put it
   through the machine 2 to 3
   times at this setting. Keep
   unused dough covered with
   plastic wrap or damp towel.
   Continue to put dough through
   machine until you have reached
   the lowest setting. Dough
   should be almost transparent
   and very elastic—the thinner
   the better. Repeat with
   remaining dough.
5. If using hand method: Knead
   dough until smooth and elastic.
   Roll paper thin on lightly floured
   surface.

6. Both methods: Cut in rectangles 2 x 3 inches. Pasta can be made into various shapes for other uses. Place in large pan of boiling, salted water and cook about 3 minutes until barely tender. Cook only a few at a time and remove from water with a strainer. Place on towels to drain.

Filling

3 tablespoons butter
4 tablespoons finely chopped onions
¾ pound finely ground veal
2 10-ounce packages frozen. chopped spinach, thawed and thoroughly squeezed dry, or 2 bags of fresh spinach, cooked, chopped and squeezed dry (should equal 1¼ cups)
½ cup freshly grated Parmesan cheese
pinch of nutmeg
3 eggs, lightly beaten
salt to taste

Besciamella Sauce

4 tablespoons butter
4 tablespoons flour
1 cup milk
1 cup heavy cream
1 teaspoon salt
⅛ teaspoon white pepper

Assembly

Besciamella sauce
stuffed cannelloni
tomato sauce
6 tablespoons freshly grated Parmesan cheese
2 tablespoons butter

Filling

1. Melt butter and cook onions until tender.
2. Add veal and cook until all liquid has cooked away.
3. Stir in spinach, cheese, and nutmeg.
4. Add eggs to veal mixture.
5. Add salt to taste.
6. Divide mixture among pasta rectangles using 1 heaping tablespoon or more for each. Fill as full as possible and roll each cannelloni the long way.

Besciamella Sauce

1. Melt butter over medium heat; stir in flour.
2. Add milk and cream and whisk until smooth.
3. Simmer 3 minutes or until whisk is heavily coated.
4. Season with salt and pepper.

Assembly

1. Pour film of besciamella sauce over bottom of large glass baking dish.
2. Add cannelloni, seam side down.
3. Cover with besciamella, followed by tomato sauce.
4. Sprinkle with cheese and dot with butter.
5. Bake, uncovered, in middle of oven until bubbly and cheese melts.
6. Brown lightly under broiler.

See next page

Freezing
1. This may be completely assembled and frozen. To serve: thaw, bring to room temperature and proceed with baking instructions.
2. All parts of this recipe may be frozen separately and assembled at a later date.

Must be done ahead

Temperature: 375°
Time: 20 minutes

Cathie S. Meisenzahl

vegetables

vegetables

VEGETABLES

orange carrots

Yield: 4 to 6 servings

A colorful addition to any dinner.

2 pounds baby carrots
¼ cup butter, melted
¼ cup brown sugar
¼ cup orange juice
   concentrate, thawed
½ cup Mandarin orange
   pieces
½ teaspoon salt

Must do ahead.

1. Boil whole carrots until tender; drain.
2. Combine remaining ingredients until well blended.
3. Place carrots in buttered baking dish and cover with sauce. Refrigerate overnight.
4. Turn carrots to coat with sauce.
5. Bake.

Temperature: 350°
Time: 20 to 25 minutes

Peggi M. Godwin

senator russell sweet potatoes

Yield: 10 servings

Our candy sweet Thanksgiving tradition.

enough sweet potatoes to
   make
3½ cups mashed sweet
   potatoes
½ cup sugar
2 eggs
1 teaspoon vanilla
½ cup milk
¼ cup butter, softened

Topping
½ cup brown sugar
⅓ cup flour
¼ cup butter, melted
1 cup chopped pecans

1. Bake sweet potatoes at 450° for 1 hour.
2. Scoop potato from shells.
3. Combine potatoes, sugar, eggs, vanilla, milk, and butter.
4. Place in large casserole.

Topping
1. Combine brown sugar, flour, butter, and pecans.
2. Place on top of potatoes in casserole.
3. Cover casserole. (This can be made a day ahead up to this point.)
4. Bake in low oven.
5. Uncover for last 10 minutes of baking.

Temperature: 450°
Time: 1 hour

Temperature: 275°
Time: 50 minutes

Tracy K. Kessler

hasselback potatoes

Yield: 4 servings

Tastes gourmet, but even the kids will like it.

4 medium oblong
　potatoes
5 tablespoons butter,
　melted
1 teaspoon salt
1 tablespoon bread
　crumbs
1 tablespoon grated
　Parmesan cheese

1. Peel potatoes or leave skins on
　and scrub with brush. With
　sharp knife slice each potato
　crosswise about every ¼ to ½
　inch, but not quite all the way
　through.
2. Place potatoes in a buttered pie
　plate.
3. Drizzle with 2 tablespoons of
　the melted butter and sprinkle
　with salt. Bake for 30 minutes.
4. Sprinkle bread crumbs over
　potatoes and drizzle with
　remaining butter. Bake for 20
　minutes.
5. Sprinkle with Parmesan cheese.
　Baste with butter from pie plate.
　Bake 10 more minutes, or until
　potatoes are tender.

Temperature: 425°
Time: 1 hour

Peggi M. Godwin

fresh bean casserole

Yield: 6 to 8 servings

Excellent use for beans and tomatoes from a garden harvest.

3 bacon slices
1 medium onion, chopped
3 cups whole fresh green
　or yellow beans, cooked
¼ to ⅓ cup mayonnaise
¼ to ⅓ cup sour cream
½ cup Cheddar cheese,
　grated
salt
freshly ground pepper
2 fresh tomatoes,
　unpeeled and quartered

1. Sauté bacon, remove and
　crumble.
2. Cook onion in same pan.
　Combine with beans and bacon
　in a 2-quart oven-proof
　casserole.
3. Blend mayonnaise, sour cream,
　and cheese. Pour over bean
　mixture and toss lightly. Add
　salt and pepper to taste.
4. Add tomato quarters. Cover
　and heat thoroughly just before
　serving.

Temperature: 325°
Time: 15 to 20 minutes

Barbara H. Hanna

146

eggplant supreme

Yield: 6 to 8 servings

A solution to the eggplant dilemma.

1 medium eggplant
salt
flour
1 egg
1 tablespoon water
bread crumbs
¼ cup oil
¼ cup butter
1 small onion, chopped
2 medium tomatoes,
    peeled, seeded, and
    chopped
6 ounces heavy cream
pepper to taste
1 teaspoon thyme
1 teaspoon rosemary
½ teaspoon oregano
8 ounces Mozzarella
    cheese
¼ cup Romano cheese

1. Slice eggplant in ¼-inch slices. Salt generously and let stand 10-15 minutes. Drain excess moisture on paper towels.
2. Lightly flour eggplant. Dip into 1 egg, beaten with 1 tablespoon water. Then coat eggplant in fine bread crumbs.
3. Sauté eggplant in 1 tablespoon of butter and 1 tablespoon of oil. Add more oil and butter as necessary.
4. Remove eggplant from pan.
5. In same pan, sauté onion and add tomatoes. Cook 2 to 3 minutes.
6. Add cream and spices to pan. Do not bring to a boil.
7. In medium-size casserole, layer eggplant with Mozzarella and half the sauce. Repeat.
8. Top with grated Romano. (This can made a day ahead up to this point.)
9. Bake uncovered.

Temperature: 350°
Time: 40 minutes

Hint: To seed a tomato, peel it, halve it, and squeeze each half gently to remove juice and seeds.

Pate S. Driscoll

lemon-mint peas

Yield: 6 servings

An early summer garden treat.

½ cup butter
1 tablespoon lemon juice
¼ teaspoon grated lemon
    peel
2 tablespoons chopped
    fresh mint leaves
4 cups fresh shelled peas

1. Cream butter, lemon juice, and lemon peel together. Add chopped mint.
2. Combine butter mixture with peas and cook over high heat for 10 minutes.
3. Serve immediately.

Polly C. Parker

147

spinach timbales

Yield: 8 servings

Not a hard job for a party dish.

¼ cup minced onion
8 tablespoons butter
3 cups cooked, drained,
  and chopped spinach (3
  10-ounce bags, fresh)
1 cup light cream
4 eggs
1 egg yolk
salt and pepper to taste
¼ teaspoon nutmeg
8 tomato slices
3 hard boiled egg yolks,
  chopped
8 6-ounce custard cups,
  greased

1. In an enamel skillet, sauté minced onion in 6 tablespoons of the butter.
2. Add spinach and toss with the butter and onion until it is well combined.
3. Add cream and simmer mixture until cream is reduced and absorbed by spinach.
4. Transfer mixture to a bowl and allow to cool for 10 minutes.
5. Add uncooked eggs and egg yolk, lightly beaten, to the spinach mixture. Add salt, pepper, and nutmeg. Mix. Fill custard cups with spinach mixture.
6. Place cups in pan with enough hot water to reach ⅔ of the way up the sides of cups.
7. Bake until puffed and set, about 25 minutes.
8. Remove cups from the pan and let stand for 5 minutes.
9. Sauté tomato slices in 2 tablespoons of the butter for 2 to 3 minutes on each side. Season with salt and pepper.
10. Arrange tomato slices on serving dish. Unmold each timbale onto a tomato slice and sprinkle with chopped hard boiled egg yolk.

Temperature: 325°
Time: 25 minutes

Margaret Beale

mama's limas

Yield: 8 servings

An old family recipe that is terrific with ham.

4 1-pound cans butter or
   lima beans
¾ cup butter, melted
1 cup sour cream
1 cup brown sugar
1 tablespoon molasses
1 teaspoon dry mustard
dash of salt

1. Drain beans.
2. Add butter, sour cream, brown sugar, molasses, dry mustard, and salt. Mixture will be soupy.
3. Turn into 3-quart casserole. (This can be made a day ahead up to this point.)
4. Bake, stirring occasionally.

Temperature: 300°
Time: 2½ hours

Hint: This recipe can easily be halved.

Gayle S. Medill

hot bean dish

Yield: 10 to 12 servings

Excellent picnic fare.

8 slices bacon
¼ cup chopped onion
1 16-ounce can pork and
   beans
1 15-ounce can kidney
   beans, drained
1 15-ounce can lima
   beans, drained
1 15-ounce can butter
   beans, drained
½ cup brown sugar
½ cup catsup
1 tablespoon
   Worcestershire sauce
1 teaspoon prepared
   mustard
2 tablespoons chopped
   green pepper
1 2-ounce jar pimiento,
   drained and chopped
½ cup cream cheese, cut
   in cubes

1. Brown bacon and onion; drain.
2. Combine all of the beans, the bacon and onion, and all other ingredients, except cream cheese, in a large bowl.
3. Pour into a greased 2½-quart casserole. Bake for 30 minutes, uncovered.
4. Fold in cream cheese, and bake for 10 more minutes.

Temperature: 350°
Time: 40 minutes

Susan L. Carpenter

blushing mushroom casserole

Yield: 6 servings

Welcome accompaniment to beef.

2 teaspoons beef base
  or 2 bouillon cubes
½ cup hot milk
7 tablespoons butter
2 tablespoons flour
½ cup cream
white pepper
1 pound mushrooms,
  sliced
2 tablespoons oil
½ teaspoon sherry
½ cup dry bread crumbs
½ cup Parmesan cheese

1. Dissolve beef base in milk.
2. Melt 1½ tablespoons of the butter. Add flour. Blend in cream, beef base mixture, and pepper. Cook and stir until thick and smooth.
3. Sauté mushrooms in oil and 3 tablespoons of the butter until brown. Drain.
4. Add mushrooms and sherry to cream sauce. Pour into a 1-quart casserole.
5. Melt remaining 2½ tablespoons butter. Mix with bread crumbs and cheese. Spread over casserole.
6. Bake until brown.

Temperature: 350°
Time: 30 minutes

Veronica A. Doty

mushrooms florentine

Yield: 4 to 6 servings

Special treatment for mushrooms.

1 pound fresh mushrooms
10 ounces beef bouillon
2 10-ounce packages
  frozen chopped spinach,
  cooked and drained
1 medium onion, chopped
2 tablespoons butter
1 cup grated sharp
  Cheddar cheese
salt
pepper

1. Poach mushroom caps in bouillon until slightly limp.
2. Chop mushroom stems. Sauté them in butter with onion until onion is transparent.
3. Put spinach in one layer in 8 x 11-inch baking dish.
4. Put mushroom caps over spinach.
5. Sprinkle mushroom stems and onion over mushroom caps.
6. Salt and pepper to taste. Top with grated cheese.
7. Bake until bubbly.

Temperature: 350°
Time: 20 to 30 minutes

Linnea O. Donahower

150

scalloped mushrooms

Yield: 8 servings

An excellent side dish with beef.

1 cup butter
5 cups plain croutons
1 pound mushrooms,
    sliced (use only caps)
1 quart light cream or half
    and half
5 tablespoons
    Worcestershire sauce
½ teaspoon salt
dash fresh pepper
½ teaspoon paprika
2 tablespoons parsley
¾ cup sherry, heated

1. Melt butter and toss with croutons to coat.
2. Alternate layers of croutons and mushrooms in 2-quart casserole, finishing with croutons.
3. Blend cream, Worcestershire sauce, salt, and pepper. Pour cream mixture over casserole.
4. Sprinkle with paprika and parsley. Bake, uncovered, 45 minutes.
5. Pour heated sherry over all; bake 15 minutes more.
6. Let stand 20 minutes before serving.

Temperature: 350°
Time: 60 minutes

Nancy B. Wolcott

squash casserole

Yield: 6 to 8 servings

Applesauce makes this lighter than most.

2 cups applesauce
¼ cup brown sugar
½ teaspoon salt
½ cup heavy cream
1¼ cups mashed, cooked
    squash, fresh or
    10-ounce package,
    frozen
⅛ teaspoon nutmeg
6 tablespoons butter,
    melted
2 eggs, beaten
½ cup soft white bread
    crumbs
½ cup slivered almonds

1. Mix together applesauce, brown sugar, salt, heavy cream, squash, nutmeg, 4 tablespoons of the melted butter, and eggs.
2. Place in buttered, 1½-quart, shallow casserole.
3. Mix together bread crumbs, remaining 2 tablespoons butter, and almonds. Sprinkle over squash. (This can be made a day ahead up to this point.)
4. Bake uncovered or freeze and bake later.

Temperature: 375°
Time: 35 minutes (if frozen, 55 to 65 minutes)

Suzanne H. Barbee

151

green onion potato casserole

Yield: 6 to 8 servings

A great new way to do potatoes to serve at a barbecue.

6 medium or 4 huge
   potatoes
1 teaspoon salt
1 cup sour cream
6 to 8 fresh green onions,
   chopped with some
   greens
1 cup shredded sharp
   Cheddar cheese
   (4 ounces)
⅓ cup melted butter

1. Peel, quarter, and boil potatoes until barely tender. Drain, cool, and grate on large side of grater. Place in large bowl.
2. Gently mix in all other ingredients, except butter.
3. Place mixture into a greased shallow pan. Top with melted butter.
4. Bake until golden.

Temperature: 400°
Time: 30 minutes

Lucy W. Cook

orange pecan yams

Yield: 4 servings

Nice company dish served with pork.

4 fresh medium yams,
   scrubbed, and dried
3 tablespoons butter
1 tablespoon freshly
   grated orange peel
½ teaspoon salt
½ teaspoon nutmeg
¼ cup chopped pecans
4 orange sections
4 pecan halves

1. Bake yams at 400° oven for 15 minutes. Reduce temperature to 375°, and continue baking 45 minutes, or until tender.
2. Scoop out yams, reserving ¼ inch shells.
3. Mash yams with butter, orange peel, salt, and nutmeg. Fold in chopped pecans.
4. Fill yam shells. Top each with orange section and pecan half. (This can be made a day ahead up to this point.)
5. To serve, bake 15 minutes at 375° or until heated through.

Temperature: 400°
Time: 15 minutes

Temperature: 375°
Time: 45 minutes

Temperature: 375°
Time: 15 minutes

Priscilla L. Minster

stuffed tomatoes

Stuffed tomatoes with a pedigree!

8 medium tomatoes
3 tablespoons flour
1 bunch scallions
1 green pepper
½ pound mushrooms
3 tablespoons butter
1 14-ounce can artichoke hearts, drained and chopped
8 ounce package shredded Mozzarella cheese
3 ounces blue cheese, crumbled

1. Remove seeds from tomatoes. Turn upside down on towel to drain for 2 hours.
2. Sprinkle inside of tomatoes with 1 tablespoon of the flour.
3. Chop scallions, green pepper, and mushroom by hand or use metal blade of food processor. Sauté in butter.
4. Add chopped artichokes to onion mixture and heat thoroughly. Thicken with remaining 2 tablespoons of flour.
5. Remove from heat and cool slightly.
6. Add Mozzarella cheese to artichoke mixture. Fill tomato shells. Put blue cheese on top.
7. Bake in shallow baking dish until tomatoes are soft.

Temperature: 350°
Time: 45 minutes

Susan G. Rhoda

barbecued onions

This is a good companion for grilled steak.

12 small white onions, peeled (1½-inch diameter)
¼ cup catsup
2 tablespoons water
1 teaspoon vinegar
¼ teaspoon salt
pinch pepper
1 tablespoon brown sugar
4 slices bacon, diced and cooked crisp

1. Parboil onions for 4 to 5 minutes. Drain and put in a buttered, shallow 1½-quart casserole.
2. Mix catsup, water, vinegar, salt, and pepper and spread over onions.
3. Sprinkle mixture with brown sugar and bacon.
4. Bake, uncovered, until tender. (Can refrigerate and bake later.)

Temperature: 375°
Time: 30 minutes

Linda W. Obourn

zwiebelkuchen
(swiss onion tart)

Yield: 9-inch pie

Whole wheat crust a treat.

Crust

1 cup whole wheat flour
6 tablespoons cold butter, diced
¼ teaspoon salt
¼ cup ice water

Filling

4 slices bacon, cooked and crumbled
8 onions, thinly sliced
½ cup butter, melted
1 cup sour cream
¼ cup flour
2 eggs, lightly beaten
1 tablespoon caraway seed
1 teaspoon salt

Crust

1. In a bowl cut butter into flour and salt until mixture resembles coarse meal. Add water and toss until blended.
2. Form the dough into a ball. Knead lightly for 5 minutes. Wrap in wax paper and chill 30 minutes.
3. Roll out dough and place in pie plate, leaving a 1-inch overhang for crimping.
4. Prick the bottom of shell, chill 30 minutes, and bake at 400° for 15 minutes. This can be done ahead and frozen.

Filling

1. Sauté onions in melted butter.
2. Sprinkle bacon in crust and cover with sautéed onions.
3. Blend flour into sour cream and combine with eggs and seasonings. Pour over onions and bake.
4. Let stand 10 minutes before serving.

Temperature: 350°
Time: 35 minutes

Peggi M. Godwin

creamed onions

Yield: 6 to 8 servings

For onion fans, this is the best.

4 or 5 large white onions,
   silver skins, peeled
salt and pepper
butter
½ pint light cream
½ pint heavy cream
Italian bread crumbs

1. Slice enough onions in ¼-inch slices to fill a medium-size greased casserole.
2. Layer onion slices in casserole.
3. Season with salt and pepper to taste, and dot generously with butter.
4. Pour heavy cream and light cream on top of onions, but do not cover.
5. Cover with generous layer of Italian bread crumbs. (This can be made a day ahead up to this point.)
6. Bake slowly. (Place casserole on top of a sheet of foil to avoid spattering oven.)

Temperature: 300°
Time: 2½ to 3 hours

Nancy McK. Sherwood

french fried onion rings

Yield: 4 servings

Super batter.

2 large Spanish onions

1. With slicing disk of food processor, slice onions. Otherwise, slice about ¼-inch thick by hand.
2. Place slices in dish of flour to dry them. This is the secret to successful onion rings.

Batter
1 cup flour
½ teaspoon salt
1 teaspoon baking powder
1 egg
¼ cup vegetable oil
1 cup milk
shortening for frying

Batter
1. Combine flour, salt, baking powder, egg, oil, and milk. Allow mixture to rest for 20 minutes.
2. Dip slices into batter to coat them.
3. Fry in hot shortening until golden brown.

Barbara S. Flannery

asparagus-tomato skillet

Yield: 6 servings

Refreshing and light.

3 slices bacon
¼ cup sliced green onion
3 tablespoons vinegar
1 tablespoon water
2 teaspoons sugar
¼ teaspoon salt
1½ pounds fresh
   asparagus
2 medium tomatoes

1. Cook bacon until crisp. Remove and crumble.
2. Sauté onion in drippings until tender.
3. Add bacon, vinegar, water, sugar, and salt. Bring to a boil.
4. Add asparagus. Cover and cook 5 minutes.
5. Cut tomatoes in eighths. Add to skillet and cook, covered, for 3 minutes.
6. Serve immediately.

Alice K. Smith

creamed celery with pecans

Yield: 6 servings

Ideal for celery lovers!

4 cups celery, cut
   diagonally into ½-inch
   pieces
3 tablespoons butter
2 tablespoons all-purpose
   flour
2 cups milk
¾ teaspoon salt
¾ cup pecan halves
½ cup bread crumbs

1. Boil celery in water to cover for about 10 minutes or until tender. Drain.
2. Melt 2 tablespoons of the butter over medium heat. Stir in flour and add milk slowly, stirring constantly, until thick and smooth. Add salt and drained celery.
3. Spoon mixture into a greased 1½-quart casserole. Top with pecans.
4. Mix bread crumbs with 1 tablespoon melted butter and sprinkle over celery mixture.
5. Bake, uncovered. (Can refrigerate, then bring to room temperature and bake.)

Temperature: 400°
Time: 15 minutes

Priscilla L. Minster

baked squash and apple casserole

Yield: 6 to 8 servings

Easy, different, with good blend of spices.

1 small butternut squash
  (2 pounds or less)
2 apples (cored, peeled,
  and sliced)
½ cup brown sugar
¼ cup cold margarine
1 tablespoon flour
1 teaspoon salt
¼ teaspoon cinnamon
¼ teaspoon nutmeg

1. Pare, seed, and cut squash into small slices.
2. Place squash and apple slices in oblong baking dish (7 x 11-inch).
3. Blend rest of ingredients with fork, fingers, or pastry cutter until crumbly.
4. Distribute over squash and apple. Prepare to here until ready to bake.
5. Cover and bake.

Temperature: 350°
Time: 45 to 50 minutes

Phyllis Connelly

creamed spinach

Yield: 10 to 12 servings

Even kids who dislike spinach will be pleasantly surprised!

6 eggs
2 pounds small curd
  cottage cheese
1 pound Cheddar cheese,
  grated
¼ pound butter or
  margarine, melted
2 10-ounce packages
  frozen spinach,
  defrosted and drained
2 tablespoons flour
¼ teaspoon salt
¼ teaspoon pepper

1. Beat eggs in large bowl.
2. Add cottage cheese, grated Cheddar, butter, spinach, flour, salt, and pepper.
3. Pour into 2-quart buttered casserole.
4. Bake one hour, uncovered.

Temperature: 350°
Time: 1 hour

Judy G. Curry

dilled zucchini

Yield: 8 servings

Something for a summertime buffet.

3 pounds zucchini, cubed
1 large onion, minced
6 tablespoons butter
2 teaspoons flour
½ cup sour cream
⅓ cup lemon juice
1 tablespoon sugar
salt to taste
1-2 tablespoons dill weed

1. Cook zucchini in steamer, over 1 inch of boiling water, until tender.
2. Sauté onion in butter. Mix in flour and sour cream.
3. Add lemon juice, sugar, and salt. Stir until blended.
4. Stir in dill weed and squash.
5. Pour into buttered casserole dish. Cover. Bake until bubbly.

Temperature: 325°
Time: 30 minutes

Kathryn P. Weider

stir-fry vegetables

Yield: 4 servings

Inexpensive and pretty vegetable dish.

¼ cup cooking oil
2 10-ounce packages frozen french-cut green beans, thawed and drained
½ pound fresh mushrooms, thinly sliced
1 green pepper, cut into thin strips
1 cup celery, thinly sliced on the diagonal
1½ cups chicken broth or bouillon
2 tablespoons cornstarch
1 tablespoon soy sauce
½ teaspoon salt
½ teaspoon garlic salt
¼ teaspoon pepper
slivered almonds
thin strips of pimiento

1. Heat cooking oil in a large skillet or wok.
2. When oil is not quite smoking-hot, add vegetables and stir quickly until tender-crisp, about 10 minutes.
3. Mix chicken broth, cornstarch, soy sauce, salt, garlic salt, and pepper in a bowl. Pour mixture over vegetables and stir until thickened.
4. Place in serving bowl and sprinkle top with slivered almonds and thin strips of pimiento. Serve immediately.
5. For variation, substitute snow peas for green beans, or add thinly sliced chicken or sirloin (stir-fried) to vegetables to make a whole meal.

Sibley's Cooks' Kitchen
Jean Summers, Home Economist

danish cauliflower

Yield: 6 to 8 servings

A very rich recipe to use in place of a starch and vegetable for one meal.

1 whole medium cauliflower, trimmed of its outer green leaves
¼ cup chopped onion
3 tablespoons butter
3 tablespoons flour
½ teaspoon dill
¾ teaspoon salt
pinch of pepper
1 cup milk
1 tablespoon lemon juice
¼ cup mayonnaise
2 egg yolks, whisked with 1 tablespoon dry vermouth
¼ pound cooked shrimp

1. Steam cauliflower for 15 to 20 minutes, until tender.
2. Sauté onion in butter until soft.
3. Add flour, dill, salt, and pepper. Blend until smooth. Add milk, heat and stir until smooth and thick.
4. Blend in lemon juice and mayonnaise.
5. Add egg and vermouth mixture.
6. Place on lowest heat, add shrimp, and heat thoroughly.
7. Put whole cauliflower head on serving dish and spoon sauce on top.
8. Place remaining sauce in dish to pass at the table.

Hint: This sauce goes well on many other vegetables too.

Nancy A. Koris

four star artichokes and mushrooms

Yield: 8 servings

Glorious with steak or chicken.

½ cup butter or margarine
2 12-ounce packages of fresh mushrooms, sliced
1 small onion, finely chopped
2 15-ounce cans artichoke hearts, drained
1¼ teaspoons salt
2 tablespoons lemon juice
1 cup fine Italian style bread crumbs

1. Melt ¼ cup of the butter and sauté mushrooms and onions until tender.
2. In a greased, 1½-quart baking dish, arrange mushrooms, onions, and artichoke hearts. Sprinkle with salt and lemon juice.
3. Melt remaining butter in skillet. Brown crumbs, stirring constantly. Sprinkle on top of vegetables. Bake.

Temperature: 350°
Time: 20 minutes

Hint: Mushrooms are at their best during the winter months.

Lucia H. Shaw

mediterranean pie

Yield: 6 servings

Especially good as an accompaniment to fish.

1 medium eggplant, peeled and sliced ¼-inch thick
1 teaspoon salt
¾ cup olive oil or vegetable oil
1 large onion, sliced
1 green pepper, cut into thin strips
1 medium zucchini, sliced
2 cloves garlic, minced
¾ teaspoon oregano
¾ teaspoon basil
½ teaspoon salt
½ teaspoon pepper
9-inch pastry shell, unbaked (extra pie crust dough for lattice top)
½ cup grated Parmesan cheese
2 medium tomatoes, seeded and cut into eighths
8 ounces shredded Mozzarella cheese
1 tablespoon milk

1. Sprinkle eggplant slices with salt and place between paper towels. Weight down with heavy cutting board for 30 minutes.
2. Heat ½ cup of the oil in a skillet.
3. Cut eggplant slices into cubes. Add to hot oil, toss. Cook until tender, stirring constantly (about 5 minutes). Remove eggplant and set aside.
4. Pour remaining oil into skillet. Add onion, green pepper, zucchini, and garlic. Cook just until tender (about 5 minutes).
5. Combine spices and salt. Set aside.
6. Line a 9-inch pie plate with pastry. Sprinkle with ¼ cup of the Parmesan cheese.
7. Spoon half the eggplant and half the vegetable mixture into pie shell. Layer with half of the tomato wedges, half of the spice mixture, and half of the Mozzarella cheese. Repeat these layers.
8. Sprinkle top with all but 1 tablespoon of remaining Parmesan cheese.
9. Make lattice top crust by criss-crossing strips of dough one over the other. Sprinkle with milk and remaining 1 tablespoon of the Parmesan cheese.
10. Bake for 25 minutes. Let stand for 15 minutes before cutting.

Temperature: 425°
Time: 25 minutes

Margo C. Shaw

stir-fried broccoli and romaine

Yield: 6 servings

Crisp and green!

1 bunch broccoli
1 medium head romaine
4 slices bacon
¼ cup water
1 teaspoon salt
1 teaspoon sugar

1. Cut broccoli into 2 x ½-inch pieces. Tear romaine into bite-sized chunks.
2. Dice bacon and fry until crisp. Add broccoli and stir fry until well coated with bacon drippings.
3. Add water, cover, and cook for 4 minutes.
4. Add romaine, salt, and sugar. Cook 3 more minutes, uncovered.
5. Serve immediately.

Alice K. Smith

 ratatouille

Yield: 8 to 10 servings

Very good served hot or cold with grilled meat.

1 pound zucchini
1 large eggplant (1¼ pounds)
1 pound red and green peppers
1 16-ounce can whole tomatoes, undrained
3 tablespoons olive oil
¼ cup chopped red onion
1 clove garlic, crushed
1 tablespoon chopped parsley
3 tablespoons tomato paste
½ teaspoon sugar
2 teaspoons salt
⅛ teaspoon dried hot red pepper
1½ teaspoons basil
1½ teaspoons marjoram
¼ cup dry vermouth or dry white wine

1. Peel zucchini and slice into ¼-inch slices. Peel eggplant and cut into cubes. Slice peppers in ¼-inch strips. Toss vegetables together in a bowl with tomatoes and their juice.
2. Heat oil in a 6-quart Dutch oven. Add onion, garlic, and parsley. Cook over medium heat until onion is transparent.
3. Add mixed vegetables, tomato paste, sugar, salt, hot pepper, basil, marjoram, and vermouth to onion mixture. Mix gently. Cook, uncovered, stirring occasionally, over medium heat for about 40 minutes, or until vegetables are just tender. If ratatouille seems too watery, cook a few minutes longer.
4. Serve hot or cold. It is delicious the next day.

Susan S. Taylor

garden casserole

Yield: 8 to 10 servings

A wonderfully healthy combination.

4 medium-size potatoes, peeled
2 onions, sliced
1 medium-size zucchini
4 or 5 tomatoes
3 carrots, pared
1 cup Rhine wine
salt and pepper
¼ cup butter, melted
1 cup small bread cubes
2 cups grated Cheddar cheese

1. Slice potatoes thin and spread over bottom of a medium-size, ungreased casserole.
2. Place onions, in rings, over potatoes.
3. Cut zucchini in half, remove seeds, and cut in small chunks. Spread over previous layer.
4. Cut tomatoes in small chunks. Place over squash.
5. Slice carrots thin and place throughout casserole.
6. Pour wine over entire casserole. Add salt and pepper to taste.
7. Cover dish and bake for 1 hour, or until vegetables are soft but crisp.
8. Mix bread cubes with melted butter until all are coated.
9. Sprinkle grated cheese and bread cubes over entire casserole.
10. Return to oven. Bake, uncovered, for 15 minutes longer.

Temperature: 375°
Time: 1 hour, 15 minutes

William M. Fox

dutch lettuce

Yield: 4 servings

Unusual combination with surprising results.

6 medium potatoes, peeled and quartered
⅓ to ½ pound bacon
1 large head of lettuce, broken into small pieces
1 tablespoon vinegar
salt
pepper
2 hard boiled eggs

1. Boil potatoes. While potatoes are cooking, fry bacon until crisp.
2. Add lettuce pieces slowly to bacon drippings. Stir and fold until lettuce is wilted.
3. Add vinegar, salt, and pepper.
4. Mash potatoes, adding salt to taste. Fold into bacon and lettuce mixture while hot.
5. Serve immediately, garnishing with egg slices.

Ellen W. Cooper

dilly vegetables

Yield: 6 to 8 servings

A new taste and texture.

2 10-ounce packages
  frozen broccoli
1 10-ounce package
  frozen peas
1 8-ounce package sharp
  shredded cheese
2 tablespoons butter or
  margarine
2 tablespoons flour
1½ cups milk

1. Cook vegetables separately,
   according to package
   directions.
2. Place broccoli in a 1½-quart flat
   baking dish. Top with cheese,
   and sprinkle on peas. Set aside.
3. Melt butter in a medium
   saucepan. Whisk in flour until
   smooth.
4. Gradually add milk, stirring
   constantly, and bring to a boil.
   Reduce heat. Simmer 1 minute.
5. Pour white sauce over
   vegetables.

Topping
2 tablespoons butter
½ cup fine bread crumbs
½ teaspoon onion salt
½ teaspoon dill weed

Topping
1. Melt butter in saucepan. Add
   bread crumbs, onion salt, and
   dill weed. Sprinkle over
   vegetables.
2. Bake, or refrigerate and bake
   later.

Temperature: 350°
Time: 25 minutes

Anne C. Burnham

tomato-carrot casserole

Yield: 6 servings

Very pretty and tasty.

3 tablespoons butter
½ cup chopped celery
2 to 3 medium sliced
  onions
½ to 1 cup grated carrot
1 teaspoon salt
pepper
3 to 4 large sliced
  tomatoes
8 ounces shredded
  Cheddar cheese
½ cup bread crumbs,
  buttered

1. Heat butter, sauté celery and
   onions, covered, for 5 minutes.
2. Add carrots and salt.
3. Put all in greased 1-quart
   casserole.
4. Add pepper and cover with
   tomatoes. Sprinkle cheese and
   buttered crumbs over top. (This
   can be made a day ahead up to
   this point.)
5. Bake.

Temperature: 350°
Time: 30 minutes

Beverly A. Gifford

asparagus pie

Yield: 8 servings

Easy, yet delicious!

1½ cups cut asparagus
spears
1 cup Cheddar cheese,
grated
1 teaspoon lemon juice
½ cup mayonnaise
1 8-inch pie crust,
unbaked
slivered almonds, toasted

1. Mix together asparagus spears,
cheese, lemon juice, and
mayonnaise.
2. Put into unbaked pie shell.
3. Sprinkle with toasted slivered
almonds. Bake.

Temperature: 350°
Time: 40 minutes

Linnea O. Donahower

year-round broccoli

Yield: 4 to 6 servings

Delicious - good for family or company.

1 pound fresh broccoli or
2 10-ounce packages
frozen, cut broccoli
2 cups frozen, whole,
small onions or 3
medium onions,
quartered
3 tablespoons butter or
margarine
2 tablespoons flour
¼ teaspoon salt
1 cup warm milk
1 3-ounce package cream
cheese, softened
½ cup shredded sharp
Cheddar cheese (2
ounces)
½ cup plain bread crumbs

1. Cut broccoli into 1-inch pieces.
Cook in boiling, salted water
until tender yet crisp; drain.
2. Cook onions in boiling, salted
water about 5 minutes; drain.
3. In saucepan, melt 2 tablespoons
of the butter; blend in flour and
salt. Add milk; cook and stir
until thick and bubbly.
4. Reduce heat, and blend in
cream cheese until smooth.
5. Place vegetables in a 1½-quart
casserole. Pour sauce over. Mix
very lightly.
6. Top with shredded cheese. (Can
be made a day ahead to here,
and refrigerated.)
7. Melt remaining tablespoon of
butter, and toss with bread
crumbs. Set aside.
8. Bake casserole, covered, for 30
minutes. Sprinkle with bread
crumbs. Bake, uncovered,
about 30 minutes more.

Temperature: 350°
Time: 1 hour

Hint: If broccoli stems are large, cut them into smaller pieces so
they become as tender as outer pieces.

Louise S. Criticos

meats

meats

flemish beef

Yield: 6 servings

Keeps them coming back for seconds!

butter
3 large onions
3½ pounds of round steak
  (1½-inch thick)
¼ cup flour
one bay leaf
½ teaspoon dried
  rosemary
2 whole cloves
1 teaspoon salt
1 teaspoon pepper
2 cups beer
parsley or chives for
  garnish

1. Butter a 9 x 13-inch covered casserole dish.
2. Cut 3 large onions into thick slices and place in the bottom of casserole.
3. Pound flour into the steak with a meat mallet.
4. Place meat on top of onions.
5. Bake uncovered in 450° oven for 40 minutes.
6. Reduce heat to 325°. Add bay leaf, rosemary, cloves, salt, pepper, and beer. Cover tightly and bake for 1½ to 2 hours, or until meat is very tender.
7. Sprinkle with chives or parsley before serving. Serve with buttered noodles, green salad, and beer.

Temperature: 450°
Time: 40 minutes

Temperature: 325°
Time: 1½ to 2 hours

Martha H. Cook

red flannel hash

Yield: 4 to 6 servings

Sunday brunch idea.

1 small onion, chopped
1 tablespoon butter or
  margarine
2 cups chopped, cooked
  corned beef
2 cups cubed, cooked
  potatoes
1 teaspoon salt
1 cup chopped beets, with
  some juice

1. Sauté onion in butter.
2. Add remaining ingredients. Heat for 20 minutes.
3. Brown under broiler for 2 minutes just before serving.

Hint: Serve with poached eggs and green salad.

Armind Rodger
Chef, Monroe Golf Club

batter-up beef pie

Yield: 6 servings

The batter bakes up to a golden, cheesy circle around the pie.

2 cups cooked beef, cut in
½ to 1-inch pieces
½ cup cooked onions
1 cup cooked carrots, cut
in chunks
1 cup cooked potatoes,
cut in 1½-inch chunks
1 cup beef gravy
¼ cup butter
1½ cups flour
2 teaspoons baking
powder
1 teaspoon salt
1½ cups milk
1 cup (4-ounce package)
grated Cheddar cheese
1 tablespoon dried
minced onion
1 tablespoon sugar

1. Combine beef, onions, carrots,
potatoes, and gravy. Set aside.
2. Melt butter in bottom of 8-inch
square baking dish in oven.
3. Combine remaining ingredients
in mixing bowl. Stir until
blended and pour into baking
dish.
4. Pour beef mixture over batter.
Do not stir.
5. Bake and serve.

Temperature: 350°
Time: 60 minutes

Hint: Leftover beef stew can be substituted for first
5 ingredients.

Priscilla L. Minster

tobey's prize flank steak

Yield: 4 to 6 servings

An easy, succulent method for this popular cut.

1½ teaspoons salt
garlic salt to taste
3 tablespoons prepared
mustard
3 tablespoons lemon juice
1 tablespoon
Worcestershire sauce
freshly ground pepper to
taste
1 to 1½ pounds flank
steak
1 large onion, sliced in
rings

Must do ahead.

1. Combine first 6 ingredients.
Pour over flank steak, covering
both sides.
2. Cover steak with onion rings,
and marinate in a closed
container overnight.
3. Remove onion rings and enough
marinade to make it easy to
grill.
4. Grill for 6 minutes on each side.
5. Slice thin, on the diagonal.

Sue M. Hanson

sirloin supper

Yield: 4 servings

Successful for years and years.

1 pound sirloin steak cut in ¼-inch strips
1 garlic clove
3 tablespoons oil
1 cup diagonally sliced celery
1 medium onion, sliced
½ teaspoon ginger
1 tablespoon sugar
2 teaspoons cornstarch
¼ cup soy sauce
½ cup water
½ cup diced green pepper
6 halved cherry tomatoes
½ cup toasted slivered almonds

1. Quickly brown steak strips with garlic in 2 tablespoons of the oil.
2. Remove meat from pan and discard garlic clove.
3. In same pan, heat remaining 1 tablespoon of the oil. Add celery and onion, cover, and cook 1 minute.
4. Add ginger, sugar, cornstarch, soy sauce, water, green pepper, and meat to onion and celery mixture. Cover and heat 1 minute.
5. Add tomato halves and heat one more minute.
6. Serve over hot cooked rice. Garnish with toasted almonds.

Hint: This recipe doubles or triples easily.

Gayle S. Medill

roast barbecue

Yield: 12 servings

Double or triple this for an après ski or theater party.

3 pounds chuck roast
2 tablespoons shortening
1 large onion, chopped
2 tablespoons vinegar
2 tablespoons lemon juice
¾ cup water
½ cup chopped celery
2 cups catsup
3 tablespoons Worcestershire sauce
2 tablespoons brown sugar
1 tablespoon prepared mustard
2 tablespoons chili powder
1 teaspoon salt
¼ teaspoon pepper

1. Trim meat and brown in shortening.
2. Add the remaining ingredients. Bring to a boil; reduce heat to low.
3. As soon as meat is tender enough (approximately 2 to 3 hours), use two forks and shred or pull meat apart.
4. Continue cooking until meat is very tender. (Cooking time frequently varies from 3 to 6 hours.)
5. Serve on buns.

Nancy M. Frank

savory sauerbraten— in the crock pot

Yield: 8 servings

Much easier than the 3-day variety and just as good.

1 chuck roast, about 4 pounds
salt and pepper
2 onions, sliced
1 10¾-ounce can condensed beef broth
⅓ cup liquid brown sugar
⅓ cup cider vinegar
8 gingersnaps
noodles

1. Sprinkle roast on all sides with salt and pepper.
2. Place roast in crock pot, add onion, broth, brown sugar, and vinegar.
3. Cover tightly, cook 5 to 6 hours on high, turning occasionally.
4. Remove roast and set aside.
5. Add crumbled gingersnaps to the sauce in the crock pot. Stir until sauce thickens.
6. Slice meat and spoon sauce over slices.
7. Serve with noodles.

Kristine K. Hoppe

 beef wellington

Yield: 6 to 8 slices

Absolutely elegant to serve, sensational to taste!

Pastry
½ cup shortening
½ cup butter
4 cups unbleached flour
1 teaspoon salt
1 egg, slightly beaten
½ cup (approximately) ice water

Pastry
1. Cut shortening and butter into flour which has been combined with salt.
2. Combine egg and water. Mix with flour to form a ball.
3. Cover and refrigerate.

Duxelles
1 cup finely chopped mushrooms
¼ cup finely chopped shallots
3 tablespoons butter
2 tablespoons flour
3 to 4 tablespoons heavy cream
¼ teaspoon dry tarragon
2 to 3 tablespoons finely chopped prosciutto (ham)
3 tablespoons Port or Madeira wine
salt, pepper, nutmeg (very little)
2 tablespoons soft butter

Duxelles
1. Place chopped mushrooms in a towel and squeeze until most of the moisture is removed.
2. Sauté shallots in butter until golden. Stir in mushrooms and flour. Cook 2 minutes.
3. Stir cream, tarragon, prosciutto, wine, and spices into mushroom mixture. Cook, over low heat, 5 minutes.
4. Cool slightly. Add soft butter.
5. Can store in refrigerator, but have at room temperature when ready to use.

168

Final Preparation

1 beef tenderloin, ends
  trimmed
cognac
salt and pepper
6 slices bacon
1 egg, slightly beaten

Final Preparation

1. Rub tenderloin with cognac and season with salt and pepper.
2. Wrap tenderloin with bacon and place in roasting pan. Roast, uncovered, at 425° for 20 minutes.
3. Discard bacon and cool roast to room temperature before next step.
4. Roll pastry dough out to a rectangle 10 inches wide and 4 inches longer than tenderloin.
5. Pat duxelles on top and bottom of meat and place meat on pastry rectangle. Wrap around, sealing seam with beaten egg.
6. Trim excess dough from ends and wrap the ends with an envelope-type seal.
7. Place seam-side down on baking sheet. Make three slits on top and decorate top with pastry flowers. Brush with beaten egg. This can be wrapped and refrigerated.

One hour before serving time:

1. Preheat oven to 425°.
2. Bake prepared tenderloin for 30 minutes or until pastry is golden and meat is rare (about 140° to 150° on meat thermometer).
3. Let sit for 10 minutes and slice. Serve hot.

Temperature: 425°
Time: 30 minutes

Sue M. Hanson

beef and broccoli

Excellent stir-fry recipe.

¼ cup soy sauce
1 tablespoon sherry
7 tablespoons peanut oil
½ teaspoon chopped
 ginger root
1 clove garlic, crushed
1 pound flank steak
1 large bunch broccoli
1 small onion
½ pound mushrooms
1 cup chicken broth
1 tablespoon cornstarch
¼ cup cold water
salt to taste

1. Mix soy sauce, sherry, 3 tablespoons of the peanut oil, ginger root, and garlic together.
2. Slice flank steak in thin strips. Cover with above mixture and marinate several hours. (Can be made a day ahead up to this point.)
3. Cut broccoli in flowerets, quarter onion, and slice mushrooms. Set aside.
4. About 15 minutes before serving time, heat 2 tablespoons of the oil in a wok or large skillet.
5. When very hot, pour in beef mixture along with marinade. Cook, stirring constantly with wooden spoon, until beef is browned.
6. Remove wok from heat and place beef in a dish.
7. Heat remaining 2 tablespoons peanut oil in wok. When very hot, add vegetables. Toss with wooden spoon until vegetables are coated with oil.
8. Continue stirring for about 2 minutes and add chicken broth. Cover pan and steam for about 7 minutes.
9. Lower heat and add cornstarch which has been mixed with ¼ cup cold water. Continue cooking, stirring constantly, until broth is thickened.
10. Add cooked meat, stir until heated through—about 1 minute. Add salt to taste.
11. Pour into serving dish and serve immediately.

Sue M. Hanson

beef brisket

Yield: 6 to 8 servings

Tender and juicy, great for the family.

5 pounds beef brisket
liquid smoke (available in
  gourmet section)
garlic salt
Worcestershire sauce

1. Brush brisket with liquid smoke and garlic salt. Refrigerate overnight.
2. Before roasting, brush with some Worcestershire sauce.
3. Cover meat with foil and roast, in low oven, for 5 hours.
4. Uncover and coat with sauce. Reduce heat and bake for 1 hour.
5. Cut when cool.

Sauce
2 tablespoons brown
  sugar
2 tablespoons vinegar
2 teaspoons
  Worcestershire sauce
½ cup catsup
1 teaspoon dry mustard
½ teaspoon salt
½ teaspoon pepper
½ teaspoon chili powder

Sauce
1. Mix all ingredients.
2. Simmer for 15 minutes before pouring over brisket.

Must do one day ahead.

Temperature: 275°
Time: 5 hours

Temperature: 225°
Time: 1 hour

Hint: When carving brisket, always slice across the grain of the meat.

Nancy C. Alderman

As a newlywed, when Belle was told to baste the brisket she sewed the hot meat with black thread. Her mother was a dressmaker so, to her, the word baste meant sewing, not spooning sauce over meat. By the time her fingers were hot and she was crying in pain, she realized she was doing something wrong.

chili tostada

Yield: 6 servings

Great winter buffet for serving large groups!

1½ pounds ground beef
1 large onion, chopped
2 28-ounce cans tomato
    sauce
1 15-ounce can red beans
    and sauce
½ cup canned corn
½ cup chopped celery
1 chopped green pepper
1½ teaspoons salt
1 teaspoon garlic
3 to 4 tablespoons chili
    powder

Chili
1. Brown ground beef and onion;
   drain excess fat.
2. Add remaining ingredients, and
   simmer for 1 hour.

Accompaniments
1 pint sour cream
1 pound shredded sharp
    yellow cheese
1 head lettuce, shredded
1 large package tortilla
    chips
1 avocado, cubed

Arranging the Buffet
1. Place chili in tureen surrounded
   by accompaniments.
2. In individual bowls, layer a
   handful of corn chips, chili, then
   any or all accompaniments.

Cynthia L. Stockman

italian meatloaf

Yield: 10 servings

A little extra oomph!

2 pounds ground meat,
    combination of beef,
    pork, and veal
2 eggs
½ cup seasoned Italian
    bread crumbs
1 cup tomato-vegetable
    juice
1 teaspoon oregano
¼ teaspoon pepper
½ teaspoon salt
2 small onions, minced
8 thin slices boiled ham
½ pound Mozzarella
    cheese, grated
catsup, optional

1. Combine all ingredients except
   cheese and ham.
2. Flatten meat mixture on
   foil-lined jelly roll pan.
3. Place ham slices evenly on top
   of meat mixture. Sprinkle with
   grated cheese.
4. Holding one end of foil, roll up
   meat like a jelly roll.
5. Remove foil. Slide meat roll to
   center of pan. Pat seams closed.
6. Spread catsup over top, if
   desired. Bake.
7. Remove from oven, and allow to
   sit in a warm spot for five
   minutes before slicing.

Temperature: 350°
Time: 1 hour

Sheila N. Prezzano

tenderloin roast

Yield: 6 servings

An experienced chef's failsafe recipe.

1 5-pound beef tenderloin, trimmed by butcher
vegetable oil

1. Pre-heat oven.
2. Coat tenderloin with oil. Place in roasting pan.
3. Cook at 450° for 35 minutes for medium rare meat. Average tenderloin is 5 pounds and should serve 6 people. The cooking time is the same, even if the weight varies by a few ounces.
4. Remove from oven and place on cutting board for 10 minutes to allow juices to settle.
5. Slice and serve.
6. Have people add salt and pepper to taste. Salt on meat before cooking will dry it out.

Temperature: 450°
Time: 35 minutes —
sitting 10 minutes

Hint: Serve this with Sauce for Tenderloin.

Jane N. Clifford

sauce for tenderloin (or sirloin or roast beef)

Yield: 4 to 8 servings

A Miami chef's secret.

1 6-ounce bottle sauce Robert made by Escoffier and available at gourmet stores
6 ounces heavy cream
1 teaspoon dry mustard
¼ cup granulated sugar (or more to taste)

1. Whisk all ingredients together, in a saucepan, over medium heat. (Do *NOT* allow to boil.)
2. When well blended, simmer for 10 to 30 minutes. This can simmer for quite awhile and will darken as it simmers.
3. Serve hot, as a gravy.
4. (Can be stored in the refrigerator for at least a week, and reheated, but it is better fresh.)

Jane N. Clifford

tenderloin sauté

Yield: 4 servings

A special recipe from a renowned chef.

8 tablespoons butter
8 ½-inch thick slices
  tenderloin, flattened
  with side of heavy
  cleaver
2 cloves garlic, crushed
  and minced
2 to 3 cups sliced fresh
  mushrooms
1 tablespoon lemon juice
1 cup canned artichoke
  hearts, quartered
salt
freshly ground pepper
chopped fresh parsley

1. Melt 6 tablespoons of the butter
   in a heavy skillet.
2. Sauté tenderloin and garlic to
   just under desired degree of
   doneness (medium rare).
   Remove from pan. Keep warm.
3. Add remaining 2 tablespoons
   butter to pan. Deglaze by
   stirring.
4. Add mushrooms, lemon juice,
   and artichoke hearts. Sauté 3
   minutes, *no longer!*
5. Replace meat in skillet. Add salt
   and pepper to taste. Sprinkle
   with parsley. Stir once.
6. Serve hot, spooning pan juices
   over each portion.

Hint: An egg slicer works well for slicing mushrooms.

Donald Antinore
Chef, Irondequoit Country Club

moussaka

Yield: 10 servings

A company casserole favorite.

Meat Sauce
2 tablespoons butter or
  margarine
1 cup finely chopped
  onion
1½ pounds ground chuck
  or lamb
1 clove garlic, minced
1 teaspoon oregano
1 teaspoon basil
¾ teaspoon cinnamon
1 teaspoon salt
pepper
2 8-ounce cans tomato
  sauce
2 tablespoons dry bread
  crumbs

Meat Sauce
1. Melt butter and sauté the onion,
   meat, and garlic, stirring until
   brown.
2. Add herbs, spices, and tomato
   sauce. Bring to a boil.
3. Reduce heat. Simmer,
   uncovered, about ½ hour.
4. Just before assembling
   casserole, mix bread crumbs
   into sauce.

Eggplant

2 eggplants, unpeeled
½ cup melted butter or
  margarine
salt and pepper

Eggplant

1. Halve eggplants lengthwise. Cut
   each half across into ½-inch
   slices.
2. Place slices in bottom of broiler
   pan. Sprinkle with salt and
   pepper and brush with butter.
3. Broil 4 inches from heat four
   minutes on each side.

Cream Sauce

2 tablespoons butter or
  margarine
2 tablespoons flour
salt and pepper to taste
2 cups milk
2 eggs, beaten

Cream Sauce

1. Melt butter and stir in flour, salt,
   and pepper.
2. Add milk gradually. Bring to a
   boil, stirring until thick. Remove
   from heat.
3. Beat small amount of cream
   sauce into eggs. Blend egg
   mixture into remaining sauce.
   Mix well and set aside.

Topping

½ cup grated Parmesan
  cheese
½ cup grated Cheddar
  cheese

To Assemble

1. In a 2-quart shallow baking dish,
   layer half of eggplant,
   overlapping slightly.
2. Sprinkle with 2 tablespoons of
   the combined cheeses.
3. Pour meat sauce over eggplant.
4. Sprinkle with 2 more
   tablespoons of the cheeses.
5. Layer remaining eggplant over
   top.
6. Pour cream sauce over all.
7. Sprinkle with remaining
   cheeses.
8. Bake until brown and top is set.

Temperature: 350°
Time: 35 to 40 minutes

Suzy M. Hengerer

peach of a flank steak

Yield: 6 servings

A favorite of men!

1 one-pound can of cling
  peach halves
1 cup chili sauce
½ cup vinegar
¼ cup Worcestershire
  sauce
2 cloves garlic, minced
2 beef bouillon cubes
¼ cup butter
2 1½-pound flank steaks
parsley for garnish

1. Drain peaches, reserving syrup.
   Set aside.
2. Combine, in saucepan, syrup,
   chili sauce, vinegar,
   Worcestershire sauce, minced
   garlic, bouillon cubes, and
   butter. Simmer for 10 minutes.
3. Score steak by making shallow,
   diagonal cuts in a diamond
   pattern.
4. Place steak and peaches in a
   large dish. Cover with marinade
   mixture from Step 2. Marinate
   overnight in refrigerator.
5. Transfer steak, only, to greased
   pan. Broil 5 to 8 minutes, two
   inches from heat, basting twice
   with marinade.
6. Turn steak. Add peaches cut
   side up and baste. Broil 5 to 8
   minutes longer.
7. Arrange diagonally sliced steak
   and peach halves on platter.
   Garnish with parsley. Serve with
   warm marinade.

Must do ahead.

Temperature: Broil
Time: 10 to 16 minutes

Priscilla L. Minster

beef bourguignon

Yield: 6 servings

A company stew.

3 tablespoons shortening
2 pounds round steak, cut
  into 2-inch cubes
1 teaspoon salt
¼ teaspoon marjoram
¼ teaspoon thyme
⅛ teaspoon pepper
1½ tablespoons flour
¾ cup beef bouillon
1½ cups red burgundy
  wine
4 large onions, sliced

1. Brown meat in 2 tablespoons of
   the shortening in a dutch oven.
   Remove from heat.
2. Sprinkle salt, marjoram, thyme,
   and pepper over meat.
3. Combine flour and bouillon.
   Pour over meat.
4. Heat to boiling, stirring often.
   Boil one minute.
5. Stir in wine, cover, and simmer
   about 2 hours, until meat is
   tender.

beef bourguignon continued

½ pound fresh
  mushrooms, sliced
1 15-ounce can of
  artichoke hearts,
  drained
fresh chopped parsley to
  garnish

6. Add more bouillon and wine, if
   necessary. Liquid should always
   just cover meat.
7. Sauté onions and mushrooms in
   remaining tablespoon of
   shortening until tender.
8. Gently stir onions, mushrooms,
   and artichoke hearts into stew.
9. Cook, uncovered, for 15
   minutes, or until heated
   through. Sauce may be
   thickened at this time.
10. Sprinkle with parsley, just
    before serving.

Time: 2 hours, 15 minutes

Lucia H. Shaw

steak and bacon tournedos

Yield: 4 servings

Our favorite barbeque . . . we even get the grill out in the winter.

1½ pounds flank steak
instant meat tenderizer
  (non-seasoned)
10 slices bacon
½ teaspoon freshly
  ground black pepper
½ teaspoon garlic salt
½ teaspoon seasoned salt
2 tablespoons chopped
  fresh parsley

1. Pound steak until it is uniformly
   ½-inch thick.
2. Use meat tenderizer as directed
   on label.
3. Cook bacon until almost done,
   but *NOT CRISP.*
4. Sprinkle meat with pepper,
   garlic salt, and seasoned salt.
5. Score steak diagonally making
   diamond shaped cuts. Turn
   steak, scored side down.
6. Place bacon strips lengthwise on
   steak. Sprinkle with parsley.
7. Starting at narrow end, roll up
   steak, jelly-roll style.
8. Skewer with 8 wooden sticks,
   metal skewers, or trussing pins
   at 1-inch intervals.
9. Cut into 8 1-inch slices with
   serrated knife. (Can be done
   ahead to this point and
   refrigerated until ready to grill.)
10. Grill 15 minutes, over medium
    coals, turning once. Serve
    immediately.

Time: 15 minutes

Arlene A. Wright

grilled steak with wine sauce

Yield: 4 servings

Great London Broil—heavenly for onion lovers!

1 flank steak or
1 top round steak
salt and pepper to taste
1 teaspoon thyme
soy sauce, for basting
French bread, optional

1. Brush steak with soy sauce. Sprinkle well with salt, pepper, and thyme. Let stand for at least one hour. Meanwhile, prepare sauce.
2. Just before grilling, brush again with soy sauce. Grill over hot fire, 3 to 4 minutes on each side for rare steak.
3. Carve on diagonal into thin slices.

Sauce
1¼ cups chopped shallots
　or green onions
1¼ cups red wine
6 tablespoons butter
salt to taste
2 tablespoons chopped
　fresh parsley

Sauce
1. Combine shallots and red wine in saucepan. Bring just to boiling.
2. Add butter and salt. Stir until butter is melted.
3. Add fresh parsley.
4. Serve warm over steak slices. Pass extra sauce. Accompany this with French bread.

Lucia H. Shaw

veal madelon

Yield: 4 servings

A piquant dish with gourmet aspirations.

1 clove garlic, minced
2 tablespoons butter
2 pounds boneless veal,
　cut in bite-size chunks
2 tablespoons flour
1 teaspoon salt
¼ teaspoon pepper
2　¼ x 2-inch lemon peels
1 cup hot water
1 cup heavy cream

1. Sauté garlic in butter.
2. Remove garlic and brown veal in same butter.
3. Sprinkle veal with flour, salt, and pepper; continue browning.
4. Add lemon peels and water, mix, and cover. Simmer until tender, adding more water if needed.
5. Remove lemon peels. Stir in cream; heat through.

Temperature: Simmer
Time: 1 hour

Hint: Serve with hot, buttered noodles.

Peggi M. Godwin

veal stroganoff

Yield: 4 servings

A festive company dinner everyone will rave about!!

½ cup chopped onion
1 clove garlic, minced
6 tablespoons butter
6 veal cutlets, ½-inch
    thick
1 teaspoon salt
dash of pepper
1 cup sour cream
½ pound mushrooms,
    sliced
3 to 4 tablespoons brandy
noodles

1. In a skillet, cook onion and garlic in 4 tablespoons of the butter until tender.
2. Add veal cutlets, cooking 6 to 7 minutes, turning a couple of times.
3. Add salt, pepper, and sour cream. Simmer, covered, 10 minutes or more until tender.
4. Sauté mushrooms in remaining 2 tablespoons butter for 2 to 3 minutes.
5. Add brandy to mushrooms, and pour over veal.
6. Serve with noodles.

Barbara D. Newman

 veal royale

Yield: 6 to 8 servings

Serve this with rice, as the sauce is superb.

2 pounds veal, sliced thin
1 cup flour
½ teaspoon paprika
½ teaspoon salt
½ teaspoon sage
⅓ cup oil
⅓ cup butter
½ cup currant jelly
4 tablespoons catsup
1 10-ounce can
    consommé
⅓ cup dry sherry
pinch of cayenne pepper
pinch of garlic salt
pinch of pepper
1 to 2 cups sliced
    mushrooms, enough to
    cover veal

1. Dry veal on paper towel. Dredge slices in mixture of flour, paprika, salt, and sage.
2. Heat butter and oil together in a frying pan until *very* hot. Water should bead when sprinkled in pan.
3. Brown veal slices very quickly and remove them to a 9 x 13-inch casserole dish.
4. In same frying pan, combine currant jelly, catsup, consommé, sherry, cayenne, garlic salt, and pepper. Stir and bring to a boil. Pour this mixture over veal.
5. Add mushrooms to casserole.
6. Cover with foil and bake, or refrigerate, and bake later.

Temperature: 325°
Time: 60 minutes or

Temperature: 400°
Time: 30 minutes

Susan R. van der Stricht

veal kidneys in wine sauce

Yield: 1 serving

Delicious as a luncheon dish or appetizer.

1 veal kidney (veal is best and most tender)
1 tablespoon butter
2 tablespoons brandy, warmed
¼ cup dry white wine or vermouth
½ teaspoon Dijon mustard
¼ cup port wine
3 tablespoons cream or milk
½ tablespoon flour
parsley
salt and pepper

1. For each serving, cut out fat and remove membrane from 1 kidney. Cut into bite-size slices.
2. Melt butter in a small skillet. Sauté kidney slices over medium heat until browned.
3. Add brandy. Ignite. Flambé until flame dies out.
4. Add the white wine. Cover. Cook over low heat for 3 minutes. Do not overcook. Transfer kidneys, using a slotted spoon, to a small dish and keep warm.

Sauce:

1. Cook liquid in skillet until reduced to almost nothing.
2. Stir in mustard and port wine. Season with a little salt and pepper. Cook over low heat until port is slightly reduced.
3. Combine cream with flour. Stir into sauce. Keeping heat low, cook and stir until sauce is slightly thickened. Continue to cook for 5 minutes.
4. Pour sauce over warm kidney slices. Sprinkle with parsley.
5. Best when served immediately, however, leftovers can be frozen and reheated slowly.

Susan S. Taylor

veal cordon bleu

Yield: 6 servings

The spectacular sauce makes this so right for a special dinner party.

1½ pounds boneless veal round, ¼-inch thick
6 slices Swiss cheese
6 thin slices cooked ham
2 tablespoons flour

1. Pound veal until thin. Cut into 6 pieces.
2. On each piece, place one slice cheese and one slice ham. Roll up, and secure with toothpicks.

veal cordon bleu continued

½ teaspoon salt
1 teaspoon paprika
½ pound fresh
  mushrooms, sliced
⅓ cup butter
1 cup dry white wine
1 cup beef gravy
½ cup sour cream

3. Dust each with flour mixed with salt and paprika.
4. Sauté mushrooms in butter until golden. Remove mushrooms from pan, and reserve.
5. Lightly brown meat in same skillet. Add ½ cup of the wine, and cook slowly until liquid is almost evaporated.
6. Slowly mix in gravy and remaining wine. Add mushrooms.
7. Cover skillet, and bake.
8. Just before serving, stir in sour cream.

Temperature: 400°
Time: 10 minutes

Nancy C. Alderman

veal scallops

Yield: 4 servings

Akin to those in gourmet restaurants.

1 pound veal (6 thin
  slices)
½ cup minced onion
2 tablespoons butter
2 tablespoons oil
salt
pepper
1 cup sour cream
½ cup shredded Gjetost
  cheese

1. Pound veal, lightly, between two pieces of wax paper, using a smooth mallet. Dry scallops with paper towel.
2. Sauté onion in heavy skillet using one tablespoon oil and one tablespoon butter. Remove from pan and set aside.
3. Brown veal, using the remaining tablespoon of oil and butter. Remove from pan, set aside, and sprinkle with salt and pepper.
4. Reduce heat and return onions to skillet. Add sour cream and cheese. Stir constantly, until cheese is melted. *Do not boil.*
5. Return veal to skillet and heat, basting with sauce. Serve.

Hint: Gjetost (ye-tost) cheese is a brown Norwegian cheese, heavy and a little sweet. Can be found in most stores that stock imported cheese.

Lorraine E. Beasom

181

veal français

*A house specialty of the Wild Winds Restaurant,
Wild Winds Farm, Naples, New York.*

2 eggs
6 tablespoons grated
  Parmesan cheese
6 tablespoons chopped,
  fresh parsley
2 lemons
paprika
6 2-ounce portions veal
  steak
flour
6 tablespoons clarified
  butter
dry sherry

1. Beat eggs in a bowl. Add 1
   tablespoon of the cheese and 2
   tablespoons of the parsley. Mix.
2. Cut 1 of the lemons in half and
   slice 3 thin slices from each half.
   Cover half of each slice with
   paprika and other half with
   parsley; reserve for garnish.
3. Dip veal in flour, then in egg
   mixture.
4. Heat butter in large pan until
   very hot. Sauté veal until
   golden brown, turning once.
5. Add remaining cheese to veal.
6. Squeeze juice of one lemon into
   pan.
7. Add enough sherry to barely
   cover veal. Cook, reducing pan
   liquid to approximately
   one-third.
8. Place veal on serving plates.
   Cover with sauce and garnish
   with reserved lemon slices.
   Serve immediately.

Hint: If more sauce is desired, add a little wine or broth (chicken
or beef) to sauce before pouring over veal.

*Eleanor Clapp
Wild Winds Farms, Naples, N.Y.*

lamb shanks and white beans

A robust recipe like a thick soup.

4 lamb shanks
¼ cup flour
¼ cup olive oil
3 medium onions, sliced
3 large cloves garlic,
  minced
1 teaspoon rosemary
dash of salt
2 teaspoons black pepper

1. Rub lamb shanks with flour.
2. Brown meat on all sides in oil in
   heavy pan. Remove when
   browned.
3. Sauté onion and garlic in same
   pan about 5 minutes.
4. Add rosemary, salt, pepper, and
   tomatoes, with their liquid, to
   onion and garlic.

1 one-pound, 1-ounce can
  Italian peeled tomatoes
2 tablespoons seasoned
  bread crumbs
2 tablespoons grated
  Parmesan cheese
2 1-pound, 4-ounce cans
  cannellini beans (white
  kidney beans)
rind of 1 lemon, cut in
  slivers
1½ tablespoons chopped
  fresh parsley (optional)

5. Add lamb; cover; cook slowly
   for 2 hours. (Can be done ahead
   to this point.)
6. Add bread crumbs and cheese.
   Cook 5 more minutes.
7. Heat beans in their own liquid.
   Place them in a warm serving
   dish with lamb in center.
8. Sprinkle lemon peel and parsley
   over all. Serve in bowls.

Hint: Noodles or rice can be substituted for beans.

Katrina H. Looby

lamb and eggplant casserole

Yield: 4 to 6 servings

Harvest autumn's vegetable bounty for your table.

1 to 1½ pounds ground
  lamb
2 tablespoons oil
1 onion, chopped
1 clove garlic, minced
4 tomatoes, skinned and
  sliced
1½ teaspoons salt
½ teaspoon freshly
  ground pepper
1 tablespoon chopped
  basil, fresh if possible
½ teaspoon oregano
1- to 1½-pound eggplant,
  peeled, sliced, salted,
  and drained
1 green pepper, cut in
  strips
1 zucchini, sliced
¼ to ½ pound
  mushrooms, sliced
1 cup rice, uncooked
1½ cups tomato sauce
3 tablespoons Feta
  cheese, crumbled

1. Brown lamb in oil. Drain lamb
   and set aside.
2. In same pan, sauté onions and
   garlic in small amount of oil
   until golden. Drain.
3. Place ½ of the tomato slices on
   the bottom of a 2½- to 3-quart
   casserole.
4. Add in layers ½ each of the
   seasonings, eggplant, green
   pepper, zucchini, mushrooms,
   lamb, onions, and garlic.
5. Repeat the layers with the
   remaining seasonings,
   vegetables, and meat.
6. Combine rice and tomato sauce.
   Pour this mixture over casserole
   ingredients.
7. Top casserole with remaining
   tomato slices and the Feta
   cheese.
8. Bake covered.

Temperature: 350°
Time: 1 hour covered then 10
minutes uncovered

Patricia S. Driscoll

183

gourmet lamb stew

Yield: 6 servings

Delicious blending of flavors.

2 pounds shoulder lamb,
   cubed
¼ cup flour
1 teaspoon salt
pepper
3 tablespoons bacon fat
   or butter
2 medium onions,
   coarsely chopped
2 stalks celery, chopped
1 carrot, coarsely
   chopped
½ to 1 cup sliced
   mushrooms
1 cup raw rice
2 tomatoes, skinned and
   chopped
1 small bay leaf
½ teaspoon oregano
½ teaspoon basil
1 cup consommé
1 cup dry white wine
2 teaspoons parsley

1. Shake meat cubes in a bag with flour, salt, and pepper until coated.
2. Melt fat in frying pan. Brown lamb cubes well on all sides. Transfer to large covered casserole.
3. Sauté onions, celery, carrot, and mushrooms very lightly, in remaining fat, in frying pan. Add more fat or butter, if necessary. Transfer vegetables to casserole, using a slotted spoon.
4. Brown rice lightly in same fat.
5. Add rice, tomatoes, and herbs to casserole.
6. Pour consommé and wine into frying pan. Scrape up all brown glaze. Add to casserole. Stir well.
7. Bake, covered, stirring once or twice during cooking.
8. Before serving, stir lightly. Sprinkle with parsley.

Temperature: 325°
Time: 1 ½ hours

Jane N. Clifford

lamb shish kabob with hot or cold marinade

Yield: 6 to 8 servings

Grill cherry tomatoes, green peppers, and mushrooms skewered with the lamb.

4 pounds lamb, cut into 1½-inch cubes (or whole butterflied leg of lamb)

1. Prepare marinade of your choice.
2. Pierce meat. Place in enamel or glass pan. Pour marinade over meat. Marinate 4 hours or overnight.
3. Thread meat onto skewers. Grill 10 to 15 minutes, basting with marinade.

Marinade I
4 onions, peeled and sliced
½ teaspoon pepper
1 tablespoon salt
½ cup sherry
2 tablespoons olive oil
2 tablespoons oregano
1 teaspoon rosemary

Marinade II
½ cup olive oil (or salad oil)
½ cup lemon juice
1 teaspoon salt
1 teaspoon marjoram
1 teaspoon thyme
1 clove garlic, minced
½ cup dried onion flakes
¼ cup chopped fresh parsley

Marinades I and II
1. Combine all ingredients.

Marinade III
3 tablespoons Worcestershire sauce
3 tablespoons steak sauce
2 splashes soy sauce
½ cup catsup
5 tablespoons oil
1 tablespoon sugar
1 tablespoon wine vinegar
1 medium onion, grated
1 teaspoon salt
few drops Tabasco

Marinade III
1. Combine all ingredients.
2. Heat to boiling.

Must do ahead

Lucia H. Shaw
Susan L. Carpenter
Donna Torpey

185

roast leg of lamb with marinades

Yield: 8 to 10 servings

Choose either marinade for beautifully seasoned, moist lamb.

5 to 6 pound leg of lamb

Marinade I
1 cup dry red wine
½ cup orange juice
¼ cup chili sauce
¼ cup water
1 tablespoon chili powder
2 tablespoons olive oil
1 large onion, finely
  chopped
2 cloves garlic, minced
1 tablespoon fresh
  oregano
1 teaspoon cumin seed
1 tablespoon brown sugar
salt and pepper

Marinade I
1. Combine all ingredients.

Marinade II
1 cup dry red wine
½ cup chili sauce
2 tablespoons lemon juice
2 tablespoons cider
  vinegar
½ cup grated carrots
¼ cup chopped fresh
  parsley
½ cup beef broth
2 teaspoons salt
2 tablespoons oil
½ teaspoon pepper
1 tablespoon sugar
1 bay leaf
1 clove garlic, minced
1 cup minced onion

Marinade II
1. Combine all ingredients.

1. Prepare marinade of choice.
2. Place lamb in glass or enamel
   pan. Pour marinade over meat.
   Marinate overnight, turning
   meat occasionally.
3. Roast meat 30 minutes at 425°.
4. Reduce heat to 350°, continue
   roasting 1¼ hours, basting
   occasionally.
5. Thicken Marinade II to serve
   with meat.

Temperature: **425°**
Time: **30 minutes**

Temperature: **350°**
Time: **1¼ hours**

Must do ahead

Alice K. Smith
Mary Kay Taber

pork with cream mustard sauce

Yield: 6 servings

A little bit different, a little bit special.

pork tenderloin cut into
   twelve 1½-inch thick
   slices
flour
salt and pepper
4 tablespoons butter
½ cup chopped onion
8 peppercorns
⅓ cup vinegar
2 cups heavy cream
⅓ cup Dijon mustard
2 tablespoons butter
½ teaspoon salt

1. Roll pork slices to ½-inch thickness. Dust pieces with flour, salt, and pepper.
2. Brown on both sides in butter. When thoroughly cooked, remove from pan and keep warm.
3. Add onion to drippings, and cook until transparent.
4. Stir in peppercorns and vinegar and bring to a boil.
5. Remove from heat and stir in heavy cream. Return to heat and cook until thickened.
6. Remove from heat and discard peppercorns. Stir in mustard, butter, and salt.
7. Pour over pork and serve immediately.

Paula S. Howk

honey pork chops

Yield: 4 to 6 servings

This recipe is not delicate and can sit in a warm oven waiting to be served.

6 1-inch thick pork chops

Marinade
½ cup honey
¼ cup cider vinegar
2 tablespoons soy sauce
2 tablespoons crystallized
   ginger, coarsely
   chopped
½ clove garlic, minced
freshly ground pepper

Must do ahead.

1. Mix all marinade ingredients together in a baking dish and add chops, turning to cover with marinade.
2. Refrigerate for about 8 hours, turning the pork chops occasionally.
3. Bake in same dish, turning the chops during baking.
4. Skim fat from marinade. Serve marinade with pork chops. If not serving immediately, baste while you keep it warm.

Temperature: 350°
Time: 1 hour, 15 minutes

Jeanne P. Massey

babi kecap (pork with soy sauce)

Yield: 4 to 6 servings

An Indonesian recipe served as one dish on a rice table.

1 red onion, finely chopped
4 garlic cloves, minced
6 slices fresh ginger, minced, or 1 teaspoon ground ginger
1 teaspoon crushed red pepper
4 tablespoons peanut oil
½ cup soy sauce
½ cup cream of coconut (thin slightly with milk, about 2 tablespoons)
2 pounds boneless pork
pepper
rice

1. Sauté onions, garlic, ginger, and crushed red pepper in one tablespoon of the peanut oil for a minute or two over medium-high heat, stirring to prevent burning.
2. Add soy sauce and coconut milk. Remove from heat.
3. Cut pork into 1-inch cubes and sprinkle with pepper. Sauté pork in the remaining 3 tablespoons oil, until evenly browned.
4. Combine spice mixture with pork in a 4-quart pan. Cook, uncovered, over medium heat until meat is tender (about 1 hour). Add more coconut milk if necessary.
5. Serve over rice or egg noodles.

Hint: Use leftover cream of coconut for piña coladas.

Susan N. Woehr

genesee valley pork chops

Yield: 4 servings

Especially hearty served with mashed potatoes.

3 tablespoons butter
4 center cut pork chops
2 16-ounce cans tomatoes
1 cup beer or ale
salt and pepper to taste
1 tablespoon caraway seeds (optional)
1 16-ounce can sauerkraut, drained

1. Melt butter and quickly brown chops (375° if using an electric frying pan).
2. Add the tomatoes and their liquid, the beer, salt, pepper, and caraway seeds.
3. Cover pan and lower heat to simmer for 25 minutes.
4. Add sauerkraut and continue to simmer, covered, 10 minutes.

Pamm E. Ferguson

roast pork loin with apple topping

Yield: 4 to 6 servings

A familiar flavor combination that even the kids will like.

2 tablespoons flour
1½ teaspoons salt
1 teaspoon dry mustard
1 teaspoon caraway
  seeds
½ teaspoon sugar
¼ teaspoon black pepper
¼ teaspoon ground sage
4 to 5-pound pork loin
  roast

1. Mix together flour, salt, mustard, caraway seeds, sugar, pepper, and sage.
2. Rub mixture over surface of pork.
3. Set fat side up in roasting pan. Bake for 1½ hours.

Topping
1½ cups applesauce or
  minced apple
½ cup brown sugar
¼ teaspoon cinnamon
¼ teaspoon mace
¼ teaspoon salt

Topping
1. Mix all ingredients. Spread over top of roast.
2. Bake 1 hour longer, adding water to bottom of pan, if necessary.

Temperature: 325°
Time: 1½ hours, then 1 hour more

Hint: Garnish with spiced apple rings or miniature crab apples.

Phyllis Connally
Schutt's Cider Mill

chinese spareribs

Yield: 4 servings

One of my children's favorite meats!

½ cup dark corn syrup
½ cup pineapple juice
¼ cup soy sauce
2 tablespoons sherry
2 teaspoons ground ginger
¼ teaspoon dry mustard
⅛ teaspoon garlic powder
4 pounds lean spareribs,
  separated

1. Mix all ingredients, except ribs. Pour in large baking dish. Add ribs, cover, and marinate overnight.
2. Drain ribs and reserve marinade. Place in shallow baking pan and cover.
3. Bake at 350° for 1 hour. Remove ribs, discard fat from pan, and return ribs to pan.
4. Return to oven and bake for 30 minutes more, basting frequently with marinade, and turning as needed.

Must do one day ahead.

Temperature: 350°
Time: 1½ hours

Sheila N. Prezzano

real polish sausage

Yield: 5 to 6 pounds

An old family recipe, served at all special events.

1 lean pork butt (5 to 6 pounds)

garlic cloves (1 per pound of pork butt)

salt (1 tablespoon per pound of meat)

fresh ground pepper (½ teaspoon per pound of meat)

2 to 3 cups water

hog casings (available in meat departments)

sawed-off top of a beverage bottle (smooth the cut edges)

1. Cut pork butt into 1-inch cubes.
2. Using the metal blade of the food processor, or by using a food grinder, process ½ to ¾ cup of cubes at a time. Meat should look like ground beef.
3. Mince garlic. Combine with all of the meat.
4. Add salt, pepper, and enough water to make the sausage mixture feel like soft mud pies. Mix thoroughly. Refrigerate this mixture overnight.
5. Remove hog casings from the salt in which they are packed. Soak in a bowl of water for 30 minutes. Rinse each casing by letting water flow through it. Check for holes in the casings. Casings should be 18 to 24 inches long without holes.
6. To make sausage, gather one casing on the end of the beverage bottle, allowing 3 inches of casing to extend. This unfilled portion of each casing should be knotted after links are completed. You will need to knot both ends.
7. With one hand holding and controlling the release of the casing, begin pushing meat into the wide end of the beverage top using your other thumb. You will soon learn to control both to prevent large air pockets from forming in the casing. Overpacking will cause the casing to break. Should breakage occur, cut the casing at that point and begin again. The size of the links can vary.
8. After stuffing, tie ends of casing. Links can be wrapped and frozen up to 3 months.

9. To cook sausage, bring it to a boil in a large pot of water. Simmer for 50 minutes. Drain. Brown in a frying pan or on the grill.
10. Serve on rolls or with sauerkraut.

Alice K. Smith

sweet and sour pork kabobs

Yield: 6 servings

Charlie Chan's number one dinner!

½ cup apricot preserves
½ cup tomato sauce
¼ cup brown sugar
⅓ cup dry red wine
2 tablespoons lemon juice
2 tablespoons cooking oil
2 teaspoons grated onion
2 pounds lean, boneless pork, cut in 1½-inch pieces
4 large carrots, cooked and cut in 1-inch pieces
2 green peppers, seeded and cut in 1½-inch pieces
pineapple chunks, fresh or canned
salt and pepper to taste

1. Combine preserves, tomato sauce, brown sugar, wine, lemon juice, oil, and onion in saucepan. Boil, uncovered, 10 to 15 minutes.
2. Thread pieces of pork on 4 skewers. Season with salt and pepper.
3. Thread pieces of carrots, pepper, and pineapple alternately on 4 additional skewers. Season with salt and pepper. Set aside.
4. Grill and turn meat only over medium coals for 10 minutes.
5. Add other skewers to grill. Brush all with sauce and grill for 15 minutes more, turning occasionally.
6. Brush pork and vegetable/fruit with sauce just before serving.
7. Remove from skewers. Arrange on a serving platter or divide among individual plates. Good with rice.

Time: 15 to 25 minutes

Lucia H. Shaw

191

buffy's ham rolls

Yield: 6 servings

Super for a buffet supper.

1 10-ounce package frozen, chopped spinach, cooked, drained, and cooled
1 7-ounce package seasoned stuffing
1 8-ounce container sour cream
1 pound boiled ham, sliced

1. Combine spinach, stuffing, and sour cream.
2. Spoon about 1½ tablespoons of spinach mixture on each ham slice and roll up.
3. Place ham rolls in shallow baking dish. Prepare sauce.

Sauce
2 cups milk
2 tablespoons butter
2 tablespoons cornstarch
1½ cups grated Cheddar cheese
dash of sherry
bread crumbs

Sauce
1. Over medium heat, combine milk, butter, and cornstarch.
2. Stir and cook until thickened; add cheese and sherry.
3. When cheese is melted, pour sauce over ham rolls. Sprinkle top with bread crumbs.
4. Bake covered, then uncovered.

Temperature: 350°
Time: 15 minutes covered, then 15 minutes uncovered

Pamela B. Mele

simmered ham with sauerkraut

Yield: 4 servings

A welcome way to take the chill off a late autumn day.

4 slices bacon, diced
1½ pounds fully cooked ham
2 cups chopped onion
1 tablespoon firmly packed brown sugar
⅛ teaspoon ground cloves
¼ teaspoon pepper
1 large apple, pared and thinly sliced (enough to equal 1 cup)
1 32-ounce can sauerkraut, well drained

1. Fry bacon pieces until crisp. Remove from pan with a slotted spoon. Drain on paper towel. Set aside. Discard all but 2 tablespoons of the drippings.
2. Trim excess fat from ham. Cut into cubes or pieces. Brown on all sides in the bacon drippings. Remove from pan.
3. Add onions to pan. Cook, stirring until onions are limp.
4. Stir in sugar, cloves, pepper, apple, and sauerkraut.
5. Add ham pieces to vegetables.

simmered ham with sauerkraut *continued*

1 cup apple juice or cider
2 tablespoons chopped
  parsley

6. Pour in apple juice. Simmer,
   covered, over low heat until
   apples are tender (about 20
   minutes).
7. Garnish with parsley and bacon.

Hint: Dice the bacon with scissors before cooking.

Mary W. Schwertz

sweet mustard

Yield: 1 cup

Serve with ham, or mix with mayonnaise for coleslaw.

1 cup sugar
2 tablespoons dry
  mustard
2 eggs
1 scant cup vinegar
1 tablespoon butter or
  margarine

1. In a small saucepan, mix sugar
   and dry mustard thoroughly.
2. Add eggs, one at a time, stir in
   carefully.
3. Gradually add vinegar.
4. Cook on stove over medium
   heat. When heated through, add
   butter or margarine, and mix
   well.
5. Remove from heat, and cool.
   Store, covered, in refrigerator.

Peggy Patterson

barbeque sauce superior

Yield: 1½ cups

Make a big batch, it's so good.

2 tablespoons brown
  sugar
1 tablespoon paprika
1 teaspoon salt
1 teaspoon prepared
  mustard
¼ teaspoon chili powder
⅛ teaspoon cayenne
  pepper
2 tablespoons
  Worcestershire sauce
¼ cup vinegar
1 cup tomato juice
½ cup water

1. Combine all ingredients in a
   saucepan. Bring to a boil.
2. Simmer until slightly thick.
3. Brush on meat of your choice,
   and grill. Baste as meat cooks.

Kristine K. Hoppe

quick bearnaise sauce

Yield: ¾ to 1 cup

A great way to dress up a steak for last minute company.

2 tablespoons white wine
1 tablespoon tarragon
vinegar
2 teaspoons tarragon,
chopped
2 teaspoons chopped
shallots or scallions
¼ teaspoon freshly
ground black pepper
½ cup butter
3 egg yolks
2 tablespoons lemon juice
¼ teaspoon salt
pinch of cayenne pepper

1. Combine wine, vinegar,
   tarragon, shallots, and pepper in
   saucepan.
2. Bring ingredients to a boil. Cook
   rapidly until almost all the liquid
   disappears.
3. In a small saucepan, heat butter
   until it bubbles. Do not allow
   butter to brown.
4. Place egg yolks, lemon juice,
   salt, and cayenne in electric
   blender or food processor.
   Cover and flick motor on and off
   at high speed. Gradually add
   hot butter while blending at high
   speed.
5. Add herb mixture, cover, and
   blend on high speed four
   seconds.
6. Serve immediately.

**Hint: As a change from spooning sauce directly onto meat or
fish, scoop out small fresh tomatoes, scallop edges, and fill with
bearnaise sauce. Serve on each plate beside meat or fish.**

Patsy M. Gilges

bordelaise sauce

Yield: 1½ cups

A mushroom-wine blend to enhance meats.

2 tablespoons butter
¼ cup sliced mushrooms
1½ tablespoons
cornstarch
1 cup cold beef bouillon
1½ tablespoons red wine
1 tablespoon lemon juice
¼ teaspoon tarragon
leaves
dash of pepper

1. Melt butter. Sauté mushrooms
   until golden.
2. Blend cornstarch into bouillon.
   Add to mushrooms.
3. Bring mixture to a boil, stirring
   constantly.
4. Stir in wine, lemon juice, and
   seasonings; simmer 5 minutes.

Cristy B. Richardson

 ## rosy ham sauce

Yield: 1 cup

Serve in cut glass or silver bowl with ladle—elegant!

1 10½-ounce jar of red currant jelly
1 tablespoon horseradish or more to taste

1. Heat jelly until melted over medium heat.
2. Add horseradish and stir.
3. Serve warm or at room temperature.

Hester G. Hellebush

mighty mighty mustard

Yield: 1½ cups

Very potent!

1 cup white vinegar
1 cup dry mustard
2 eggs, beaten
½ cup sugar
pinch of salt

1. Whisk vinegar and mustard in glass bowl. Cover, and let stand overnight.
2. The next day, stir in remaining ingredients over low heat. Bring mixture to a slow boil, stirring constantly.
3. Cook mixture until it thickens and coats a spoon.
4. Cool, and refrigerate. (Keeps up to one month.)
5. This can be used on sandwiches or as a dip for beef stick chunks, cheese.

Must do part ahead.

Judy U. Murray

Every time Judy serves this very potent mustard, folks implore her for the recipe. Until now she gracefully declined all requests except those of two close friends who swore silence. Now, at last, she has made the secret public so we can all enjoy her nostril flaring condiment.

toad hill mint sauce

Yield: 1 cup

Mom always made this sauce for lamb and now my family won't eat lamb without it.

1 cup sugar
¼ cup vinegar
¼ cup water
¾ to 1 cup finely chopped
  fresh mint

1. Bring sugar, vinegar, and water to a boil in a small saucepan.
2. Boil 3 to 4 minutes.
3. Pour over mint. Serve with lamb chops, roast, or patties.

Hint: It's easy to make several jars of this sauce in the summer for later use. Store jars on a cool shelf. When tightly capped, this will keep for a year.

Priscilla L. Minster

fresh mint jelly

Yield: 6 to 8 small jars

This has a delicate flavor, the perfect addition to any lamb meal.

1 cup mint leaves with
  stems
½ cup white vinegar
1 cup water
3½ cups sugar
4 to 6 drops green food
  coloring
¼-inch by ¼-inch cube of
  butter or margarine
3 fluid ounces fruit pectin
1 square of paraffin

1. Pick only the topmost mint leaves and stems. Do not remove leaves from stems. Pack tightly to make the one cup measure.
2. Rinse mint. Cut up into very small pieces. Crush with bottom of a glass for a few seconds.
3. Place mint, vinegar, water, and sugar in a 3- or 4-quart saucepan.
4. Bring to a boil over highest heat, stirring as it cooks. Add four to six drops of food coloring as soon as mix is nearly boiling.
5. Add butter and fruit pectin, stirring constantly. Bring to a full boil. Boil hard for ½ minute.
6. Remove from heat.
7. Pour through a medium fine sieve into a pitcher. Press with spoon to extract all liquid and make little specks of mint fall into jelly.
8. Pour into sterilized jars, or run jars through dishwasher. Wash jelly off top rims of jars. Seal with ¼ inch of paraffin which has been melted in a disposable coffee can.

Nancy M. Frank

196

poultry

poultry

POULTRY

Chicken

Almond Chicken Fingers, p 198
Bahamian Chicken Breasts, p 198
Baked Chicken Teriyaki, p 205
Chicken Breasts with Basil
    Sauce, p 197
Chicken Gumbo, p 217
Chicken Ham Cheese Wheel,
    p 202
Chicken-Herb Pie, p 208
Chicken Italian in Foil, p 197
Chicken Marceil, p 206
Chicken Marengo, p 209
Chicken Parmesan, p 207
Chicken Ragout, p 208
Chicken Ratatouille, p 212
Chicken Saltimboca, p 199
Chicken-Shrimp Casserole, p 203
Chicken and Spice, p 215
Chicken and Vegetables in Cream
    Sauce, p 204
Chicken Wellington, p 212
Chicken with Cashews, p 216
Coq au Vin, p 215
Fowl Play, p 218
Hot Chicken Salad, p 216
Naples Valley Chicken, p 206
Orange-glazed Chicken, p 200
Picnic Chicken, p 207
Piquant Chicken and Ribs, p 199
Popover Chicken Tarragon, p 211
Rolled Chicken Washington,
    p 200
Sherried Chicken Breasts, p 210
Skillet Tomato Chicken, p 205
Soy Sauced Chicken, p 201
World's Fair Chicken, p 214

Turkey

Pastel de Montezuma, p 219

GAME

Cornish Hens Wellington, p 221
Pheasant in Sour Cream, p 222
Pheasant Supreme, p 220

Stuffings

Chestnut Stuffing, p 218
Cornish Hen Dressing, p 219
Dill Bread Stuffing, p 222

Sauces

Cornell Barbeque Sauce, p 210
Indian Summer Sauce, p 209
Wine Marinade, p 201

chicken italian in foil

Yield: 4 servings

Great for camping or homemade TV dinners.

2 large potatoes
¼ teaspoon salt
2 green peppers, sliced
2 tomatoes, cut in wedges
4 boneless chicken
  breasts
salad oil
4 tablespoons catsup
1 teaspoon oregano
2 tablespoons butter,
  melted

1. Cut potatoes lengthwise into
⅛-inch slices and place on an
18 x 12-inch double layer of foil.
Sprinkle with salt.
2. Add peppers and tomatoes.
3. Lay chicken on top of vegetables and brush with salad oil.
4. Mix catsup, oregano, and butter.
Pour over chicken.
5. Wrap foil securely around
chicken and vegetables.
6. Bake until tender for 1 hour or
grill 5 inches from coals for 25
to 30 minutes on each side.

Temperature: 400°
Time: 1 hour

Pamela B. Mele

chicken breasts with basil sauce

Yield: 4 servings

Surprise your unexpected guests!

2 whole chicken breasts
½ cup dry white wine
2 egg yolks
¼ cup heavy cream
¼ teaspoon salt
1 tablespoon chopped,
  fresh parsley
1 teaspoon basil
1 tablespoon lemon juice

1. Bone, skin, and split chicken
breasts.
2. Place in skillet with wine. Cover
and cook over medium heat
until done (about 10 to 12
minutes). Remove from heat and
set aside.
3. In a separate bowl, whisk yolks,
cream, salt, ¼ cup of cooking
liquid, parsley, and basil.
4. Pour egg yolk mixture into a
small saucepan and cook over
low heat, stirring constantly
until sauce thickens slightly.
Remove from heat and add
lemon juice.
5. Remove breasts from pan using
slotted spoon. Place on warmed
serving platter.
6. Pour sauce over breasts just
before serving.

Must serve immediately.

Ann B. Irwin

almond chicken fingers

Yield: 6 servings

Prepare this elegant meal right at the table.

1 teaspoon salt
1 cup flour
3 boneless chicken
  breasts, cut into small
  strips
3 ounces clarified butter
2 ounces almond liqueur
1 chicken bouillon cube,
  dissolved in 1 cup hot
  water
½ teaspoon garlic powder
white pepper to taste
1 cup mushrooms,
  sautéed
1 pint heavy cream
1 cup rice, cooked
½ cup chopped parsley

1. Lightly salt and flour chicken fingers.
2. Sauté them in butter in a large pan until the chicken turns white.
3. Warm the liqueur, and flame it over the chicken.
4. Add the chicken bouillon, garlic powder, pepper, mushrooms, and bring to a boil. Cook over moderate heat until liquid is reduced to half the original amount.
5. Add heavy cream; heat through but do not boil.
6. Check seasoning. Serve over rice, garnished with parsley.

Must serve immediately.

Hint: Clarify butter by melting butter and removing foam that forms on top. This butter will be less likely to burn.

John W. McCarthy
Sherlock's Restaurant

bahamian chicken breasts

Yield: 4 to 6 servings

So tender and light!

4 whole chicken breasts
4 teaspoons lime juice
⅛ teaspoon salt
⅛ teaspoon pepper
2 tablespoons butter
pinch of bay leaf or 1
  small whole bay leaf
lemon rind slices for
  garnish

1. Skin and bone chicken breasts. Pound to flatten.
2. Soak chicken at least 15 minutes in lime juice, salt, and pepper.
3. Melt butter in skillet or in chafing dish at table until it foams. Do *not* let butter brown. Add bay leaf.
4. Sauté breasts about 5 to 7 minutes on *each* side. For larger breasts, sauté 10 to 15 minutes per side.
5. Pour sauce over chicken, garnish with slices of lemon rind, and serve.

Must serve immediately.

Lucius R. Gordon

piquant chicken and ribs

Yield: 6 to 8 servings

An indoor barbeque with outdoor flavor.

¼ cup chopped onion
1 tablespoon oil
½ cup water
1 tablespoon vinegar
1 tablespoon
  Worcestershire sauce
¼ cup lemon juice
¼ teaspoon salt
¼ teaspoon paprika
6 tablespoons brown
  sugar
½ cup chili sauce
½ cup catsup
½ cup molasses
1 chicken, cut up
6 to 8 sliced pork ribs
  (country style)

1. Sauté onion in oil until transparent.
2. Add all other ingredients except chicken and ribs. Cook over medium heat until blended.
3. Simmer on low heat for 30 minutes, stirring occasionally.
4. Arrange chicken and ribs in large casserole. Pour on sauce and bake.

Temperature: 350°
Time: 1 hour

Polly C. Parker

chicken saltimboca

Yield: 4 to 6 servings

This doubles (or triples) easily—perfect for a do-ahead dinner party.

3 whole chicken breasts,
  split, boned, and
  skinned
1 teaspoon salt
6 thin slices ham
1 medium tomato, peeled,
  seeded, and chopped
6 slices Swiss cheese
½ teaspoon dry sage
⅓ cup dry bread crumbs
2 tablespoons Parmesan
  cheese
2 tablespoons minced
  parsley
4 tablespoons melted
  butter

1. Flatten chicken breasts between sheets of waxed paper.
2. Sprinkle each piece with salt.
3. Top each with a slice of ham, chopped tomato, Swiss cheese, and a dash of sage.
4. Roll jelly roll fashion, securing with toothpicks.
5. Combine crumbs, Parmesan cheese, and parsley.
6. Dip chicken in melted butter, roll in crumb mixture, and place in buttered baking dish.
7. Bake uncovered.

Temperature: 350°
Time: 40 to 45 minutes

Cecy R. Szuba

199

orange-glazed chicken
Yield: 4 servings

Serve on a bed of rice—generously ladle on the sauce.

6 chicken breast halves,
   boned, skinned
½ teaspoon salt
¼ cup butter or
   margarine
2 tablespoons flour
⅛ teaspoon cinnamon
dash of ginger
1½ cups orange juice
½ cup slivered almonds,
   toasted
½ cup seedless raisins
1 cup mandarin oranges
   or fresh orange sections

1. Sprinkle chicken with ¼ teaspoon of the salt.
2. Brown chicken in melted butter. Remove from pan and set aside.
3. Blend flour, remaining salt, cinnamon, and ginger into pan drippings to make a smooth paste.
4. Gradually add orange juice, stirring constantly. Cook and stir until sauce thickens.
5. Return chicken to pan. Add almonds and raisins. Cover and cook over low heat, about 45 minutes, or until chicken is tender.
6. Add orange sections and heat through.

Joanne K. Gianniny

rolled chicken washington
Yield: 4 servings

A delightful way to serve an old favorite!

½ cup chopped fresh
   mushrooms or 1
   3-ounce can
2 tablespoons butter
2 tablespoons flour
½ cup light cream or half
   and half
dash of pepper
¼ teaspoon salt
1¼ cup shredded sharp
   Cheddar cheese
2 chicken breasts, boned
   and halved
1 egg, slightly beaten
bread crumbs

1. Sauté mushrooms in butter for 5 minutes.
2. Blend in flour, then light cream, pepper, and salt. Cook and stir until thickened. Remove from heat.
3. Add Cheddar cheese gradually. Turn mixture into a 9-inch pan and chill thoroughly.
4. Shape cheese mixture into 4 sticks. Roll chicken breasts around the sticks and secure with toothpicks.
5. Dip breasts into flour, then egg, and coat with bread crumbs.
6. Bake. Remove toothpicks before serving.

Temperature: 325°
Time: 1 hour

Ann P. Merley

soy sauced chicken

Yield: 4 to 6 servings

A good do-ahead company dish.

1 medium onion, sliced
1 clove garlic, chopped or pressed
1 4-ounce can mushrooms, drained
2 tablespoons salad oil
3 pounds frying chicken, cut up or chicken breasts
flour for dredging
¼ cup soy sauce
¼ cup catsup
¼ cup white wine
¼ cup sliced, pitted black olives, optional

1. Cook onions, garlic, and mushrooms in oil until onion is soft. Using a slotted spoon, transfer them to a buttered 3-quart casserole.
2. Dredge chicken in flour. Brown chicken in same skillet, adding more oil, if necessary. Transfer pieces to casserole.
3. Mix soy sauce, catsup, and wine. Pour over chicken. (Can be refrigerated until baking time.)
4. Bake covered.
5. Garnish with black olives.

Temperature: 350°
Time: 45 minutes

Mary W. Schwertz

wine marinade

Yield: 1½ to 2 quarts

For added flavor and tenderness.

1 quart Rhine or Sauterne wine
4 ounces vinegar
4 onions, chopped
4 green stalks of celery, chopped
3 carrots, sliced
1 clove garlic, chopped
2 bay leaves
1 tablespoon chopped parsley
1 pinch basil
1 small pinch thyme
1 teaspoon tarragon
2 teaspoons salt
1 teaspoon red pepper
1 teaspoon monosodium glutamate
3 to 4 ounces salad or olive oil

1. Mix together all ingredients except oil.
2. Place meat in marinade.
3. Pour oil over marinade. It will stay on top of the marinade and prevent the meat from discoloring.
4. Marinate meat from 3 hours to 2 days in refrigerator. Use marinade to baste during cooking and to flavor gravy.
5. The white wine recipe should be used for fish, poultry, and lighter meats. It also can be used to poach fish as a bouillon. To create a red wine marinade to be used for darker meats and game, replace white wine with a quart of burgundy, add ½ cup sherry, and replace the tarragon with 1 teaspoon of oregano.

Charles M. Fournier
Gold Seal Vineyards, Inc.

chicken ham cheese wheel

Yield: 6 servings

An elegant company dish that can serve as an hors d'oeuvre when cut into bite-size pieces.

Filling

2 eggs, slightly beaten
2 cups shredded Swiss cheese
2 cups chopped cooked chicken
1 cup cubed cooked ham or sliced ham in strips
½ cup sliced black olives
4 scallions, thinly sliced
½ teaspoon salt
½ teaspoon freshly ground pepper

Crust

1 package active dry yeast
⅔ cup warm water (110° to 115°)
2 to 2¼ cups flour
½ teaspoon sugar
½ teaspoon salt
2 tablespoons cooking oil

Filling

1. Combine all ingredients, cover, and refrigerate.

Crust

1. Soften yeast in water.
2. Combine 1 cup of the flour, sugar, and salt in a large mixing bowl.
3. Beat in softened yeast and oil.
4. Stir in enough remaining flour to make a moderately stiff dough. Knead dough 5 to 8 minutes on a floured surface until smooth and elastic.
5. Place dough in greased bowl, turning to grease the top. Cover and let rise in a warm place until doubled, about 1 hour.
6. Punch down. Divide into 2 equal pieces. Roll each on a lightly floured surface into a 13-inch circle.
7. Place one circle on a greased 12-inch pizza pan. Spread with filling. Cover with remaining circle.
8. Trim and flute edges. Prick top crust with fork. Cover with foil and bake for 45 minutes.

Glaze
1 slightly beaten egg
1 tablespoon water
1 teaspoon poppy seeds

Glaze
1. Combine egg and water. Brush on baked pie.
2. Sprinkle with poppy seeds. Return pie to oven for additional 15 minutes. Bake uncovered.
3. Serve warm or cold.

Temperature: 400°
Time: 60 minutes

Hint: Make ahead and freeze. Pack it frozen in your picnic hamper, and it will stay safely cool until serving time.

Nicole R. Doolittle

chicken-shrimp casserole

Yield: 8 servings

A special company dish!

4 whole chicken breasts, boiled and boned and halved
1 pound cooked shrimp
2 13-ounce cans artichoke hearts, drained
7 tablespoons butter
3 medium-sized onions, chopped
½ pound fresh mushrooms, sliced
5 tablespoons flour
4 cups milk, heated
salt and pepper to taste
2 tablespoons tomato paste
1 tablespoon Worcestershire sauce
¼ cup white wine (or dry sherry)
½ cup grated Parmesan or Romano cheese

1. Place cooked chicken breasts on bottom of greased, large glass baking dish.
2. Top with shrimp and artichokes.
3. Sauté onions and mushrooms in 2 tablespoons of the butter. Spread over chicken mixture.
4. Melt remaining 5 tablespoons of butter and add flour. Whisk and cook for 1 to 2 minutes.
5. Slowly add warmed milk, stirring constantly. Cook until it is smooth and thick.
6. Stir in tomato paste, Worcestershire sauce and wine.
7. Pour over chicken mixture and sprinkle with grated cheese. Bake.

Temperature: 350 degrees
Time: 45 minutes

Susan Rhoda

203

chicken and vegetables in cream sauce

Yield: 8 servings

Can easily be doubled or tripled.

3 whole chicken breasts, split, boned, and skinned
6 chicken thighs, boned and skinned
juice of 2 to 3 fresh limes
salt and freshly ground pepper
flour seasoned with salt, pepper, and paprika for dredging
½ cup butter
½ clove garlic, minced
¾ teaspoon rosemary, crushed
2 tablespoons chopped parsley
1 large stalk of celery, chopped
6 slender carrots, sliced lengthwise
3 small white onions, sliced
12 ounces mushrooms, sliced
3 tablespoons flour
½ cup dry white wine, heated
1 cup chicken broth, heated
½ to 1 cup heavy cream

1. Dip each piece of chicken in lime juice and sprinkle with salt and pepper.
2. Dredge in seasoned flour and sauté in butter until browned, about 10 to 15 minutes. Reserve pan for later use.
3. Put half the chicken pieces in the bottom of a 3-quart covered casserole. Sprinkle with garlic, rosemary, and parsley.
4. Put in remainder of chicken and sprinkle with celery. Lay carrots and onions over all.
5. In butter used to brown the chicken sauté the mushrooms for about 5 minutes. Stir in flour and cook over low heat for 1 to 2 minutes. Remove from heat. Add the wine and chicken broth.
6. Return sauce to heat. Add enough cream to make it the consistency of a thick, cream soup. Bring just to boiling, stirring constantly. Salt to taste.
7. Pour sauce over chicken and vegetables. Cover and bake until carrots are tender. Good served with rice.

Temperature: 325°
Time: 2 hours

Hint: Can be assembled early in the day, refrigerated, and then baked in the evening.

Jeanne P. Massey

skillet tomato chicken

Yield: 8 servings

A different and delicious combination.

½ cup butter
6 whole chicken breasts,
   skinned, and boned,
   and halved
1 large onion, sliced
2 cloves garlic, minced
2 tablespoons flour
1 teaspoon salt
1 one pound 12-ounce
   can plum tomatoes,
   drained
1 cup sour cream
½ cup grated Parmesan
   cheese

1. Melt butter in large skillet.
   Sauté chicken until tender.
   Remove chicken and set aside.
2. In same skillet, cook onion and
   garlic until transparent.
3. Blend in flour and salt. Add
   tomatoes and chicken.
4. Cover and cook 35 minutes on
   low heat.
5. Add sour cream and Parmesan
   cheese. Heat gently, but do *not*
   boil.
6. Serve over hot noodles, if
   desired.

Betty B. Iwan

baked chicken teriyaki

Yield: 4 to 6 servings

Economical chicken with an Oriental flair.

½ cup soy sauce
½ cup dry sherry
2 tablespoons sugar
2 small cloves garlic,
   minced
several thin slices of fresh
   ginger root, minced or 1
   teaspoon powdered
   ginger
3 pound frying chicken,
   cut in pieces or 4 to 6
   chicken breasts

1. Blend soy sauce, sherry, sugar,
   garlic, and ginger in a shallow
   pan.
2. Add chicken pieces. Marinate all
   day in refrigerator, turning
   chicken once.
3. Remove chicken from marinade,
   reserving the liquid. Arrange
   chicken, skin side down, in a
   single layer in a 3-quart, shallow
   baking dish.
4. Bake chicken, uncovered at
   400° for 15 minutes. Turn skin
   side up, bake 10 additional
   minutes.
5. Reduce heat to 350°. Pour half
   of the marinade over the
   chicken. Bake 10 minutes. Pour
   on remaining marinade. Bake 10
   more minutes.

Must do ahead.

Temperature: 400°
Time: 25 minutes

Temperature: 350°
Time: 20 minutes

Emily M. Henderson

naples valley chicken

Yield: 4 to 6 servings

Gleaned from the vineyards of Western New York.

4 tablespoons margarine
4 to 6 boneless chicken
  breast halves
½ pound fresh
  mushrooms, sliced
½ cup chopped onion
1 cup dry white wine
1 cup chicken bouillon
1 tablespoon chopped
  parsley
dash of garlic powder
1½ teaspoons oregano
1 teaspoon salt
dash of pepper
4 tablespoons flour
½ cup water

1. Brown chicken breasts in melted margarine, remove and set aside.
2. Sauté mushrooms and onions in the same pan until tender.
3. Return chicken to pan. Add wine, bouillon, parsley, garlic powder, oregano, salt, and pepper. Cover chicken and simmer 40 minutes.
4. Remove chicken. Blend flour and water into pan juices. Stir until thickened.
5. Return chicken to pan. Heat through or refrigerate until serving time, then reheat.

Hint: Good served with spinach noodles.

Marcia W. McDowell

chicken marceil

Yield: 6 to 8 servings

Great for a brunch; use up that leftover chicken.

1 cup uncooked rice
4 cups cubed, cooked
  chicken
½ cup butter
¼ cup dry sherry
1 tablespoon cornstarch
½ teaspoon curry powder
1 pint light cream
¼ teaspoon salt
½ pound grated Swiss
  cheese
¼ teaspoon paprika

1. Cook rice according to directions on package.
2. Sauté cooked chicken in butter until lightly browned. Cool.
3. Prepare cream sauce by mixing sherry, cornstarch, and curry powder together until cornstarch is dissolved. Pour in cream and mix well. Cook over medium heat, stirring constantly, until sauce is thickened and smooth.
4. Combine chicken, rice, salt, cream sauce, and 1½ cups of the grated cheese in a casserole dish.
5. Sprinkle remaining cheese and paprika on top. Heat until bubbly.

Temperature: 350°
Time: 25 to 30 minutes

Carolyn H. Saum

206

chicken parmesan

Yield: 6 to 8 servings

Kids will love this combination.

2 eggs, lightly beaten
1 teaspoon salt
dash of pepper
4 whole chicken breasts, split, skinned, and boned
1 cup fine, dry, unseasoned bread crumbs
½ cup vegetable oil
4 cups tomato sauce
½ teaspoon basil
½ teaspoon oregano
1 tablespoon parsley
dash of garlic powder
2 tablespoons butter
½ cup grated Parmesan cheese
8 ounces Mozzarella cheese, sliced or grated

1. Combine eggs, salt, and pepper. Dip chicken breasts in egg, then into bread crumbs.
2. Heat oil in electric skillet to 360°. Brown chicken on both sides and remove to casserole dish.
3. Stir tomato sauce and herbs in a pan. Heat until boiling and then simmer for 10 minutes.
4. Stir in butter and pour sauce over chicken.
5. Sprinkle with Parmesan cheese. Cover and bake 30 minutes.
6. Uncover, put Mozzarella cheese on top, and bake 10 minutes more uncovered.

Temperature: 325°
Time: 40 minutes

Nancy B. Wolcott

picnic chicken

Yield: 4 servings

A piquant herb butter bastes this chicken as it bakes.

1 shallot or green onion, minced
1 clove garlic, minced
2 teaspoons fresh parsley, minced
½ cup butter, softened
1 teaspoon dill weed
1 teaspoon oregano
1 teaspoon salt
4 pieces chicken (breasts or legs)

1. In a bowl or food processor, combine all ingredients except chicken.
2. Slip 2 tablespoons of this herb butter mixture underneath the skin of each chicken piece.
3. Bake until brown, basting with pan juices, if desired.

Temperature: 350°
Time: 50 to 60 minutes

Ann B. Irwin

chicken-herb pie

Yield: serves 6 people

A beautiful lattice-topped pie.

generous quantity of
    pastry for 9- or 10-inch
    pie or our Flakiest Pie
    Crust (see index)
2 tablespoons butter or
    margarine
2 tablespoons flour
1 teaspoon salt
⅛ teaspoon pepper
⅛ teaspoon ground thyme
½ cup chicken broth
½ cup light cream
2 tablespoons sherry or
    white wine
2 cups cubed cooked
    chicken
1 10-ounce box frozen
    peas, thawed slightly
1 pound can sliced
    carrots, drained
1 8-ounce can small whole
    onions, drained

1. Use ⅔ of pastry to line pie plate. Reserve remaining ⅓ for lattice crust.
2. In large saucepan, melt butter over low heat. Blend in flour, salt, pepper, and thyme. Cook over low heat, stirring, until smooth and bubbly. Remove from heat.
3. Add broth, cream, and wine to mixture in saucepan. Stir well. Return to heat, stirring constantly. Bring to a boil, and boil for one minute. Remove from heat.
4. Add chicken and vegetables. Mix well.
5. Fill pastry shell with mixture. Add pastry lattice on top.
6. Bake until browned.

Temperature: 425°
Time: 35 to 40 minutes

Hint: To serve more people: use a 9 x 13-inch pan, double the pastry, and use 1½ times the chicken and vegetables.

Lucia H. Shaw

chicken ragout

Yield: 4 servings

Serve over hot buttered noodles.

¼ cup butter
2 onions, sliced
1 clove garlic, minced
2½-pound frying chicken,
    cut up
3 large tomatoes,
    chopped
1½ cups white wine
1 teaspoon tarragon
salt and pepper to taste
2 green peppers, cut in
    strips
3 tablespoons minced
    parsley

1. Melt butter in large skillet. Sauté onions and garlic. Remove with slotted spoon, and set aside.
2. Brown chicken thoroughly in same skillet.
3. Return onions and garlic to skillet. Add tomatoes, wine, tarragon, salt, and pepper. Cover, and simmer for 15 minutes.
4. Add green pepper. Cook 20 minutes.
5. Blend in parsley before serving.

Peggi M. Godwin

chicken marengo
Yield: 8 to 10 servings

A spicy way to add interest to chicken.

1 pound Italian sausage
2 tablespoons butter
2 broiler/fryer chickens,
  cut in pieces
1 16-ounce can tomato
  purée
1 6-ounce can
  mushrooms
1 10½-ounce can pitted
  ripe olives, sliced
¼ cup liquid drained from
  olives
1 tablespoon parsley
  flakes
1½ teaspoons celery
  flakes
1½ teaspoons Italian
  seasoning
1 teaspoon minced onion
½ teaspoon salt
¼ teaspoon black pepper
¼ teaspoon garlic salt
1 bay leaf

1. Cut sausage into bite-size
   pieces. Brown in a large covered
   skillet or dutch oven. Remove
   sausage, pour off grease.
2. Melt butter in the same pan.
   Sauté chicken pieces until
   brown. Remove chicken.
3. Add tomato purée to drippings
   and blend.
4. Add remaining ingredients and
   blend.
5. Return chicken and sausage to
   the pan. Spoon sauce over both.
6. Cover. Simmer for 1 to 1½ hours
   or until chicken is tender.

Linda G. Stenstrom

 indian summer sauce
Yield: about 4 cups

A wonderful orange sauce for poultry or pork roast.

2 tablespoons sugar
2 ounces red wine vinegar
3 tablespoons currant
  jelly
3 tablespoons orange
  marmalade
1 cup orange juice
grated rind of 1 lemon
grated rind of 2 oranges
salt
3 cups brown sauce
  (gravy, homemade or
  store bought)
4 ounces Cointreau

1. Slowly simmer all ingredients
   until sauce thickens. (If you are
   using brown sauce from a
   package, prepare according to
   package directions, then add to
   remaining ingredients.)
2. Cook pork tenderloin, or duck,
   or Cornish hen according to
   directions. Add orange sauce
   during last half hour.
3. Serve remaining sauce at the
   table.

Lynn P. Natapow

sherried chicken breasts

Yield: 6 servings

Experiment with your favorite cheeses for delicious variations.

4 whole chicken breasts,
  skinned and boned
¼ to ½ cup margarine
½ cup sliced mushrooms
3 scallions, chopped
¼ cup dry sherry
½ cup chicken broth
½ cup grated Mozzarella
  cheese
3 tablespoons grated
  Parmesan cheese

1. Sauté chicken breasts in a large skillet using 2 tablespoons of the margarine. Add more margarine as necessary.
2. Cook chicken 15 minutes, over low heat. Remove chicken from skillet. Place in a single layer in a greased baking dish.
3. Melt 2 additional tablespoons of the margarine in the same skillet. Sauté mushrooms and scallions until the mushrooms are lightly colored.
4. Spoon the mushrooms and scallions over the chicken, reserving pan drippings. Add sherry and broth to drippings. Blend well, scraping pan. Simmer 2 to 3 minutes.
5. Pour the sauce over the chicken. Sprinkle with Mozzarella and Parmesan.
6. (Can be refrigerated until baking time.) Bake uncovered.

Temperature: 350°
Time: 20 minutes

Nancy F. Reale

cornell barbecue sauce

Yield: enough for 10 broiler chicken halves

This recipe was originated by a professor in the Cornell Agriculture School years ago.

¾ cup oil
2 cups vinegar
1½ tablespoons salt
1 tablespoon poultry
  seasoning
½ teaspoon pepper

1. Combine all the ingredients in a heavy saucepan.
2. Bring mixture to a boil, and cook five minutes. Cool.
3. Brush sauce on chicken. Baste often as it cooks on grill.

Julie G. Ball

popover chicken tarragon

Yield: 6 servings

A pleasant deviation: try it!

3 whole chicken breasts, split, boned, and skinned
4 tablespoons cooking oil
1½ cups milk
1½ cups flour
¾ teaspoon tarragon
¾ teaspoon salt
3 eggs, beaten

1. Brown chicken in 3 tablespoons of the cooking oil.
2. Season with salt and pepper.
3. Place in a greased 9 x 13-inch pan.
4. Stir together milk, remaining 1 tablespoon cooking oil, flour, tarragon, and salt.
5. Add eggs to flour mixture. Mix well until smooth.
6. Pour over chicken and bake.

Mushroom Sauce
4 tablespoons butter
½ to ¾ cup sliced mushrooms
2 tablespoons flour
½ teaspoon salt
dash of pepper
1 cup milk

Mushroom Sauce
1. Melt 2 tablespoons of the butter in a heavy saucepan. Sauté mushrooms 2 to 3 minutes. Remove them using a slotted spoon and reserve.
2. In the same pan, melt remaining butter. Stir in flour, salt, and pepper.
3. Add milk gradually. Cook, stirring constantly, until thickened and smooth.
4. Add mushrooms and heat through.
5. Spoon over chicken when serving.

Temperature: 350°
Time: 45 to 60 minutes

Marilyn Wehrheim

chicken ratatouille

Great way to use your garden vegetables.

¼ cup corn oil
2 whole chicken breasts, skinned, boned, and cut in 1-inch pieces
2 small zucchini, unpeeled and thinly sliced
1 small eggplant, cut in 1-inch cubes
1 large onion, sliced
1 green pepper, cut in 1-inch squares
½ pound mushrooms, sliced
1 16-ounce can tomato wedges or 2 fresh tomatoes, cut in wedges
2 teaspoons garlic salt
1 teaspoon MSG, optional
1 teaspoon basil
1 teaspoon parsley
½ teaspoon pepper
hot, cooked rice

1. Heat oil in a large frying pan. Add chicken and sauté about 2 minutes on each side.
2. Add zucchini, eggplant, onion, green pepper, and mushrooms to chicken. Cook, stirring occasionally, until vegetables are tender but still crisp; about 15 minutes.
3. Carefully stir in tomatoes.
4. Add seasonings and simmer, covered, for 5 minutes, or until chicken is tender.
5. Serve ratatouille in a casserole with hot, fluffy rice.

Mary Kay Mahar

chicken wellington

An easy way to impress your guests.

Chicken Preparation
3 cups water
1½ cups dry white wine
1 medium carrot, thinly sliced
1 medium onion, thinly sliced
1 bay leaf
12 whole black peppercorns
4 whole allspice
½ teaspoon thyme
½ teaspoon salt
3 sprigs parsley
6 small chicken breasts, split, skinned, and boned

Chicken Preparation
1. Combine all ingredients, except chicken, in a large, heavy saucepan. Simmer, covered, for 15 minutes.
2. Poach chicken in liquid for 15 minutes.
3. Reserve liquid. Cool, cover, and chill chicken.

Mushroom Filling and Assembly

1 pound sliced mushrooms

2 green onions, thinly sliced

1 tablespoon butter

2 10-ounce packages frozen patty shells, thawed

Mushroom Filling and Assembly

1. Sauté mushrooms and green onions in melted butter, stirring until liquid evaporates and mixture is lightly colored. Cool, cover, and chill.
2. For each piece of chicken, roll out a thawed patty shell on a floured board to make an 8-inch circle.
3. Spoon 1 tablespoon mushroom filling in the center, and set chicken on top. Enclose in pastry. Place Wellingtons with folded side down on an ungreased baking sheet. Cover and chill.
4. Bake Wellingtons uncovered on lowest rack of the oven for 10 minutes. Move pan to highest rack, and bake 10 minutes more or until pastry is golden brown. Serve with sherry sauce.

Sherry Sauce

poaching liquid

1 tablespoon water

1 tablespoon cornstarch

3 egg yolks

3 tablespoons dry sherry

Sherry Sauce

(This may be made ahead and reheated in a double boiler.)

1. Strain poaching liquid. Boil uncovered over high heat until reduced to 2 cups.
2. Stir together water and cornstarch. Add to poaching liquid and stir until sauce thickens and boils.
3. Beat egg yolks with sherry.
4. Stir a tablespoon of hot poaching liquid into the yolk mixture and whisk. Repeat. Then add egg yolk mixture to the poaching liquid, whisking constantly.
5. Cook, stirring constantly, until thickened.

Temperature: 425°
Time: 20 to 25 minutes

Gail W. Catlin

213

world's fair chicken

Yield: 8 servings

Extremely pretty dish to serve.

4 chicken breasts, split
2 tablespoons butter
salt and pepper to taste
1¼ cups orange juice
½ cup currants
¼ cup chopped chutney
½ cup blanched, split
    almonds
½ teaspoon curry powder
½ teaspoon cinnamon
dash of thyme
rice

Garnish
bananas
mandarin orange sections

Condiments
sliced green onions
crumbled crisp bacon
coconut chips

1. Arrange chicken, skin side up, in a greased, shallow baking pan. Dot with butter and sprinkle with salt and pepper.
2. Bake at 425° for 20 minutes or until golden brown.
3. While chicken bakes, place the next seven ingredients in a saucepan. Simmer 10 to 15 minutes.
4. When chicken is brown, pour sauce over it. Reduce the oven temperature to 350°. Bake another 60 minutes or until tender.
5. Serve on bed of hot rice, garnished with banana slices and orange sections.
6. Accompany with condiments served in small bowls.

Temperature: 425°
Time: 20 minutes

Temperature: 350°
Time: 60 minutes

Sheila N. Prezzano

chicken lovers' marinade

Yield: 2½ cups

Steak lovers' marinade, pork lovers' marinade, etc.

1 cup soy sauce
2 large onions, chopped
2 cloves garlic, halved
¼ cup browning and
    seasoning sauce (like
    Kitchen Bouquet)
2 teaspoons Beau Monde
    seasoning

1. Combine soy sauce, onions, and garlic in a blender or food processor. Blend until mixture is smooth.
2. Stir in remaining ingredients.
3. Store marinade in a covered container in the refrigerator, or use marinade immediately.
4. For a delicate flavor, marinate chicken for 15 minutes on each side; baste chicken with marinade while cooking.
5. For a heartier flavor, marinate chicken for 1 hour on each side; baste while cooking.

Bonnie W. Hindman

214

chicken and spice

Yield: 8 servings

A great choice with pasta for an Italian dinner.

¼ cup olive oil
2 cloves garlic, quartered
8 medium chicken breast
  halves, boned
1½ pounds Italian
  sausage
2 cups dry white wine
1½ pounds fresh
  mushrooms, sliced
1 teaspoon salt
½ cup water
2 tablespoons cornstarch

1. In a large skillet, cook garlic in hot olive oil until golden. Discard garlic.
2. Brown chicken and sausage in same skillet over medium high heat.
3. Pour off and discard all but 2 tablespoons of the pan drippings.
4. Add wine, mushrooms, and salt. Heat to boiling.
5. Cover and reduce heat. Simmer 30 minutes or until chicken is tender.
6. Arrange chicken and sausage on a warm platter.
7. Blend water and cornstarch. Stir gradually into hot pan drippings. Cook over medium heat until thickened.
8. Spoon sauce over chicken and sausage. Serve. (Can be refrigerated and reheated at 350° for 30 minutes.)

Carol Michna

coq au vin

Yield: 6 to 8 servings

A scrumptious, foolproof way to show off your cooking skill.

½ cup butter
1 cup flour
10 to 12 chicken pieces
  (boned, if desired)
½ cup brandy
12 ounces whole, fresh
  mushrooms
5 green onions, diced
1 bay leaf, crumbled
1 clove garlic, minced
2 cups white wine
5 slices raw bacon, cut
  into ½-inch pieces
¼ cup chopped, fresh
  parsley
1 teaspoon thyme

1. Melt butter in a heavy skillet.
2. Dredge chicken in flour. Brown in butter.
3. Place browned chicken in a foil-lined baking dish. Reserve butter in skillet.
4. Pour brandy over chicken and flame.
5. Mix together remaining ingredients. Distribute evenly around chicken.
6. Pour on reserved butter. Bake.

Temperature: 350°
Time: 2 hours

"B" Armstrong

chicken with cashews

Yield: 6 servings

Good buffet dish served in large casserole or chafing dish.

4 whole chicken breasts
¾ cup oil
6 tablespoons soy sauce
3 teaspoons salt
pepper to taste
2 tablespoons sherry
2 cloves garlic, chopped
1 cup sliced water
   chestnuts
1 cup chopped bamboo
   shoots
2 green peppers, diced
2 scallions, chopped
1 teaspoon MSG
½ teaspoon sugar
4 tablespoons cornstarch
8 tablespoons water
2 cups toasted cashews

1. Cut chicken into bite-size pieces.
2. Marinate chicken in 6 tablespoons of the oil, 2 tablespoons of the soy sauce, 2 teaspoons of the salt, pepper, and sherry for half a day.
3. Discard marinade. Stir fry chicken in 4 tablespoons of the oil and set aside.
4. Stir fry garlic, water chestnuts, bamboo shoots, peppers, and scallions in remaining 2 tablespoons oil.
5. Add remaining 4 tablespoons soy sauce, MSG, sugar, remaining teaspoon salt, and cook 2 minutes. (Can prepare ahead to this point.)
6. Just before serving, mix cornstarch and water. Add to vegetables. Heat through.
7. Combine vegetable mixture with chicken and cashews. Heat and serve with rice.

Must do ahead.

Sue B. Moscato

hot chicken salad

Yield: 8 to 10 servings

Crunchy favorite from a Finger Lake winery.

4 to 5 pounds chicken
   (4 cups cubed, cooked
   chicken)
4 cups chopped celery
2 teaspoons salt
½ teaspoon tarragon,
   optional
¼ cup grated onion
1 tablespoon lemon juice

1. Cut chicken into ¾-inch cubes. Cut dark meat slightly smaller.
2. Combine chicken with next 8 ingredients. Allow to stand at least one hour; taste. Adjust salt.
3. Spoon mixture into a buttered, shallow glass, 2-quart casserole. (Refrigerate or continue.)

hot chicken salad   *continued*

2 cups mayonnaise
¼ cup extra dry vermouth
1 cup sliced, blanched, toasted almonds
1 cup crushed corn flakes
½ cup freshly grated Parmesan or Romano cheese

4. Top with cornflakes and cheese. Bake until heated through and lightly browned.

Temperature: 350°
Time: 25 to 30 minutes

Hint: To serve, mound salad onto baked slices of acorn squash.

The Taylor Wine Company, Inc.
Hammondsport, NY

chicken gumbo   Yield: 9 servings

A delicious one-dish or buffet meal!

¼ cup butter
2 onions, sliced
½ green pepper, diced
2 cloves garlic, minced
2 tablespoons flour
1 one-pound can tomatoes
2 10-ounce packages frozen okra
1 6-ounce can tomato paste
4 cups cooked, cubed chicken
3 beef bouillon cubes
3 cups water
4 teaspoons Worcestershire sauce
1½ teaspoons chili powder
⅛ teaspoon ground cloves
pinch of dried basil
¼ teaspoon pepper
1 bay leaf
1 teaspoon salt

1. Melt butter in a dutch oven. Sauté onions, green pepper, and garlic until soft.
2. Blend in flour. Cook over low heat, stirring constantly for 1 to 2 minutes.
3. Stir in remaining ingredients.
4. Cover, and simmer for 45 minutes.
5. Serve in bowls.

Hint: This is outstanding served over parslied rice in soup bowls.

Dale G. Fennie

fowl play

Yield: 4 to 6 servings

An easy, layered casserole you can assemble ahead.

1 10-ounce package frozen or fresh broccoli, cooked and drained
1 Bermuda onion, thinly sliced
2 large tomatoes, thinly sliced
3 whole chicken breasts, boned, halved, and skinned
salt and pepper
1 6-ounce can mushrooms, drained
½ pound bacon strips, cooked and drained
2½ cups sharp grated Cheddar cheese
¼ cup sherry, optional

1. Cover the bottom of a deep, 2½-quart casserole with broccoli.
2. Layer remaining ingredients over broccoli as follows: onion slices, ½ of the tomato slices, chicken breasts, salt and pepper, mushrooms, ½ of the tomato slices, bacon, cheese, and sherry.
3. Cover casserole with foil, and bake. Remove foil, reduce temperature and bake until done.

Temperature: 450°
Time: 45 minutes, then

Temperature: 375°
Time: 45 minutes

Lynn P. Natapow

chestnut stuffing

Yield: stuffing for a 20-pound turkey

A family heirloom, passed down through several generations.

4 cups chestnuts, about 2 pounds (do *not* use roasted chestnuts)
4 cups diced celery
1 pound butter
4 teaspoons salt
1 teaspoon white pepper
4 cups milk or turkey stock, the stock in which the giblets and neck have cooked
4 quarts dry, coarse bread crumbs

1. Hull chestnuts, and blanch in boiling water about one minute to loosen inner skins.
2. Remove inner skins. This is more easily accomplished if the chestnuts are kept warm in the water and worked with a few at a time.
3. Chop chestnuts finely.
4. Sauté celery in butter until translucent.
5. Add salt, pepper, and chestnuts. Cook for about 5 minutes.
6. Add milk or stock.
7. Fold mixture into bread crumbs.
8. Stuff into turkey. Roast.

Jeanne P. Massey

pastel de montezuma   Yield: 8 to 10 servings

Good way to use up all your leftover turkey.

6 cups cooked turkey or
  chicken cut into
  2½-inch pieces
1 pint sour cream
8 to 10 corn tortillas cut
  in 1½-inch pieces
1½ pounds Monterey
  Jack cheese, shredded

Green Sauce
1 one-pound can
  tomatoes, drained
1 small onion, chopped
2 cloves fresh garlic
1 4-ounce can green
  chiles
1½ teaspoons coriander
1 teaspoon salt
½ teaspoon sugar

1. Arrange half of the turkey in
   lightly greased 9 x 13-inch pan.
2. Purée all green sauce
   ingredients in blender or food
   processor.
3. Layer ingredients in the order
   given:
        ½ green sauce
        ½ sour cream
        ½ tortilla pieces
        ½ cheese
   Repeat the layers.
4. Cover with foil. Bake 40
   minutes, or refrigerate and bake
   later.
5. Uncover and bake 5 minutes
   more.

Temperature: 375°
Time: 45 minutes

Pat Reed

cornish hen dressing   Yield: Fills 4 to 6 birds

Can be refrigerated for several days before using.

3 tablespoons butter
½ cup uncooked rice
1 cup chicken broth
1 cup sliced mushrooms
¾ cup diced celery
3 tablespoons minced
  onion
3 tablespoons minced
  parsley
¼ teaspoon black pepper
1 teaspoon dill weed
salt to taste

1. In a small saucepan, melt 2
   tablespoons of the butter.
   Brown the rice in the butter.
2. In a separate pan, bring the
   broth to a boil.
3. Add the hot broth to the rice
   and cover. Steam for 15
   minutes.
4. Melt remaining tablespoon of
   butter. Add mushrooms, cover
   pan, and cook slowly for 10
   minutes.
5. In a large bowl, combine
   mushrooms, rice, and remaining
   ingredients.
6. Rub cavity of hens with salt.
   Spoon stuffing into birds. Cook
   birds immediately after stuffing.

"B" Armstrong

pheasant supreme

This method assures a moist and tender result.

8 whole pheasant breasts, halved
salt and white pepper to taste
2 cups (1 pound) butter
4 cups dry white wine
1 pound mushrooms, sliced
1½ cups chopped onion
10 leeks, chopped
3½ cups sour cream
optional garnish - choose one:
chopped parsley
chopped chives
pimiento
cayenne pepper

1. Sprinkle pheasant with salt and pepper.
2. Melt 1½ cups of the butter in a very large skillet. Add 3 cups of the wine.
3. Poach pheasant breasts in wine-butter sauce until juices run clear. Keep warm while completing sauce. (Breasts can also be refrigerated up to 1 day. When ready to serve, cover, warm in poaching liquid, and continue.)
4. Sauté mushrooms in remaining ½ cup butter. Remove mushrooms and set aside.
5. Sprinkle onion and leeks with salt and pepper. Sauté in same butter until clear.
6. Add remaining 1 cup wine and sour cream to onion and leeks. Cook until thick.
7. Blend onion mixture in blender until smooth. Return to skillet and add mushrooms.
8. Place breasts on warmed serving platter. Blend wine-butter poaching liquid into onion mixture. Heat through but *do not boil.*
9. Pour over warm pheasant breasts, garnish, and serve.

Hint: Serve with dry white wine, spinach, and stuffing balls or wild rice.

Jane Knup

We're still trying to find the probable dog lover who labeled an ingredient "canine" pepper. After searching the spice rack we realized that cayenne pepper was the intended item.

 **cornish hens wellington**

Yield: 6 generous servings

The pièce de résistance of a special meal.

6 Cornish hens (1 pound each)
seasoned salt
pepper
3 eggs, separated
1 6-ounce package long grain and wild rice
2 to 4 tablespoons grated orange peel
2 10-ounce packages frozen patty shells, thawed, or
1 17¼-ounce package frozen puff pastry, thawed, or
12 x 16-inch sheet of your favorite puff recipe
2 10-ounce jars currant jelly
1 tablespoon prepared mustard
3 tablespoons port wine
¼ cup lemon juice
1 jar spiced crabapples or watercress for garnish

1. Thaw hens. Rinse and pat dry. Sprinkle each cavity with seasoned salt and pepper.
2. Brush outside of birds with egg whites; refrigerate.
3. Cook rice as directed on package. Add orange peel.
4. Remove birds from refrigerator. Spoon rice into cavity of each bird. Return to refrigerator.
5. Divide chosen pastry into 6 portions. Roll out each portion fairly thin to cover each bird.
6. Remove birds from refrigerator. Cover each with pastry, tucking extra underneath.
7. Brush pastry with slightly beaten egg yolks. (At this time, birds can be refrigerated. Bring to room temperature before baking.)
8. Place birds on large cookie sheet. Bake.
9. Mix jelly, mustard, wine, and lemon juice in a small saucepan over low heat.
10. Serve warm sauce over birds. Garnish with spiced crabapples or watercress.

Temperature: 375°
Time: 1 to 1¼ hours

Hint: Roll dough between sheets of plastic wrap for easier handling. Dampen counter to prevent plastic wrap from slipping.

Ann P. Cowles

🍎 pheasant in sour cream

Yield: 6 to 8 servings

Delicious served over wild rice!

3 2-pound pheasants
garlic salt
salt
pepper
flour
4 tablespoons butter
1 8-ounce carton sour
   cream
2 cups water
2 to 3 tablespoons sherry

1. Skin and bone pheasant breasts and thighs.
2. Sprinkle one side of pheasant pieces with garlic salt; the other with salt and pepper.
3. Dust both sides lightly with flour.
4. Melt butter in a large skillet. Brown both sides of pheasant over medium heat. Remove, and set aside.
5. Blend sour cream with pan drippings in skillet. Stir in water and sherry.
6. Add pheasant. Simmer 30 minutes.

Hazel McCray

dill bread stuffing

Yield: for 16- to 20-pound turkey

Distinctive flavor everyone will love.

3 pounds onions, chopped
2 large bunches celery, chopped
1 pound butter
2 1-pound loaves of dill bread, cubed (do not use heals of bread)
salt and pepper to taste

1. Melt ¼ pound butter in large skillet. Sauté onions until transparent. Remove, and set aside.
2. In same pan, melt ¼ pound butter. Sauté celery. Remove, and set aside.
3. In same pan, melt ¼ pound butter. Over medium heat, brown half of the bread cubes. Remove and set aside. Repeat, using remaining bread cubes and butter.
4. Mix all ingredients together in large bowl.
5. Salt and pepper to taste.

Hint: Extra stuffing can be used to make stuffed tomatoes. Combine it with tomatoes' pulp and crumbled bacon to taste. Fill tomatoes. Bake at 300° for 15 to 20 minutes. Use these as a garnish for your turkey platter.

Wanda G. Webster

fish & seafoods

fish & seafoods

FISH

SEAFOODS

sole filled with shrimp mousse

Yield: 6 servings

Great served with rice placed in the center of the mold.

8 sole fillets (2 pounds), thawed and dried thoroughly if frozen
2 tablespoons lemon juice
salt and pepper

Mousse

1 pound small cooked shrimp
2 egg whites (reserve yolks for sauce)
1 cup heavy cream
1 tablespoon chopped parsley
1 teaspoon salt
2 tablespoons sherry

Sauce

6 tablespoons butter
¼ cup flour
1 cup light cream
2 egg yolks, beaten
¼ pound sliced mushrooms
1 tablespoon catsup

1. Brush sole on both sides with lemon juice and sprinkle with salt and pepper.
2. Lightly butter a 5 cup oven-proof ring mold. Line with fillets, dark side up, narrow ends toward the center and overhanging both rims.
3. Prepare mousse. Put shrimp, egg whites, cream, parsley, salt, and sherry into a blender or food processor. Blend at high speed until smooth.
4. Pour mousse over fillets and fold ends of fish over filling.
5. Dot exposed fish with butter, cover loosely with foil, set in pan of hot water, and bake.

Sauce

1. While fish is baking, prepare the sauce. Melt 4 tablespoons of the butter and add flour. Whisk for 1 to 2 minutes. Slowly add cream and heat until the sauce is thickened.
2. Stir a tablespoon of hot liquid into egg yolks, and then slowly add yolks to hot mixture, whisking constantly.
3. Sauté mushrooms in remaining 2 tablespoons of butter. Add to sauce along with the catsup.
4. Remove ring from oven when done, pour any liquid into the sauce and unmold onto serving platter.
5. Pour sauce over and serve.

Serve immediately

Temperature: 350 degrees
Time: 45 minutes

Violet E. Kapusta

223

filet of sole
with cheese sauce
Yield: 4 servings

A wonderfully simple dish—can be dressed up for company.

1½ pounds filet of sole
1 cup milk
¾ teaspoon salt
dash of pepper
2 tablespoons butter
2 tablespoons flour
2 tablespoons sherry
¼ cup grated cheese

1. Poach fish in milk, salt, and pepper in shallow buttered pan in oven.
2. Drain and reserve poaching liquid.
3. Melt butter in small saucepan; add flour and poaching liquid. Cook until thickened.
4. Add sherry and cheese; pour over fish.
5. Brown under broiler.

Temperature: 350°
Time: 30 minutes for poaching

Hint: Garnish with fresh parsley and almonds for company.

Hester G. Hellebush

filets of sole
fournier
Yield: 4 to 6 servings

A wine connoisseur's favorite.

2 tablespoons butter, melted
1 tablespoon chopped shallots (or onions)
1 cup chablis
2 pounds filets of sole (or filets of your choice)
6 medium mushrooms, sliced (or a 4-ounce can of mushroom pieces, drained)
½ teaspoon pepper
¾ teaspoon salt
1 teaspoon chopped fresh parsley
1 small bay leaf
pinch of thyme
1 tablespoon flour
1 cup heavy cream

1. Sauté shallots 2 minutes in butter. Add chablis while stirring.
2. Fold each filet in half and place side by side in skillet.
3. Add mushrooms and seasonings.
4. Poach fish slowly, until it flakes easily. Do not overcook.
5. Carefully remove filets to a warm platter and keep warm.
6. Remove bay leaf from stock.
7. Blend flour into cream and add to stock using wire whisk. Stir and simmer until thickened.
8. Pour over fish and serve.

Charles M. Fournier
Gold Seal Vineyards, Inc.

224

🍎 rolled filet of sole

Yield: 4 servings

Even if you're not a seafood cook, try this.

2 pounds fresh filet of
  sole
1 teaspoon salt
¼ teaspoon pepper
½ pound sharp Cheddar
  cheese, grated
1 medium onion, chopped
1 egg, beaten
2 tablespoons water
3 slices bread, crumbed
¾ cup melted butter
fresh parsley and lemon
  wedges for garnish

1. Wipe each fillet and sprinkle
   with salt and pepper.
2. Sprinkle cheese and onion on
   each fillet. Roll jelly-roll style
   and secure with toothpick.
3. Dip each rolled fillet in egg and
   water wash. Coat with bread
   crumbs.
4. Place in well-buttered dish. Pour
   melted butter over top and
   bake.
5. Place under broiler until bread
   crumbs brown (1 to 2 minutes).
6. Serve garnished with parsley
   and lemon wedges.

Temperature: 400°
Time: 25 to 30 minutes

Elinor Nicholas

flounder filets in foil

Yield: 4 servings

Clean up is a snap! Great for boaters.

1 tablespoon chopped
  shallots or green onions
1 tablespoon butter
½ pound mushrooms,
  chopped
3 tablespoons dry white
  wine
1 tablespoon lemon juice
1 tablespoon chopped
  parsley
4 flounder filets
fresh ground pepper

1. Sauté shallots in butter until
   soft.
2. Add mushrooms, and cook for 5
   minutes.
3. Stir in wine, lemon juice, and
   parsley. Continue to cook over
   moderate heat until most of the
   liquid has evaporated.
4. Place each filet on a lightly
   buttered piece of heavy-duty
   foil. Season with pepper, and
   spoon mushroom mixture over
   each filet.
5. Draw edges of foil together, and
   seal. Bake until fish flakes.
   Serve in foil packets.

Temperature: 400°
Time: 20 minutes

Celia G. Riley

crab stuffed sole

Yield: 6 to 8 servings

Cheese topping adds different and piquant accent.

2 pounds filets of sole
(8 pieces)

Stuffing
¼ cup chopped onions
¼ cup butter
6 ounces mushrooms,
chopped
13 ounces crab (canned
or frozen)
½ cup crushed saltines
2 tablespoons parsley
½ teaspoon salt

Sauce
3 tablespoons butter
2 tablespoons flour
¼ teaspoon salt
1½ cups milk
⅓ cup dry sherry
4 ounces Swiss cheese,
grated
½ teaspoon paprika

Stuffing
1. Sauté onions in butter until
   tender.
2. Stir in mushrooms and sauté
   several minutes.
3. Add crab, crushed crackers,
   parsley, and salt.
4. Spread this mixture on each
   filet, roll, and place seamside
   down in a 9 x 13-inch baking
   dish.

Sauce
1. Melt butter in small saucepan.
   Blend in flour and salt.
2. Add milk and stir until smooth.
3. Add sherry and stir 3 to 5
   minutes until sauce thickens.
4. Pour sauce over filets. (You may
   make this a day ahead or early
   in the morning. Wrap tightly and
   refrigerate until ready to bake.)
5. Bake, uncovered, until sauce
   bubbles. Sprinkle with grated
   cheese and paprika, and bake 5
   minutes more until cheese melts.
6. Garnish and serve.

Temperature: 350°
Time: 25 to 30

Donna Y. Torpey

mustard sauce

Yield: ⅔ cup

*Particularly good with cold crabmeat, shrimp, corned beef,
or lamb.*

2 tablespoons minced,
fresh dill or 1
tablespoon dry dill
weed
1 tablespoon dry mustard
3 tablespoons sugar
½ teaspoon salt
2 tablespoons vegetable
oil or olive oil
1 tablespoon vinegar
½ cup sour cream

1. Combine all ingredients. Blend
   well.
2. Cover and refrigerate. Keeps
   one week in refrigerator.

Nancy M. Giles

soy-grilled fish

Yield: 4 to 6 servings

Great for summer vacation!

¼ cup soy sauce
2 tablespoons dry sherry
2½ teaspoons sugar
½ teaspoon ginger
1 clove garlic, crushed
4 to 6 small, whole
   panfish, cleaned
2 tablespoons oil

1. Combine soy sauce, sherry, sugar, ginger, and garlic.
2. Brush on fish and let stand 30 minutes.
3. Grease grill or place fish in a hinged basket. Brush fish with remaining marinade.
4. Cook over hot coals for 5 minutes. Brush with oil. Turn and grill 10 minutes longer, basting and turning once or twice, until fish flakes easily with a fork.
5. Serve with seasoned rice and additional soy sauce.

Emily M. Henderson

stuffed lake trout

Yield: 4 to 6 servings

A fisherman's catch.

3 cups crumbled
   seasoned stuffing mix
1 teaspoon salt
¼ teaspoon pepper
¼ teaspoon dried thyme
¼ teaspoon dried
   rosemary
¼ cup butter
1 medium onion, chopped
   fine
⅓ cup milk
1 cup grated sharp cheese
1 4-pound fish prepared
   for stuffing
melted butter and white
   wine for basting
lemon wedges

1. Combine crumbs, salt, pepper, thyme, and rosemary and set aside.
2. Melt butter in skillet and sauté onions.
3. Combine thoroughly contents of skillet with crumb mixture.
4. Stir in only enough milk to moisten. Add cheese and mix well.
5. Stuff fish about ¾ of capacity. Skewer and lace with dental floss.
6. Line pan with brown paper and grease well.
7. Place fish in pan and brush with melted butter and white wine. Bake and serve with lemon wedges.

Must serve immediately.

Temperature: 350°
Time: 45 to 50 minutes

Hint: Soak fish in ice water ½ hour before cooking to remove fishy taste.

Paula S. Howk

salmon steaks

Super when grilled outdoors!

4 salmon steaks sliced
  ¾-inch thick
½ cup lemon juice
½ cup corn oil
1 tablespoon brown sugar
1 tablespoon grated onion
1 teaspoon dry mustard
1 teaspoon salt

1. Place salmon in a flat glass dish.
2. Combine remaining ingredients and pour over fish. Let salmon marinate for 2 hours or longer, even overnight.
3. Place salmon in a baking dish and bake, basting frequently with the marinade. Fish is done if it flakes easily. *OR* barbecue salmon on a well greased grill about 5 minutes on each side, basting with marinade. Grill should be very hot to avoid sticking.

Must do ahead

Temperature: 350 degrees
Time: 20 minutes

Hint: Serve with bearnaise sauce for an additional treat.

Violet E. Kapusta

salmon kulibiaka

A spectacular entrée, served hot or cold!

Pastry
12 ounces cream cheese
¾ pound butter
3 cups flour
½ teaspoon salt

Court Bouillon
1 cup dry white wine
1 quart water
1 medium onion, sliced
6 to 8 parsley sprigs
¼ teaspoon salt
4 peppercorns
1 bay leaf
4 whole allspice
4 shakes hot pepper
  sauce
2 cloves garlic, mashed
2½ pounds fresh salmon

Pastry
1. Mix chilled cream cheese and butter by hand.
2. Sift flour and salt together. Work with pastry cutter into butter until dough is formed.
3. Divide into 2 parts, one slightly larger than the other. Wrap and chill at least 3 hours (can go overnight).

Court Bouillon
1. Place all ingredients, except salmon, in a 2½ to 3-quart stainless steel pan. Simmer 20 to 30 minutes and strain.
2. Place salmon in strained liquid. Heat to simmer (don't boil) and cook 8 to 10 minutes per pound until fish flakes.
3. Cool salmon in bouillon. Remove fish from liquid; skin and de-bone.

Filling and Assembly

½ cup soft butter
1 cup cooked rice
½ cup finely chopped
  fresh dill
2½ cups finely chopped
  onions
2 teaspoons sugar
juice of 2 lemons
3 tablespoons capers
salt and pepper for each
  layer
4 carrots, cooked al dente
  and chopped
2 hard-boiled eggs, finely
  chopped
2 egg yolks combined with
  1 tablespoon water
2 tablespoons melted
  butter with ½ teaspoon
  curry

Sauce

½ pint heavy cream
1 pint sour cream
1 tablespoon capers

Filling and Assembly

1. Stir 2 tablespoons of the butter
   into rice; add dill.
2. Fry onions in remaining butter
   with the sugar. Cover and cook
   on low heat until wilted, not
   brown.
3. Mix the salmon with lemon juice
   and capers.
4. Preheat oven.
5. Roll out smaller piece of dough
   in round or oval shape
   (depending on shape of serving
   platter) to ⅛-inch thickness.
   Place on buttered, edgeless
   cookie sheet.
6. Spread rice/dill mixture to
   within ½ inch of edge. Season
   with salt and pepper.
7. Cover with salmon. Season with
   more salt and pepper.
8. Cover salmon with onions,
   carrots, and chopped eggs,
   seasoning each layer.
9. Roll out larger piece of dough to
   cover. Pinch edges of top and
   bottom pastry together.
10. Beat egg yolks with water.
    Brush top of pastry with egg
    wash. Slash top crust in
    pattern.
11. Bake until golden brown.
12. Remove from oven. Mix melted
    butter with curry and pour
    into slashes.
13. Transfer to serving platter.
    Serve with the following sauce.

Sauce

1. Whip cream until stiff and fold
   into sour cream.
2. Add capers, combining
   thoroughly.
3. Refrigerate until serving time.

Temperature: 400°
Time: 25 to 35 minutes

**Hint: All parts may be prepared one day ahead. Assemble when
ready to bake or a couple of hours ahead.**

Patricia S. Driscoll

salmon pie with cucumber sauce

Yield: 9-inch pie

Good luncheon dish.

Sauce
1 medium cucumber, unpared
1 tablespoon grated onion
¼ cup mayonnaise
2 teaspoons cider vinegar
1 tablespoon chopped parsley
1 cup sour cream
Salt and pepper to taste
1 9-inch unbaked pie shell

Filling
2 beaten eggs
½ cup milk
1 tablespoon butter, melted
¼ cup chopped onion
2 tablespoons chopped parsley
½ teaspoon grated lemon peel
¾ teaspoon basil
¼ teaspoon salt
1 16-ounce can salmon

Make sauce ahead

Sauce
1. Seed cucumber. Grate and drain well.
2. Combine with remaining sauce ingredients.
3. Chill well.

Filling
1. Combine eggs, milk, and melted butter.
2. Add all remaining ingredients except salmon.
3. Break salmon into chunks, removing skin and bones. Add to first mixture.
4. Pour into unbaked pie shell.
5. Bake. Serve with cold sauce over pie.

Temperature: 400°
Time: 25 minutes

Susan S. Taylor

salmon croquettes

Yield: 5 large patties

Just like Grandma's.

1 15½-ounce can red salmon
1 medium onion, diced
1 egg, slightly beaten
3 slices white bread, crumbled
2 tablespoons flour
salt and pepper to taste
¼ cup cooking oil
tartar sauce

1. Drain salmon; break into smaller bits with a fork. Remove bones and skin.
2. Add onion, egg, bread, flour, salt, and pepper.
3. Form into patties.
4. Heat oil and cook patties a few minutes at medium heat. Reduce to low heat and continue to cook until brown on both sides (5 to 7 minutes on each side).
5. Serve with tartar sauce.

Hazel McCray

230

baked fish with tomatoes

Yield: 8 servings

Especially good when tomatoes are in season.

4 tablespoons butter or margarine
2 tablespoons chopped onion
4 tablespoons chopped parsley
pinch of thyme
1 bay leaf
salt and pepper
6 large tomatoes, thickly sliced
2 pounds fresh or frozen fish fillets
1 clove garlic, finely chopped
½ cup fine bread crumbs
4 tablespoons grated Parmesan, Swiss, or Cheddar cheese

1. Melt 2 tablespoons of the butter in large frypan.
2. Add onion, parsley, thyme, bay leaf, salt, and pepper; sauté until golden.
3. Add tomato slices and cook uncovered until juice from tomatoes is almost evaporated. Shake pan occasionally to avoid sticking.
4. Spoon tomatoes into large baking dish.
5. Arrange fish on top and season with salt and pepper. When using frozen fish it should be thawed.
6. Mix garlic with bread crumbs and cheese; sprinkle over fish and dot with remaining butter.
7. Bake uncovered until fish flakes evenly and top is golden brown.

Temperature: 375°
Time: 30 minutes

Ann E. Evans

poor man's lobster

Yield: 4 servings

An economical substitute for lobster in any seafood dish.

1½ pounds monkfish filets
1 cup butter or margarine, melted
salt
pepper
paprika
lemon slices
parsley sprigs

1. Arrange fish in shallow pan. Pour half of the melted butter over the filets.
2. Sprinkle with salt, pepper, and paprika to taste. Bake until fish flakes with fork.
3. Garnish with parsley. Serve with lemon slices and remaining butter for dipping.

Temperature: 375°
Time: 15 to 25 minutes

Hint: Choose lighter colored filets. They are milder and more tender.

Bobbie Gerner

231

lobster thermidor

Yield: 8 servings

This elegant dish can also be economical by substituting monk fish.

2 or more lobster tails
  (should be at least 12
  ounces of lobster meat)
4 tablespoons butter
½ pound mushrooms,
  sliced
4 tablespoons flour
1 teaspoon dry mustard
1 teaspoon salt
dash of cayenne pepper
⅛ teaspoon nutmeg
1 cup milk
1 cup cream
2 egg yolks, slightly
  beaten
1 tablespoon lemon juice
3 tablespoons sherry
½ cup bread crumbs
2 tablespoons freshly
  grated Parmesan cheese
2 tablespoons melted
  butter

1. Poach lobster and remove from shell. To poach, place lobster in pan and cover with water. Bring it to a boil and cook for 5 minutes. Simmer 15 minutes, then plunge meat into ice water to arrest further cooking. If substituting monk fish, simmer for 10 minutes or until opaque.
2. Dice meat and set aside.
3. Melt butter and sauté mushrooms until brown.
4. Blend in flour, mustard, salt, cayenne, and nutmeg.
5. Stir in milk and cream gradually. Cook and stir over medium heat until mixture thickens and comes to a boil.
6. Stir small amount of cooked mixture into egg yolks. Add to sauce and remove from heat.
7. Stir in lemon juice, sherry, and lobster. (Can be refrigerated after this step.)
8. When ready to bake, spoon mixture into seafood shells, individual casseroles, or large casserole.
9. Combine bread crumbs, Parmesan cheese, melted butter. Sprinkle over seafood.
10. Bake. Should you choose to bake this in a casserole, serve it in individual puff pastry shells.

Temperature: 400°
Time: 15 minutes

Patsy M. Gilges

apple crabmeat ramekins

Yield: 4 to 6 servings

Apple adds nice texture.

6 tablespoons butter
¼ cup chopped onions
6 tablespoons flour
½ teaspoon salt
dash freshly ground
  pepper
½ teaspoon paprika
2 cups milk
½ cup light cream
½ cup sliced fresh
  mushrooms
2 6-ounce packages
  frozen crabmeat,
  thawed and flaked
2 medium apples, pared,
  cored, and sliced
½ cup dry white wine
2 tablespoons chopped
  parsley
¾ cup buttered bread
  crumbs

1. Sauté onions and mushrooms in melted butter 3-5 minutes. Do not brown. Remove with slotted spoon and reserve.
2. Blend flour, salt, pepper, and paprika into same batter.
3. Add milk and cream; stir over low heat until thickened.
4. Combine onions, mushrooms, and crabmeat with sauce.
5. Poach apple slices in wine until tender but still firm. Drain.
6. Add apple slices and parsley to sauce. Mix well. (Can refrigerate and reheat slowly at serving time.)
7. Spoon hot mixture into ramekins. Scatter buttered bread crumbs on top.
8. Broil 4 inches from heat source until crumbs are browned.

Temperature: Broil
Time: 4 minutes

Gail H. Lewis

quick crab casserole

Yield: 4 to 5 servings

Super easy and super good.

6 slices bread, cubed
1 pound crab meat
½ pound sharp Cheddar
  cheese, grated
¼ cup margarine, melted
3 eggs, beaten
½ teaspoon dry mustard
2 cups milk
dash of salt

Must do ahead.

1. Line bottom of greased 11 x 7-inch casserole dish with bread.
2. Layer crab on top of bread. Crumble cheese, and place on top of crab. Pour melted margarine over top.
3. Beat eggs, mustard, milk, and salt together. Pour over casserole. Refrigerate overnight.
4. Bake covered.

Temperature: 350°
Time: 1 hour

Susan L. Carpenter

seafood paella

Yield: 4 servings

A best seller at The Village Grill.

2½ pounds king crab
2 dozen steamer clams in shells
¾ pound butter, melted
¼ cup sherry
2 teaspoons paprika
juice of ½ lemon
20 medium, fresh scallops
16 pieces (under 15 size) shrimp, cleaned and shelled

1. Steam clams and crab until clams open, about 6 to 12 minutes.
2. Combine butter, sherry, paprika and lemon in a large frying pan.
3. Sauté scallops and shrimp in sauce until cooked. Add clams and crab.
4. Serve over wild rice with extra butter sauce as a dip for the seafood.
5. Garnish with parsley and lemon.

Hint: To steam seafood, place on rack in kettle with 1 cup hot water. Cover tightly and steam.

The Village Grill
Penfield, New York

neptune's spears

Yield: 4 servings

An elegant and different blend of great flavors.

12 jumbo shell-on shrimp
1 pound fresh monk fish
12 fresh sea scallops
8 large mushroom caps
¾ to 1 cup white wine
1 teaspoon dry mustard
1 tablespoon prepared mustard
1 teaspoon salt
¼ teaspoon pepper
¼ cup *fresh* lime juice
¼ cup brown sugar
paprika

1. Remove shells from shrimp and devein.
2. Cut monk fish into 8 large pieces.
3. Place scallops, monk fish, and shrimp in shallow dish and marinate in wine for 30 to 60 minutes.
4. Prepare sauce in a small bowl: combine both mustards, salt, pepper, lime juice, and brown sugar.
5. Alternate seafood and mushrooms on skewers, spinning mushrooms gently so as not to split them. Can refrigerate covered until ready to cook.
6. Baste with sauce and broil, turning and re-basting often.
7. Sprinkle with paprika and serve over a bed of rice.

Temperature: Broil
Time: 10 to 15 minutes

Donald R. Wilson

seafood bisque casserole

Yield: 4 servings

The first time this was served to us, my husband said, "Get that recipe!"

½ pound shrimp
½ pound crabmeat
½ pound fresh scallops
1 tablespoon chopped shallots
7 tablespoons butter
10 tablespoons sherry
½ teaspoon salt
¼ teaspoon pepper
3 tablespoons flour
1½ cups milk
bread crumbs
Parmesan cheese

1. Sauté seafood and shallots in 4 tablespoons of the butter. Cook 5 minutes.
2. Sprinkle with 6 tablespoons of the sherry, salt, and pepper.
3. In another pan melt the remaining 3 tablespoons butter. Add flour to make a paste. Add milk and the remaining 4 tablespoons of sherry; stir until smooth.
4. Combine sauce and seafood mixture and place in a casserole or individual ramekins.
5. Sprinkle with bread crumbs and Parmesan; bake.

Temperature: 400°
Time: 30 minutes

Peggi M. Godwin

scallops and mushrooms elegant

Yield: 4 servings

Great for a special luncheon.

½ pound fresh mushrooms
3 tablespoons butter
2 tablespoons flour
1 cup heavy cream or half and half
1 tablespoon dry vermouth
salt and pepper to taste
1 pound fresh or frozen sea scallops, quartered (or bay scallops, whole)
bread crumbs
butter

1. Slice mushrooms and cook in butter until limp—about 5 minutes. Blend in flour.
2. Add cream slowly, stirring until a thin sauce is made.
3. Add vermouth, seasonings, and scallops.
4. Place in small, lightly buttered casserole. Top with bread crumbs and dot with butter.
5. Cover and bake.

Temperature: 375°
Time: 10 to 15 minutes

Lucia H. Shaw

gruyère and scallops
Yield: 6 to 8 servings

A beautiful seafood entree.

2 pounds scallops, washed and drained
1 teaspoon plus 1 tablespoon fresh lemon juice
1 cup water
4 tablespoons butter
5 ounces fresh mushrooms, sliced
¼ cup minced fresh onion
⅓ cup flour
1 cup light cream
½ cup whole milk
1 cup grated Gruyère cheese
½ cup dry white wine
1 tablespoon chopped fresh parsley

1. Combine scallops with the 1 teaspoon lemon juice and water. Bring to boil.
2. Cover and simmer 2 to 3 minutes until tender. Drain on paper towels and set aside.
3. Saute mushrooms and onions in melted butter. Blend in flour.
4. Gradually add light cream and milk and stir until thick.
5. Lower heat. Add cheese, stirring until melted.
6. Add the 1 tablespoon lemon juice, wine, and parsley.
7. Carefully fold scallops into sauce mixture. Blend well.
8. Turn into 1½-quart casserole and brown lightly under broiler.

Hint: Serve with fresh asparagus, broiled tomatoes, French bread, and white wine.

Cindy Bartlett

christmas eve oysters
Yield: 4 servings

A tradition in our house in place of oyster stew.

1 pint shucked oysters
1 pound bacon
1 medium onion, finely chopped
1 green pepper, finely chopped
1 red pepper, finely chopped
2 tablespoons Worcestershire sauce

1. Layer oysters, with their liquid, in the bottom of a shallow baking dish.
2. Fry bacon until crisp. Remove bacon and crumble.
3. Sauté onion in bacon fat until golden.
4. Top oysters with bacon, onion, and peppers. Sprinkle Worcestershire sauce on top.
5. Bake, basting a few times with oyster liquid, just until oysters start to curl.

Serve immediately

Temperature: 375°
Time: about 30 minutes

Hint: Oysters simple to open: wash in cold water, place in plastic bag, then place in freezer for an hour prior to shucking.

Patricia S. Driscoll

shrimp scampi

Yield: 6 servings

Serve on rice as entrée or with toothpicks as appetizer.

2 pounds large shrimp
½ lemon
2 celery stalks
½ cup butter
3 cloves garlic, finely
   chopped
dash of onion powder
dash of oregano
1 tablespoon basil
1 teaspoon dry mustard
3 tablespoons olive oil
3 tablespoons lemon juice
1 teaspoon parsley
½ teaspoon salt
dash freshly ground
   pepper

Must do ahead

1. Cook shrimp in boiling water with lemon and celery as directed on package, *do not overcook.* Drain.
2. Melt butter in a small saucepan and add remaining ingredients.
3. Place shrimp in a 10 x 13-inch glass baking dish. Pour butter mixture over and mix well.
4. Cover tightly with plastic wrap and place in refrigerator overnight. Can freeze.
5. Bring shrimp to room temperature. Heat oven and bake covered with foil.

Temperature: 300° to 325°
Time: 25 minutes

Cathie S. Meisenzahl

shrimp and artichoke supreme

Yield: 4 servings

Excellent served with curried rice.

1 15-ounce can artichoke
   hearts, quartered
1 pound cooked shrimp
3 tablespoons butter
3 tablespoons flour
1 pint light cream
1 tablespoon lemon juice
2 tablespoons catsup
1 tablespoon sherry
1 teaspoon
   Worcestershire sauce
½ teaspoon paprika
½ pound soft yellow
   American cheese or
   pimento cheese,
   shredded

1. Grease a 1½-quart casserole; layer artichoke hearts and shrimp. Set aside.
2. In a saucepan melt butter; add flour and stir. Add cream and stir over medium heat until mixture boils.
3. Remove from heat and add remaining ingredients. Stir until cheese is melted. You may have to return to low heat to melt cheese.
4. Pour sauce over shrimp and artichoke hearts.
5. Bake or freeze at this point. If frozen, bring to room temperature before baking.

Temperature: 325°
Time: 35 to 45 minutes

Elizabeth G. Garrett

shrimp in white wine and cream

Yield: 4 servings

A rich dish. Garnish prettily with thin lemon twists.

1 shallot, minced
3 tablespoons butter
1½ pounds raw shrimp, shelled and deveined
pinch of thyme
1 bay leaf
salt and pepper to taste
2 tablespoons brandy
¾ cup dry white wine
1 cup heavy cream
2 egg yolks
1 teaspoon lemon juice
1 teaspoon chopped parsley
1 teaspoon chervil
1 teaspoon tarragon

1. In a heavy saucepan sauté shallot in butter until golden.
2. Add shrimp, thyme, bay leaf, salt, and pepper. Simmer 7 to 8 minutes, turning shrimp occasionally.
3. Warm brandy. Light it and pour it flaming over the shrimp. Shake pan back and forth until flame dies.
4. Add white wine and simmer 5 minutes.
5. Remove shrimp with a slotted spoon to a heated serving dish and keep warm. Reduce pan juices to ⅓ their original quantity.
6. Combine cream, egg yolks, lemon juice, parsley, chervil, and tarragon. Add to saucepan; stir well. *Do not let boil.*
7. When sauce is hot and slightly thickened, pour it over shrimp, and garnish with parsley sprigs.

Serve immediately

Patsy M. Gilges

charleston seafood gumbo

Yield: 3 quarts

For a casual stew type dinner or elegantly over rice.

1 stick butter or margarine
1 cup chopped onion
½ cup chopped green pepper
½ cup chopped celery
1 pound sliced frozen okra
2 tablespoons flour
1 quart chicken stock, fresh or canned
1 6-ounce can tomato paste

1. Sauté onion, green pepper, and celery in butter until soft, not brown. Stir while cooking.
2. Add okra. Cook 2 to 3 minutes.
3. Stir in flour. Slowly add chicken stock.
4. Add tomato paste, tomatoes, and all seasonings.
5. Bring to a boil, reduce heat and simmer 30 minutes. Refrigerate or freeze at this point.
6. Reheat slowly.

charleston seafood gumbo *continued*

2 cups Italian style
    canned or fresh
    tomatoes, chopped
1 bouquet garni made of:
    3 bay leaves and 1
    bunch parsley tied with
    a string
½ teaspoon thyme
2 teaspoons salt
pinch cayenne
½ teaspoon Tabasco
1 pound raw shrimp
1 pound raw scallops
1 pint raw oysters
1 tablespoon
    Worcestershire

7. Just before serving, add shrimp and scallops. Cook 5 minutes. Add oysters, cook 3 minutes.
8. Add Worchestershire and correct seasonings to taste.

Hint: Substitute monk fish, cod, and broken salad shrimp for a less expensive version.

"Sam" E. Lawless

shrimp mediterranean   Yield: 4 to 6 servings

Attractive served in shells.

¼ cup butter
¼ cup olive oil
½ cup fresh sliced
    mushrooms
8 shallots, minced
4 cloves garlic, minced
1 cup undrained canned
    tomatoes, coarsely
    chopped
¼ cup lemon juice
1 teaspoon salt
pepper to taste
¼ cup chopped parsley
2 to 4 tablespoons tomato
    paste
1½ pounds cooked shrimp
    (lobster may be used)

1. In butter and oil, sauté mushrooms, shallots, and garlic.
2. Add tomatoes and their liquid, lemon juice, salt, pepper, and parsley. If mixture appears thin, add enough tomato paste to thicken. Simmer uncovered 15 minutes.
3. Add cooked shrimp or lobster just before serving.
4. Spoon over bed of rice or noodles or serve with Italian bread.

Lynn P. Natapow

coquilles st. jacques

Yield: 4 servings

Magnifique either as an appetizer or main course.

½ cup sherry
1½ cups water
1 pound bay scallops or
   larger scallops cut up,
   washed
½ teaspoon salt
⅛ teaspoon pepper
1 medium onion, chopped
1 tablespoon parsley
2½ tablespoons butter
juice of ½ lemon
½ pound mushrooms,
   sliced
2 tablespoons flour
½ cup heavy cream,
   heated
paprika

1. Bring sherry and ½ cup of the water to a boil, in a medium saucepan. Add scallops, salt, and pepper. Poach for 5 to 7 minutes.
2. Remove scallops to casserole or individual dishes. Reserve poaching liquid.
3. Sauté onions and parsley in ½ tablespoon of the butter for 5 to 8 minutes.
4. Boil remaining cup of water; add lemon juice and mushrooms. Simmer for 5 minutes. Drain.
5. Melt remaining 2 tablespoons butter, add the flour, stirring constantly, and cook for 1 to 2 minutes. With a whisk, blend in reserved poaching liquid; cook until sauce thickens.
6. Add onions, parsley, mushrooms, and hot cream. Check seasonings.
7. Pour sauce over scallops, and sprinkle with paprika. Cover and refrigerate, or bake immediately.

Temperature: 350°
Time: 25 to 30 minutes

Jane N. Clifford

cioppino

Yield: 6 to 8 servings

Serve this in bowls so you don't miss any of the delicious sauce.

1 large onion, thinly sliced
1 green pepper, sliced
5 green onions, with 3
   inches of top, sliced
   diagonally
2 large cloves garlic
⅓ cup olive oil
⅓ cup chopped fresh
   parsley

1. Sauté onion, pepper, green onions, and garlic, in olive oil, for 5 minutes in a large frying pan.
2. Add parsley, tomato purée, tomato sauce, wine, water, and seasonings. Cover tightly and simmer 1 hour.

1 one-pound can tomato
purée
1 8-ounce can tomato
sauce
8 ounces white or red
wine
8 ounces water
½ bay leaf
3 teaspoons salt
¼ teaspoon pepper
⅛ teaspoon rosemary
⅛ teaspoon thyme
1½ pounds crab (legs and
claws) in shell
1 dozen clams, in shell
1 pound large shrimp, in
shell

3. Remove garlic and discard. (At
this point, sauce can be frozen
and reheated.)
4. Arrange crab, which has been
cut into 3-inch pieces, on
bottom of Dutch oven. Do not
remove shells.
5. Scrub clams to remove sand
and place on top of crab pieces.
6. Cut shrimp down the back using
scissors and remove vein. Wash,
but do not remove shells.
Arrange on top of other
seafood.
7. Pour well-heated sauce on top
of seafood. Cover and simmer
20 to 30 minutes, or until clam
shells open.

Nancy F. Reale

shrimp florentine

Yield: 2 casseroles, 6 servings each

Makes two casseroles—serve one, freeze the other.

4 10-ounce packages
frozen, chopped
spinach, thawed and
drained
3 pounds shrimp, cooked,
shelled, and deveined
½ cup butter or
margarine
½ cup flour
3 cups milk
1 cup dry white wine
½ cup chopped scallions
salt and pepper to taste
paprika
2 cups (8 ounces) grated
Cheddar cheese

1. Spread spinach in bottom of two
9 x 13-inch casseroles. Arrange
shrimp on top of spinach.
2. Melt butter in a saucepan, and
stir in flour. Gradually add milk,
stirring constantly.
3. Blend in wine and scallions.
Cook over low heat, still stirring
constantly, until sauce bubbles
and thickens.
4. Add salt and pepper and enough
paprika to make sauce a rosy
color. Pour over shrimp.
Sprinkle with cheese.
5. If serving immediately, bake
uncovered until bubbly. (Can be
frozen before baking.) When
ready to use, place frozen
casserole in oven.

Temperature: 350°
**Time: 35 minutes (if frozen, 1 hour
or more)**

Patsy M. Gilges

paella

Paella Valenciana is originally Spanish. There are as many variations as there are Spanish speaking countries.

3 pounds chicken pieces (legs and thighs)

1 pound hot or mild Italian sausage or chorizo (Mexican sausage), sliced

⅓ cup olive oil

⅓ cup water

2 dozen well scrubbed little neck clams, in their shells

1½ pounds large shrimp, peeled and deveined

1 large onion, minced

2 large garlic cloves, minced

3 medium tomatoes, quartered

3 cups uncooked long grain rice (not instant rice)

3 cups chicken broth

1 tablespoon salt

¼ teaspoon cayenne pepper

½ teaspoon pepper

¼ teaspoon saffron

1 16-ounce package frozen green peas, thawed but uncooked

1. Fry chicken and sausage in oil for 15 minutes, until evenly browned.
2. Remove sausage and set aside.
3. Add water and cook chicken, covered, for 20 minutes more.
4. Remove chicken and set aside.
5. Add clams and shrimp, and cook 5 minutes.
6. Remove clams and shrimp, and set aside.
7. Add onion, garlic, and tomatoes. Simmer 5 minutes.
8. Add rice, broth, and seasonings. Cook, stirring occasionally, until rice is done, about 35 minutes.
9. In a large baking dish or paella pan, layer ½ of the rice mixture, all of the chicken and sausage, and the remaining rice, peas, clams, and shrimp which have been combined.
10. Bake, until heated through, and serve.
11. This can be assembled one day ahead and refrigerated, then brought to room temperature and baked until heated through, about 30 minutes.

Temperature: 350°
Time: 20 to 30 minutes

Jane F. Bailey

desserts

desserts

crêpes frangipane

Yield: Filling for 10 crêpes

Very different . . . light and sweet.

1 cup sugar
¼ cup flour
1 cup milk
2 eggs
2 egg yolks
3 tablespoons butter,
   melted
2 teaspoons vanilla
½ teaspoon almond
   extract
½ cup ground blanched
   almonds, lightly toasted
10 crêpes
confectioners sugar

1. Combine sugar and flour in a saucepan. Add milk, cooking and stirring until thick. Continue cooking 1 to 2 minutes longer, stirring constantly.
2. In a small bowl, beat eggs and egg yolks slightly. Stir small amount of the milk mixture into eggs, and then return all of the egg mixture to the saucepan.
3. Bring just to the boiling point, stirring constantly, and remove from heat. Stir in butter, vanilla, almond extract, and almonds.
4. Cool to room temperature.

To Serve

1. Spread about 2 tablespoons of almond cream filling on unbrowned side of each crêpe.
2. Roll up, and place fold side down in a buttered 9 x 13-inch baking dish. Brush crêpes with melted butter, and bake.
3. Sift confectioners sugar on top of the crêpes and serve warm.

Temperature: 350°
Time: 20 to 25 minutes

Caroll A. Meyers

peaches in port

Yield: 6 to 8 servings

Use fresh or frozen for an elegant, light finale.

6 fresh peaches, peeled
   and sliced
4 tablespoons sugar
1 tablespoon lemon juice
½ cup port wine
½ cup heavy cream
pinch salt
1 tablespoon
   confectioners sugar

1. Sprinkle peach slices with sugar. Mix thoroughly.
2. Add lemon juice and wine. Chill 1 to 3 hours.
3. Whip cream with salt and confectioners sugar. Spoon peaches and juice into individual dishes.
4. Serve with a dollop of whipped cream.

Linda G. Stenstrom

apple beignets

Yield: 8 servings

Popular European dessert or snack.

1¼ cups flour
¼ teaspoon salt
1 package dry yeast
½ cup apple juice
½ cup flat beer
1 tablespoon olive oil
1 egg white, stiffly beaten
4 cups salad oil
5 medium apples, peeled,
   cored, and sliced into
   ½-inch slices (or ¾
   pound of dried apples,
   plumped in ½ cup apple
   juice)
confectioners sugar

1. Stir flour, salt, and yeast together.
2. Mix in the apple juice, beer, and olive oil.
3. Cover the bowl and let stand 4 hours at room temperature.
4. Fold in the egg white to complete batter.
5. Heat salad oil in deep fat fryer or electric frying pan.
6. Place apples in large bowl. Pour batter over apple slices, coating both sides.
7. Drop slices into hot oil; cook until lightly browned, turning frequently.
8. Remove from oil and drain well.
9. Transfer to paper towels to further drain. Cool slightly.
10. Sprinkle with confectioners sugar. Serve warm.

Temperature: 400°
Time: 10 minutes

Sue N. Woehr

chocolate crêpes

Yield: 12 6-inch crêpes

Incredibly satisfying!

Batter
6 tablespoons flour
6 tablespoons cocoa
¼ teaspoon salt
2 eggs
2 egg yolks
1 tablespoon sugar
¼ cup vegetable oil
⅓ cup milk

Batter
1. Mix all ingredients in a blender or food processor.
2. Refrigerate batter 1 to 2 hours.
3. Make crêpes: pour 2 tablespoons batter into heated skillet. Rotate pan so batter covers bottom. Cook 45 to 60 seconds. Invert pan, let crêpe drop out. Fill unbrowned side.

Filling
1 quart vanilla or
   peppermint ice cream
chocolate sauce

Filling
1. Fill with slices of ice cream.
2. Top with your favorite chocolate sauce. (Serve our Yummy Chocolate Mocha Sauce, see index.)

Peggi M. Godwin

rote gruetzl

Yield: 6 servings

A light holiday dessert.

1 10-ounce package
    frozen raspberries,
    slightly thawed
½ cup red currant jelly
1½ cups plus 2
    tablespoons cold water
3½ tablespoons minute
    tapioca
½ pint heavy cream,
    either whipped or
    unwhipped

1. Combine all ingredients, except
   cream, in a saucepan.
2. Bring to a boil over medium high
   heat, stirring constantly.
3. Pour into a bowl and let mixture
   sit 20 minutes.
4. Stir thoroughly. Refrigerate 8
   hours or overnight.
5. Serve with cream.

Nancy M. Frank

easy fruit cobbler

Yield: 6 to 8 servings

One of my childhood favorites.

¼ cup butter or
    margarine
½ cup sugar
1 cup flour
¼ teaspoon salt
2 teaspoons baking
    powder
½ cup milk
2 cups fresh or canned
    blueberries, cherries,
    blackberries, or
    peaches
¼ to ½ cup sugar
¼ teaspoon cinnamon
1½ cups water or a
    compatible fruit juice or
    juice from a can of fruit
(can add 2 tablespoons
    bourbon which is
    especially good with
    blueberries)

1. Cream the butter and sugar
   until fluffy.
2. Mix flour, salt, and baking
   powder. Add to creamed
   mixture alternately with milk,
   beating until smooth.
3. Pour the mixture into a lightly
   greased, shallow 2-quart
   casserole, spreading evenly.
4. Wash fruit (if fresh). Drain
   thoroughly, reserving juice, if
   canned.
5. Spoon fruit over the batter.
6. Mix sugar and cinnamon, and
   sprinkle evenly over the fruit.
   Note: Sugar may be omitted, if
   using canned fruit in heavy
   syrup.
7. Pour fruit juice or water over
   the top.
8. Bake. During baking, fruit and
   juice go to the bottom, and
   cake-like layer forms on top.
9. Serve warm with ice cream or
   fresh cream.

Temperature: 375°
Time: 45 to 50 minutes

Frances G. Tully

strawberries in red wine

Yield: 4 servings

An easy, delicious summertime dessert.

1 cup dry red wine
½ cup sugar
¼ teaspoon vanilla
1 to 2 cups fresh
    strawberries, hulled just
    before preparation

1. Mix wine and sugar in small saucepan. Heat to boiling, stirring constantly to dissolve sugar. Reduce heat. Simmer, covered, 5 minutes.
2. Remove from heat. Stir in vanilla. Cover, and cool to room temperature.
3. Refrigerate for up to 5 days.
4. Pour wine syrup over prepared berries. Cover, and chill 1 to 2 hours.
5. Serve in champagne glasses.

Must do ahead.

*The Barry Wine Company
Conesus, New York*

berries with orange liqueur

Yield: 10 to 12 servings

Smoothly charms the madding crowd.

5 egg yolks
½ cup sugar
½ cup orange-flavored
    liqueur
1 cup heavy cream
2 tablespoons sugar
fresh strawberries,
    raspberries, blueberries,
    blackberries, or mixture
    of the above

1. Cream egg yolks and sugar thoroughly.
2. Place egg mixture in double boiler. Cook over medium heat for 10 minutes. Beat constantly. Yolks should be very thick and pale yellow.
3. Remove from heat. Stir in half of the liqueur.
4. Cool and then refrigerate until thoroughly chilled.
5. Beat cream and 2 tablespoons sugar until almost stiff.
6. Fold cream into cold sauce and add remaining liqueur.
7. Spoon berries into champagne glasses or other dessert dishes. Spoon sauce over berries.
8. Garnish with mint leaves.

Patsy M. Gilges

apple cheese torte

Yield: 9-inch torte

Looks beautiful, tastes wonderful!

Crust
1 cup butter
⅔ cup sugar
½ teaspoon vanilla
2 cups flour

Crust
1. Cream butter and sugar.
2. Add vanilla and flour. Blend well.
3. Press mixture into the bottom and three-fourths of the way up the sides of an 8- or 9-inch springform pan.

Filling
1 8-ounce package cream cheese
¼ cup sugar
1 teaspoon vanilla
1 egg
5 to 6 apples, peeled and thinly sliced
⅓ cup sugar
1 teaspoon cinnamon
lemon juice
¼ cup sliced almonds

Filling
1. Beat cream cheese, ¼ cup sugar, vanilla, and egg. Pour over crust.
2. Combine sliced apples with sugar, cinnamon, and a little lemon juice. Mix well.
3. Pour apple mixture over top of cheese mixture and sprinkle with sliced almonds.
4. Using a spoon, push crust down on sides even with apples. Bake.
5. Serve warm or refrigerated.

Temperature: 450°
Time: 10 minutes, then

Temperature: 400°
Time: 25 minutes

Ronnie D. Doty

elegant grapes

Yield: 8 servings

Always elicits a gasp of pure delight!

3 cups white or red *seedless* grapes
1 lemon (juice and grated rind)
½ cup honey
½ cup brandy, warmed
French vanilla ice cream

1. Wash the grapes, and remove stems.
2. Blend lemon juice, rind, and honey in a chafing dish. Heat 5 minutes.
3. Add grapes. Heat 1 minute, or until grapes are coated with syrup, but firm.
4. Ignite the brandy and pour over grapes.
5. Serve immediately over ice cream in long-stemmed goblets.

Jean H. Whitney

apple oatmeal crinkle

Yield: 6 to 8 servings

Wholesome and delectable.

2 tablespoons flour
½ cup sugar
6 cups sliced apples

1. Combine flour and sugar.
2. Arrange apples and flour-sugar mixture forming 3 layers, in a well-greased 9-inch baking dish.

Topping
½ cup brown sugar
½ cup quick-cooking oatmeal
½ cup flour
dash of salt
¾ teaspoon cinnamon
¾ teaspoon nutmeg
¼ cup butter

Topping
1. Combine brown sugar, oatmeal, flour, salt, and spices.
2. Cut in the butter.
3. Spread this mixture over apples.
4. Bake, and serve warm with ice cream or whipped cream.

Temperature: 300°
Time: 45 minutes

Mrs. Douglas Bruno

bananas flagrante

Yield: 4 servings

Spectacular!

¼ cup butter
½ cup brown sugar
3 bananas, sliced in ¼-inch pieces
¼ teaspoon cinnamon
½ teaspoon lemon juice
1½ ounces banana liqueur
1½ ounces light rum
vanilla ice cream

1. In a chafing dish, over flame, melt butter. Add brown sugar, and stir until melted.
2. Add bananas, and sauté until tender, stirring gently.
3. Add cinnamon, lemon juice, and banana liqueur. Stir.
4. Add rum. Ignite just before serving. Stir lightly while flaming.
5. When flame dies, spoon immediately over ice cream, served in individual dessert dishes.

Hint: For a dramatic effect, lower the lights and prepare this at the table.

Norma Pealer
The Lionstone Restaurant
Geneva, New York

apple pinwheel

Yield: 6 to 8 servings

Serve by a roaring fire for the perfect fall dessert.

Pie
1 tablespoon melted
  shortening
⅓ cup milk
1 cup flour
1 teaspoon baking powder
¼ teaspoon salt
⅓ cup sugar
3 to 4 tart apples, pared,
  cored, and sliced.

Pie
1. Mix shortening and milk.
2. Sift dry ingredients together.
3. Add milk to dry ingredients. Mix
   well.
4. Spread dough in greased 9-inch
   pie pan.
5. Arrange apples in pinwheel
   design on dough.

Topping
3 tablespoons sugar
1 teaspoon cinnamon

Topping
1. Mix sugar and cinnamon
   together. Sprinkle over apples.
2. Bake.

Foamy Sauce
6 tablespoons butter or
  margarine
1 cup confectioners
  sugar
1 egg, beaten
1 teaspoon vanilla

Foamy Sauce
1. Melt butter in double boiler.
2. Stir in sugar. Add egg and
   vanilla.
3. Mix well with wire whisk until
   foamy and heated through.
4. Spoon hot sauce over pieces of
   pie. If desired, top with whipped
   cream or vanilla ice cream.

Temperature: 375°
Time: 30 minutes

Nancy W. Witmer

strawberries extraordinaire!

Yield: 20 berries

Beyond ecstasy!

20 large fresh
  strawberries
4 ounces semi-sweet
  chocolate
1 tablespoon vegetable oil

1. Wash and dry berries. Set aside.
2. Melt the chocolate in top of
   double boiler over warm, *not*
   boiling, water. Stir in oil.
3. Dip strawberries in chocolate,
   then place on waxed paper to
   cool—*do not refrigerate.*

**Hint: These may be prepared early in the day but will not keep
overnight. Do not refrigerate as they will turn white.**

Nancy S. Milbury

glazed oranges

Yield: 4 servings

Tempts the palate as dessert or side dish.

1 cup orange juice
1 teaspoon grated orange
 rind
¼ cup sugar
1 tablespoon cornstarch
4 tablespoons brandy
4 large navel oranges,
 peeled and sliced

1. Combine the first 5 ingredients. Bring them to a boil.
2. Cook until the liquid is clear and thick.
3. Pour the liquid over orange sections and chill.

Betty B. Edgerton

praline ice cream cake

Yield: 8 to 12 servings

Well worth the effort . . . fantastic!

Meringue Layer
6 egg whites
pinch of salt
¾ cup sugar
1¼ cups ground,
 blanched, almonds
2 tablespoons arrowroot
parchment paper

Meringue Layer
1. Beat egg whites and salt until they hold soft peaks. Beat in sugar, 2 tablespoons at a time.
2. Continue to beat until meringue holds very stiff peaks.
3. Fold in ground almonds and arrowroot.
4. Place parchment paper on a baking sheet. Trace the inside bottom circle of a springform pan. Make 2 circles.
5. Divide meringue evenly, filling circles.
6. Bake meringues at 275° for 25 minutes. Turn oven off, and leave meringues 8 hours, or overnight. Meringue should be crisp. If not, turn oven on to 275° for 15 minutes, or until crisp. (At this point, meringues may be tightly wrapped and stored in the freezer.)

Praline Powder
1 cup filberts (hazel nuts)
1 cup sugar
¼ cup water
⅛ teaspoon cream of
 tartar

Praline Powder
1. Place nuts on baking sheet and roast at 400° for 8 to 10 minutes. Place nuts in a towel, and rub to remove at least ¾ of the skins.

2. In a heavy saucepan bring sugar, water, and cream of tartar to a boil.
3. Continue to cook until temperature reaches 310° on a candy thermometer. Remove from heat.
4. Add filberts and spread immediately on a buttered baking sheet.
5. Let cool and pulverize in a food processor or blender. (Can be stored in an airtight container for weeks in the freezer.)

Hot Chocolate Sauce

1 12-ounce package chocolate morsels
¼ cup strong coffee, cooled
2 tablespoons cherry liqueur

Hot Chocolate Sauce

1. Melt chocolate. Stir in coffee and liqueur.
2. May be stored in refrigerator or freezer. Warm to serve.

Ice Cream

1 half-gallon vanilla ice cream, softened (homemade or very good grade commercial)
¾ cup praline powder

Ice Cream

1. Divide ice cream in half.
2. Stir praline powder into ½ of the ice cream only.

Whipped Cream

1 cup heavy cream, whipped
1 tablespoon superfine sugar

Whipped Cream

1. Add sugar to heavy cream, and beat until stiff.

To Assemble

1. Place one meringue layer in the bottom of a spring form pan.
2. Spread praline ice cream on top.
3. Place second meringue layer on ice cream. Spread with remaining ice cream.
4. Wrap tightly and freeze 1 to 2 days. (Must be frozen overnight, but no more than 2 days in advance.)
5. At serving time, release sides of springform pan and pipe whipped cream on cake. Drizzle with warmed chocolate sauce. Can serve extra sauce on each cut piece.

Cathie S. Meisenzahl

251

pamaloni's tortoni

Yield: 4 to 8 servings

Irresistible.

1 egg white
1 tablespoon powdered instant coffee
⅛ teaspoon salt
¼ cup plus 2 tablespoons sugar
1 cup heavy cream
1 teaspoon vanilla
⅛ teaspoon almond extract
¼ cup finely chopped, toasted almonds
1 bittersweet chocolate bar
2- or 4-ounce aluminum cupcake cups

1. Combine egg white, coffee, and salt, beating until stiff but not dry.
2. Gradually add 2 tablespoons of the sugar to egg white mixture, beating until glossy.
3. In another bowl, beat heavy cream, remaining sugar, vanilla, and almond extract until stiff. Add almonds.
4. Fold egg white mixture into cream mixture.
5. Fill aluminum cups, and freeze.
6. Garnish with shaved chocolate. Good with lemon cookies.

Pamm E. Ferguson

lake niagara wine sherbet

Yield: 10 to 12 servings

Cleanses your palate after a filling meal.

2 bottles (750 milliliters each) Lake Niagara wine
2 envelopes unflavored gelatin
2½ cups sugar
6 tablespoons fresh lemon juice
4 egg whites

1. Bring wine, gelatin, 2 cups of the sugar, and lemon juice to a boil.
2. Pour this mixture into 2 9-inch square cake pans or ice cube trays and freeze until partially frozen.
3. Meanwhile, beat egg whites with remaining sugar to form soft peaks.
4. Remove gelatin mixture from freezer, and pour into mixing bowl.
5. Beat until smooth, then beat in egg whites.
6. Return to cake pans or ice trays. Cover and freeze.
7. Remove from freezer. Beat sherbet again.
8. Return to pans, cover, and keep frozen until serving time.

Widmer Wine Company
Naples, New York

peppermint ice cream torte

Yield: 8 to 10 servings

Crunchy and refreshing!

Crust

1½ cups quick-cooking
  oats
⅓ cup brown sugar
⅓ cup butter, melted
2 pints peppermint ice
  cream, softened

Topping

⅓ cup margarine,
  softened
1 cup confectioners
  sugar
2 egg yolks
1 ounce baking chocolate,
  melted
2 egg whites, beaten

Crust

1. Combine the oats, brown sugar, and butter. Spread on a cookie sheet, and bake.
2. Press ¾ of this mixture into an 8-inch square pan and chill.
3. Spread 1 pint of the ice cream over the crust and freeze.

Topping

1. Cream margarine and sugar.
2. Blend in egg yolks and chocolate.
3. Fold in egg whites.
4. Spread topping over ice cream and freeze.
5. Spread the other pint of ice cream over topping, sprinkle with reserved crust mixture, and freeze.

Temperature: 350°
Time: 10 minutes

Elizabeth T. Williams

mocha ice cream cake

Yield: 9-inch cake

A festival for the senses!

1 3-ounce package lady
  fingers
½ gallon coffee ice cream,
  softened
1 quart chocolate ice
  cream, softened
2 tablespoons instant
  coffee granules
½ cup coffee-flavored
  liqueur
6 chocolate covered
  toffee bars, crushed
chocolate sauce
1 cup heavy cream,
  whipped

1. Line lady fingers around sides of a 9-inch springform pan.
2. Mix softened ice creams together.
3. Add coffee, liqueur, and crushed toffee bars.
4. Pour into a springform pan. Spread a thin layer of chocolate sauce on top. Freeze.
5. Before serving, spread cake with whipped cream.
6. Do *not* let this cake defrost before serving. Serve immediately upon removing from freezer.

Ronnie D. Doty

la grande mousse

Different, delightful, and delicious.

6 egg yolks
¾ cup sugar
2¾ cups heavy cream,
  whipped
⅓ cup orange-flavored
  liqueur
8 cleaned and fluted
  orange shells
powdered cocoa
mint leaves

1. Combine the egg yolks and sugar, beating until stiff.
2. Fold in 2 cups of the whipped cream and the liqueur.
3. Fill the orange shells with the cream soufflé mixture. (May use parfait glasses or our Chocolate Ice Cream Cups, see index.)
4. Place, covered, in freezer for at least 2 hours.
5. At serving time, top with the remaining whipped cream, sprinkle with cocoa and garnish with mint leaves.
6. Serve directly from freezer.

Hint: Use orange sections for our Glazed Oranges, see index.

Peggi M. Godwin

kona café dessert

Coconut snowballs from the Big Island.

2 pints coffee ice cream
2 to 3 ounces toasted
  coconut
coffee liqueur

1. Shape coffee ice cream into serving-size balls with ice cream scoop.
2. Roll in toasted coconut. (To toast grated coconut, spread it thinly on a baking sheet in a 325° oven for about 10 minutes. Stir frequently.) Return to freezer on a cookie sheet until serving time.
3. To serve: In dessert bowls, pour coffee liqueur generously over each ice cream ball. For special occasions, place a lighted candle in each.

Hint: Try chocolate ice cream rolled in crushed peppermint candy, then coconut.

Mary Kay Taber

lemon sherbet

Yield: 4 cups

Cool and tangy, an upbeat rendition.

1¼ cups granulated sugar
⅓ cup fresh-squeezed
  lemon juice
grated rind of 1 lemon
¼ teaspoon lemon extract
2 cups milk

1. Combine the sugar, lemon juice, rind, and extract.
2. Add the milk, and stir until sugar dissolves completely.
3. Pour into a freezing tray, and freeze until firm, at least 3 hours.
4. Remove frozen mixture to a chilled mixing bowl. Beat with electric mixer until creamy.
5. Refreeze until sherbet is firm, about 2 hours.

Pamela W. Cheek

raspberry walnut ice cream

Yield: 1 quart

Get out your napkins, this is a winner!

1 10-ounce package
  frozen raspberries,
  partially thawed
2 strips lemon rind
1 tablespoon lemon juice
⅔ cup sweetened
  condensed milk
1 cup walnuts, finely
  chopped
1 cup heavy cream,
  whipped

1. Place the raspberries, lemon rind, and lemon juice in a blender. Blend on high speed for 20 seconds, or until smooth.
2. Remove cover, and while still blending, add the milk in a steady stream.
3. Fold the walnuts into the whipped cream. Fold the cream mixture into the raspberries.
4. Place in a refrigerator tray, cover with waxed paper, and freeze 2 to 3 hours or longer.

Suzanne B. Seipel

*S*ue wanted to make her family's favorite ice cream recipe, but was missing some of the necessary ingredients She improvised, using lemon, nuts, and berries, thus originating "Homemade Raspberry Walnut Ice Cream." It has become so popular at her house, that no one ever asks for the old favorite anymore.

mom's layered raspberry dessert

Yield: 10 to 12 servings

Adds a festive touch for Christmas or Valentine entertaining.

Layer I
1 cup butter, melted
1½ cups flour
2 tablespoons sugar

Layer I
1. Mix ingredients together.
2. Spread in a greased 9 x 13-inch pan.
3. Bake. Cool completely.

Layer II
6 ounces cream cheese, softened
½ cup butter, melted
2 cups confectioners sugar

Layer II
1. Mix cream cheese and butter. Add the sugar and mix well.
2. Spread over the first layer.

Layer III
1 cup chopped pecans or walnuts

Layer III
1. Sprinkle nuts over the second layer.

Layer IV
1 3-ounce package raspberry gelatin
1 cup boiling water
2 10-ounce packages frozen raspberries in heavy syrup, thawed (strawberry gelatin and frozen strawberries may be used instead of the raspberries)
whipped cream

Layer IV
1. Mix gelatin and water. Add the raspberries. Refrigerate until gelatin has started to thicken. Spoon over layer III.
2. Chill. Cut into squares. Serve topped with whipped cream.

Temperature: 350°
Time: 30 minutes

Suzanne H. Barbee

chocolate torte royal

Yield: 8 to 10 servings

A sumptuous offering.

Meringue
2 egg whites
¼ teaspoon salt
½ teaspoon vinegar
½ cup sugar
¼ teaspoon cinnamon

Meringue
1. Cover a cookie sheet with heavy brown paper or foil.
2. Draw an 8-inch circle in the center of the paper.
3. Beat egg whites, salt, and vinegar until soft peaks form.
4. Blend sugar and cinnamon in a small bowl. Add mixture gradually to egg whites, beating until stiff peaks form and sugar has dissolved.
5. Spread meringue ½-inch thick on the paper, using circle as a guide. Mound edges to 1¾ inches high. Form trim on outside edge by indenting with the bowl of a spoon.
6. Bake at 275° for 1 hour. Turn off heat. Dry in oven for 2 hours, with oven door closed.
7. Peel off brown paper.

Filling
1 6-ounce package semi-sweet chocolate morsels
2 egg yolks, beaten
¼ cup water
1 cup heavy cream
¼ cup sugar
¼ teaspoon cinnamon
½ cup heavy cream
½ cup pecans, coarsely chopped

Filling
1. Melt chocolate over hot, *not boiling*, water. Cool slightly.
2. Spread 2 tablespoons of the chocolate over the bottom of the meringue.
3. Blend egg yolks and water into remaining chocolate. Chill until thick.
4. Combine cream, sugar, and cinnamon. Whip until stiff.
5. Spread half of the whipped cream over chocolate in the meringue.
6. Fold the remaining cream into chilled chocolate mixture. Spread in meringue.
7. Chill overnight. Garnish with whipped cream and pecans.

Janet A. Heisel

257

chocolate ice cream cups

Yield: 8 servings

Amazingly easy for such a stunning confection.

1 6-ounce package
  semi-sweet chocolate
  morsels
2 tablespoons butter
1 package, 2½-inch paper
  baking cups

1. Melt the chocolate and butter in
   a double boiler.
2. Spoon the chocolate into the
   baking cups, spreading thinly on
   the sides and bottom.
3. Place the cups in muffin tins to
   keep their shape. Chill.
4. Fill the cups with your favorite
   ice cream or mousse, and top
   with chocolate shavings.

Betty B. Edgerton

chocolate mousse

Yield: 8 servings

Delightfully smooth, rich . . . and easy.

¼ cup sugar
4 tablespoons rum
4 ounces semi-sweet
  chocolate
3 tablespoons heavy
  cream
2 egg whites, beaten stiff
1 cup heavy cream,
  whipped
whipped cream and
  shaved chocolate for
  garnish

1. Cook sugar and rum over low
   heat until sugar dissolves. Set
   aside.
2. Melt chocolate in a heavy
   saucepan. Stir in heavy cream.
3. Add the rum syrup to the
   chocolate, blending well. Cool.
4. Fold in egg whites and chocolate
   mixture into the whipped
   cream.
5. Pour the mousse into a serving
   dish or individual dessert cups.
   Chill.
6. Serve garnished with additional
   whipped cream and shaved
   chocolate.

Lucia H. Shaw

rum flan

Wonderful for a luncheon or after a heavy meal.

1½ cups sugar
2 cups heavy cream
1½ cups half and half
½ cup rum
1 vanilla bean
pinch of salt
4 eggs
6 egg yolks

1. Heat 1 cup of the sugar in a small, heavy pan over moderately high heat. Stir with a wooden spoon until melted and caramel-colored.
2. Pour caramelized sugar into eight ½-cup ramekins or custard cups, coating the bottoms and sides. Work quickly. (You may use a 1½-quart oven-proof mold rather than individual cups.) Set aside.
3. Heat cream, half and half, remaining ½ cup sugar, rum, vanilla bean, and salt in a heavy 2- or 3-quart saucepan. Let mixture simmer briskly about 15 minutes until reduced by about ½ cup. Set aside to cool.
4. Beat the eggs and yolks. Add them to the cooled milk mixture and stir well. Pour through a strainer into a pitcher, then into the caramel-coated custard cups.
5. Set the cups in a pan of warm water deep enough to reach about 1 inch up the sides of the cups. Bake in a preheated oven until done. (A knife inserted gently in the center should come out clean.)
6. Cool. Refrigerate for several hours. To serve: run a sharp knife around the sides of the cups. Invert on serving dish.

Temperature: 350°
Time: 50 to 60 minutes

Terry S. Butwid

mocha fudge pudding

Yield: 8 servings

This cake makes its own hot fudge icing!

1 cup flour
¾ cup sugar
5 tablespoons cocoa
2 teaspoons baking
  powder
¼ teaspoon salt
½ to ¾ cup chopped
  walnuts
½ cup milk
2 tablespoons melted
  butter
1 teaspoon vanilla
½ cup firmly packed
  brown sugar
1 cup strong coffee
vanilla ice cream

1. Lightly grease 8 custard cups.
2. Sift flour, sugar, 2 tablespoons of the cocoa, baking powder, and salt in a bowl. Add walnuts. Set aside.
3. In a small bowl, combine milk, butter, and vanilla.
4. In another small bowl, mix brown sugar, and remaining cocoa.
5. Combine flour mixture with milk mixture.
6. Spoon this batter into custard cups, until cups are half full.
7. Sprinkle brown sugar mixture evenly over batter.
8. Top each cup with 2 tablespoons of coffee.
9. Bake. Place on rack until ready to serve.
10. To serve, loosen and turn upside down on individual plates. Serve warm, with a scoop of ice cream.

Temperature: 350°
Time: 30 minutes

Nancy F. Reale

date nut pudding

Yield: 9 servings

Especially good served warm with vanilla ice cream.

1½ cups brown sugar
2 cups water
1 teaspoon butter
½ cup milk
1 cup flour
½ teaspoon cinnamon
2 teaspoons baking
  powder
8-ounce package dates,
  chopped
½ cup chopped walnuts

1. Boil 1 cup of the brown sugar, water, and butter for 2 minutes in an 8- or 9-inch square pan, forming a syrup.
2. Combine the remaining sugar and all other ingredients, in a separate bowl.
3. Drop the batter by spoonfuls into syrup.
4. Bake.

Temperature: 350°
Time: 40 minutes

Nancy W. Witmer

flan español

Yield: 8 servings

In Spain, sharing a flan is a traditional sign of friendship.

½ cup sugar
1 14-ounce can
   sweetened condensed
   milk
1 14-ounce can water
1 tablespoon
   coffee-flavored liqueur
pinch of salt
6 eggs

1. Melt sugar in an ungreased fireproof dish (8- or 9-inch round pie plate or 1¾-quart casserole). In order to permit the caramel to spread evenly, carefully turn dish until entire surface is covered. Set aside. Caramel will be hard.
2. In medium-sized bowl, combine milk, water, coffee liqueur, and salt. Mix thoroughly with fork or whisk. Do not use electric beater.
3. Add eggs, one at a time, mixing lightly after each. Too much beating could ruin this recipe.
4. To remove any lumps, strain mixture into prepared caramel.
5. Place baking dish into pan of hot water. Water should reach about 1 inch up the sides of the dish. Bake until set. Flan is ready when knife, inserted into center, comes out clean.
6. Set aside to cool, then refrigerate several hours.
7. To serve, invert baking dish onto a platter. Caramel will drizzle over entire flan.

Temperature: 325°
Time: 1 hour

Marie D. Campbell

pineapple saucery

Yield: 6 to 8 servings

Hawaii's inimitable topping.

1 fresh pineapple, cut into
   bite-size pieces
4 tablespoons light rum
1 cup brown sugar
1 teaspoon cinnamon
¾ cup sliced Macadamia
   nuts

1. In a saucepan or chafing dish, combine all ingredients. Heat until warm and brown sugar is dissolved.
2. Serve over vanilla ice cream.

Susan W. Smith

chocolate fudge sauce

Yield: 2 cups

A truly outstanding ice cream topping.

2 1-ounce squares
  unsweetened chocolate
1 cup sugar
½ cup butter
dash of salt
1 teaspoon vanilla
1 13-ounce can
  evaporated milk

1. Melt chocolate, sugar, and butter in a double boiler.
2. Add remaining ingredients. Mix well.
3. Place *top* of double boiler directly on heat. Bring to a boil, stirring constantly. Boil until mixture thickens, approximately 5 minutes.
4. Serve warm over ice cream.
5. This will keep for 2 to 3 weeks in your refrigerator. Reheat before serving.

Susan S. Seator

chocolate steamed pudding

Yield: 6 to 8 servings

A Christmas dinner tradition.

3 tablespoons butter or
  margarine
2½ squares semi-sweet
  chocolate
⅔ cup sugar
1 egg
2¼ cups flour
4½ teaspoons baking
  powder
1 teaspoon salt
1 cup milk
hard sauce

1. Melt butter and chocolate in large saucepan.
2. Add sugar and egg to chocolate. Beat lightly with a spoon.
3. Stir together flour, baking powder, and salt.
4. Add flour mixture alternately with milk to chocolate mixture. Mix well.
5. Pour pudding into a greased 2-quart mold. Steam 1½ to 2 hours by placing mold on a trivet in a large covered pot containing 1 to 2 inches gently boiling water.
6. Remove from mold, and serve with a hard sauce. (If made ahead, place pudding in foil, and reheat in 250° oven or in a double boiler.) May be ignited by pouring hot brandy over it and lighting it.

Hint: Serve with our Fluffy Hard Sauce (see index).

Dancy R. Duffus

chocolate soufflé

Yield: serves 4 to 6

This recipe is 75 years old, and still irresistible!

Soufflé
2 tablespoons butter
2 tablespoons flour
¾ cup milk
1½ squares unsweetened
  chocolate (1-ounce
  each)
⅓ cup sugar
2 tablespoons hot water
3 eggs, separated
½ teaspoon vanilla

Soufflé
1. In the top of a double boiler,
   melt butter. Add flour.
   Gradually add milk, and cook
   until boiling point is reached.
2. Melt chocolate in a separate
   pan. Add sugar and water to
   chocolate.
3. Combine butter and chocolate
   mixtures.
4. Beat egg yolks well. Add to
   combined mixtures. Cool.
5. Beat egg whites until stiff. Fold
   whites into chocolate mixture
   and then add vanilla.
6. Place soufflé in a 1½-quart
   ungreased baking dish. Set dish
   in a pan of hot water, and bake.
7. Serve soufflé immediately with
   golden sauce.

Golden Sauce
2 eggs
1 cup confectioners
  sugar
1 teaspoon vanilla or 2 to
  3 tablespoons rum or
  sherry

Golden Sauce
1. Beat eggs until very light.
2. Add sugar gradually.
3. Stir in flavoring.

Temperature: 350°
Time: 40 to 45 minutes

Jane R. Hanford

homemade vanilla

Yield: ¾ cup

Island formula assures success.

1 vanilla bean, chopped
  (do not grind as grinding
  will cloud the finished
  product)
6 ounces dark rum or
  bourbon

1. Cut vanilla bean into small
   pieces.
2. Add vanilla to the liquor. Store
   in an airtight jar, in the dark, for
   six months. Date the jar.

Susan B. Finnegan

fluffy hard sauce

Yield: 1 cup

A light approach to a traditionally rich sauce.

1 cup confectioners
   sugar
5 tablespoons butter
1 egg
⅛ teaspoon salt
3½ teaspoons light rum

1. Cream the sugar and butter.
   Add egg, and beat until *very*
   smooth.
2. Beat in salt and rum. (More rum
   might be needed for proper
   consistency.)

Hint: This is marvelous with steamed puddings, apple crisp, and
mince pie.

Sarah B. Foster

steamed cranberry pudding

Yield: 10 to 12 servings

A perfect ending to a traditional meal.

2 teaspoons baking soda
½ cup hot water
1 can whole berry
   cranberry sauce
½ cup molasses (dark or
   light)
1½ cups flour

1. Combine baking soda and water
   in a bowl. Add remaining
   ingredients and mix well.
2. Pour cranberry mixture into
   well-greased pudding steamer (2
   empty coffee cans may be used
   as molds.)
3. Cover steamer or cans tightly.
   Place cans on a trivet in a large
   pot containing 1 to 2 inches
   gently boiling water. Steam for 2
   hours.

Rum Sauce
2 eggs
2 tablespoons butter,
   melted
1 cup sugar
1 cup heavy cream,
   whipped
¼ cup rum

Rum Sauce
1. Beat eggs well, adding butter.
2. Add sugar gradually and
   continue beating.
3. Fold in whipped cream and rum.
4. Serve warm pudding in
   individual dessert dishes or
   champagne glasses topped with
   a generous amount of rum
   sauce.

Lee F. Wood

yummy chocolate mocha sauce

Yield: 4 cups

Rich and delicious, the ice-cream parlor variety.

1 12-ounce package
  semi-sweet chocolate
  morsels
½ cup butter
1 cup white corn syrup
4 teaspoons instant
  coffee, granules
dash of salt
2 cups confectioners
  sugar, sifted
1 cup hot water
2 teaspoons vanilla

1. Melt the chocolate and butter together, over hot water, in the top of a double boiler.
2. Add the corn syrup, coffee, and salt.
3. Add the sugar and hot water alternately, stirring after each addition. Add vanilla last.
4. Serve at once or store in a jar in the refrigerator and warm later to serve.

Time: 20 minutes

Nancy R. Murphy

This delectable sauce was discovered quite by mistake. Nancy didn't have enough time to melt the chocolate completely, so she served it anyway. Her guests loved its chunky texture so much that they asked her for the recipe and "Yummy Chocolate Mocha Sauce" was born.

hot fudge sauce

Yield: 1 cup

This sauce turns hard on ice cream!

2 ounces unsweetened
  chocolate
1 tablespoon butter
⅓ cup boiling water
1 cup sugar
2 tablespoons corn syrup
1 teaspoon vanilla *or* 2
  teaspoons rum

1. Melt the chocolate in the top of a double boiler.
2. Add the butter and blend well.
3. Add boiling water and stir.
4. Add sugar and corn syrup. Bring mixture to a boil. Without stirring, boil sauce for 8 minutes.
5. Add vanilla or rum just before serving.

Hint: This can be reheated in a double boiler.

Lucia H. Shaw

steamed berry pudding

Yield: 8 to 10 servings

Berry season treat in my family for generations.

Batter
2 tablespoons butter, melted
1 cup sugar
2 eggs
2 cups flour
2 teaspoons baking powder
½ teaspoon salt
½ cup milk

Filling
1½ to 2 cups fresh berries (blueberries, raspberries, blackberries, or cherries)
sugar to taste
2 tablespoons butter

Batter
1. Mix all batter ingredients together thoroughly in blender. Blend at high speed for 2 minutes.
2. Put ⅓ of the batter in the bottom of a well-buttered pudding steamer.
3. Put ½ of the berries on top of this layer, sprinkle with sugar, and dot with 1 tablespoon of the butter.
4. Put in another ⅓ of the batter, and top with remaining berries. Sprinkle with sugar, and dot with remaining tablespoon of butter. Cover with remaining batter.
5. Secure top of steamer. Place on a trivet in a large, covered pot containing about 1 to 2 inches gently boiling water. Steam for 1½ to 2 hours.
6. Remove steamer from pot, and take off lid. Place very briefly in a 300° oven just to dry out the pudding.
7. Remove from oven, and allow to rest for 10 minutes. Invert on a serving plate, and carefully remove steamer.
8. Serve warm with our Fluffy Hard Sauce (see index).

Jeanne P. Massey

266

pies & pastries

pies & pastries

🍎 bourbon apple pecan pie

Yield: 1 9- or 10-inch pie

Unique and out of this world!

Pastry

3 cups flour
4 tablespoons
   confectioners sugar
1 teaspoon salt
⅔ cup solid shortening
2 egg yolks
8 tablespoons water

Filling

½ to ¾ cup raisins
2 tablespoons bourbon
¼ cup butter, softened
¾ cup pecan halves
⅔ cup brown sugar
6 to 8 cups apples, pared
   and sliced
2 tablespoons lemon juice
1 tablespoon flour
½ cup sugar
½ teaspoon cinnamon
½ teaspoon nutmeg
¼ teaspoon salt
1 teaspoon grated lemon
   peel, optional
whipped cream for
   garnish

Pastry

1. Sift flour, sugar, and salt together.
2. Cut in shortening.
3. Blend yolks and water together. Add gradually to dry ingredients. Set aside.

Filling

1. Plump raisins in bourbon for several hours; drain and set aside.
2. Spread butter evenly over bottom and sides of 9- or 10-inch glass pie plate.
3. Press pecans, round side down, into butter.
4. Pat brown sugar over pecans.
5. Roll out ½ of the pastry for the bottom crust. Line pie plate with pastry, trimming edges to ½ inch.
6. Combine raisins with remaining ingredients. Fill pie crust.
7. Roll out remaining pastry; top pie, crimping edges together.
8. Prick top with a fork and bake.
9. Cool pie until filling stops bubbling. Place serving plate over pie. Invert *carefully*. Remove pie plate.
10. Garnish and serve.

Temperature: 450°
Time: 10 minutes then

Temperature: 350°
Time: 40 minutes

Hint: For perfect pie crust, use ice water and chilled shortening. Handle dough as little as possible.

Kathy Arena

french apple pie

Yield: 1 9-inch pie

A new twist on an all-American favorite.

Crust
2 cups flour
1 teaspoon salt
⅔ cup shortening
2 egg yolks
3 tablespoons cold water
1 tablespoon lemon juice

Crust
1. Sift flour and salt together.
2. Cut shortening into dry ingredients.
3. Blend egg yolks, water, and lemon juice together. Sprinkle over dry ingredients. Stir lightly until dough holds together.
4. Divide dough in half; roll out one half. Line pie plate. Set aside while preparing filling.

Filling
4 cups cooking apples, pared, cored, and sliced
½ cup brown sugar
½ cup white sugar
2 tablespoons flour
½ teaspoon cinnamon
½ teaspoon nutmeg
¼ teaspoon salt
2 tablespoons butter

Filling
1. Toss apples with sugars, flour, spices, and salt.
2. Fill crust with the apples and dot with butter.
3. Roll out remaining pastry and top pie. Bake.
4. Cool slightly. Meanwhile, prepare frosting.

Frosting
½ cup confectioners sugar
1 tablespoon milk
¼ teaspoon vanilla

Frosting
1. Combine all ingredients, stirring until smooth.
2. Frost cooled pie.

Temperature: 425°
Time: 10 minutes then

Temperature: 375°
Time: 55 minutes

Elsie Forman
Schutt's Cider Mill

genesee valley apple crumb pie

Yield: 1 9- or 10-inch pie

Delicate crust - scrumptious flavor.

Crust
⅔ cup shortening
1 teaspoon salt
¼ cup boiling water
1½ cups flour

Crust
1. Cream shortening with salt.
2. Add boiling water and mix.
3. Add flour.
4. Press crust into 9- or 10-inch pie plate.

268

genesee valley apple crumb pie *continued*

Filling
6 apples, pared, cored,
   and sliced
½ cup sugar
1 teaspoon cinnamon
pinch of salt

Crumb Topping
⅓ cup butter
½ cup sugar
¾ cup flour

Filling
1. Fill the crust with apples.
2. Sprinkle sugar, cinnamon, and
   salt on apples.

Crumb Topping
1. Cream butter with sugar and
   flour.
2. Spoon mixture on top of pie.
3. Place pie in preheated oven.
   Reduce temperature after 10
   minutes.

Temperature: 450°
Time: 10 minutes

Temperature: 350°
Time: 30 minutes

Hint: Short (2-inch) straws inserted in pie will keep juice from
running over.

Nancy W. Witmer

flakiest pie crust   Yield: 2 10-inch pie crusts

A superb crust—sure to receive raves.

2 cups sifted flour
1 teaspoon salt
⅔ cup solid shortening
2 tablespoons cider
   vinegar
2 tablespoons light cream
   or milk

1. Blend flour, salt, and shortening
   with pastry blender.
2. Add liquids and stir.
3. Chill pastry 15 minutes. Roll out
   on a well-floured board or
   pastry cloth.
4. (If using as a baked pie shell,
   you must fit dough into pie
   plate then prick dough
   thoroughly with a fork over its
   entire surface. Bake at 475° for
   8 to 10 minutes. Can be frozen if
   desired.)

Hint: Using a pastry cloth and stockinet covered rolling pin, you
will use less flour, fewer strokes, and have more tender, flaky
pie crust.

Victoria P. Gilbert

peach of a pie

Like eating a fresh peach.

1 9-inch pie crust, baked
and cooled (Try our
Flakiest Pie Crust, see
index)

Filling
9 peaches, peeled and
sliced
4 tablespoons corn starch
1 cup water
¾ to 1 cup sugar
¼ teaspoon almond
extract
pinch of salt
whipped cream for
garnish

Filling
1. Blend 3 of the peaches with
remaining ingredients in a
blender until smooth.
2. Cook over medium heat, stirring
constantly, until clear and thick.
3. Place remaining peaches in
baked pie crust.
4. Pour cooked mixture over
peaches and chill.
5. Garnish with whipped cream,
and serve.

Priscilla L. Minster

finger lakes grape pie   Yield: 1 9-inch pie

Upstate New York traditional favorite.

3 cups Concord grapes
1 cup sugar
3 tablespoons flour
1 tablespoon lemon juice
1 tablespoon butter,
melted
Pastry for 2 9-inch crusts

1. Wash, drain, and stem grapes.
2. Remove and reserve skins.
Simmer pulp for 5 minutes.
3. While hot, press pulp through
sieve to remove seeds.
4. Combine strained pulp with
skins.
5. Combine sugar and flour and
add to grapes. Blend in lemon
juice and butter.
6. Pour into a 9-inch pie crust.
Cover with top crust and slash
with your own design. Bake.

Temperature: 425°
Time: 10 minutes then

Temperature: 350°
Time: 30 minutes

Hint: 1 teaspoon grated orange rind adds zest to grape and
rhubarb pies.

Judy G. Curry

270

🍓 strawberry cheese pie Yield: 1 9-inch pie

An all-time favorite combination of flavors.

Crust
1 cup flour
2 tablespoons
confectioners sugar
¼ pound butter

Crust
1. Mix all ingredients together.
2. Pat into a 9-inch pie plate. Prick crust and bake until golden.
3. Cool.

Filling
3 ounces cream cheese, softened
1 tablespoon lemon juice
½ cup sugar
½ pint heavy cream, whipped

Filling
1. Mix all ingredients together until well blended.
2. Pour into cooled crust.
3. Chill 1 hour.

Topping
1 quart fresh strawberries
½ cup currant jelly

Topping
1. Arrange berries, points up, on pie.
2. Melt jelly; pour over berries.
3. Chill at least 2 hours.

Must do ahead.

Temperature: 350°
Time: 15 to 20 minutes

Margot C. Reed

cranberry pie Yield: 8 servings

Colorful dessert for a holiday treat.

2 cups fresh cranberries
½ cup sugar
½ cup chopped walnuts, or pecans
2 eggs
1 cup sugar
1 cup flour
½ cup butter, melted
¼ cup shortening, melted
vanilla ice cream

1. Spread cranberries in a well-greased 10-inch pie plate.
2. Sprinkle cranberries with sugar and nuts.
3. In a bowl, beat eggs, adding sugar gradually.
4. Add flour, butter, and shortening and beat well.
5. Pour mixture over cranberries and bake.
6. Serve warm or cold with vanilla ice cream.

Temperature: 325°
Time: 60 minutes

Hint: Freeze fresh cranberries to prepare this pie out of season.

Jeanne F. DesMarteau

chocolate peppermint pie

Yield: 1 9-inch pie

For the chocolate lovers in your life!

3 egg whites
dash salt
¾ cup sugar
¾ cup plus 2 tablespoons
  chocolate wafer
  crumbs, finely ground
½ cup walnuts, finely
  chopped
½ teaspoon vanilla
½ pint heavy cream
1 tablespoon peppermint
  extract
1 to 2 tablespoons sugar

1. Beat egg whites and salt until
   soft peaks form.
2. Add ¾ cup of the sugar and
   beat whites until stiff.
3. Fold in ¾ cup of the crumbs,
   nuts, and vanilla. Spread onto
   bottom and sides of a buttered
   pie plate. Bake.
4. Chill meringue 3 to 4 hours.
   (Meringue can be frozen at this
   point. Defrost in refrigerator and
   continue.)
5. Whip cream until stiff, gradually
   adding peppermint and
   remaining sugar.
6. Fill meringue with whipped
   cream. Garnish with the
   remaining chocolate crumbs.

Must do ahead.

Temperature: 325°
Time: 35 minutes

Elizabeth T. Williams

ozark pie

Yield: 8 servings

An easy, cooling summer dessert.

1 egg
¾ cup sugar
⅛ teaspoon salt
1½ teaspoons baking
  powder
¼ cup flour
½ cup tart apples, pared,
  cored, and chopped
½ cup chopped walnuts
1½ quarts vanilla ice
  cream
3 chocolate-covered
  toffee bars, frozen

1. Combine egg, sugar, salt, baking
   powder, and flour. Beat well.
2. Stir in apples and nuts.
3. Pour mixture into a well-greased
   10-inch pie pan. Bake. Cool
   completely. (Crust rises, then
   falls while cooling.)
4. Soften ice cream slightly. Spoon
   into shell.
5. Crush toffee bars and sprinkle
   over ice cream. Freeze.
6. Remove from freezer 15 minutes
   before serving.

Must do ahead.

Temperature: 350°
Time: 25 minutes

Joanne K. Gianniny

meringue mocha mousse pie

Yield: 1 9-inch pie

A melt-in-your-mouth delight!

Crust
4 egg whites
⅔ cup sugar
1 cup chopped walnuts

Crust
1. Beat egg whites until soft peaks form. Gradually add sugar, beating until stiff peaks form. Fold in the nuts.
2. Butter and flour a 9-inch pie plate. Spread egg whites over bottom and sides, forming a high edge.
3. Bake. After one hour, turn off oven. Let meringue cool in oven, with door closed, for two hours.

Filling
¼ cup light corn syrup
1 tablespoon instant coffee crystals
1 tablespoon water
½ cup semi-sweet chocolate morsels
⅔ cup sweetened, condensed milk
1 cup heavy cream
1 teaspoon vanilla

Filling
1. Mix corn syrup, coffee crystals, and water in a saucepan. Heat to boiling. Reduce heat. Add chocolate; stir until melted. Remove from heat.
2. Blend in milk. Slowly stir in cream and vanilla. Cover, and chill.
3. When chilled, whip until soft peaks form. Spoon into meringue crust.
4. Cover. Freeze several hours.
5. Serve frozen. If desired, top with additional whipped cream and chocolate curls.

Must do ahead

Temperature: 275°
Time: 60 minutes

Marilyn S. Kessler

273

williamsburg cream pie

Yield: 6 to 8 servings

Very smooth, creamy, and elegant.

1 envelope unflavored
   gelatin
½ cup cold water
5 egg yolks
1 cup sugar
¼ cup light rum
1½ cups heavy cream,
   whipped
6 individual-size graham
   cracker crusts *or*
1 9-inch graham cracker
   pie crust
grated unsweetened
   chocolate

1. Soften gelatin in cold water,
   then place over low heat and
   bring almost to a boil. Stir until
   gelatin is dissolved.
2. Beat egg yolks and sugar until
   very light.
3. Stir gelatin into egg mixture.
   Cool.
4. Gradually add rum, beating
   constantly.
5. Fold whipped cream into gelatin
   mixture.
6. Cool until mixture begins to set.
   Spoon into 6 individual crusts
   or one crumb crust. Chill until
   firm.
7. Garnish with grated
   unsweetened chocolate. If
   frozen, remove from freezer
   approximately 30 minutes
   before serving.

Must do ahead.

Pamela B. Mele

chocolate pecan pie

Yield: 1 9-inch pie

For the real chocolate lover.

3 squares unsweetened
   chocolate
3 tablespoons butter
¾ cup sugar
1 cup light corn syrup
3 eggs, lightly beaten
1 teaspoon vanilla
1 cup broken pecans
1 9-inch unbaked pie shell
½ pint heavy cream,
   whipped (optional
   garnish)

1. Bring chocolate, butter, sugar,
   and corn syrup to a boil, stirring
   constantly.
2. Add 1 tablespoon of the hot
   chocolate liquid to the eggs and
   stir. Repeat. Then, add all
   remaining chocolate to the eggs.
   Mix well.
3. Stir in vanilla and pecans.
4. Pour mixture into an unbaked
   pie shell. Bake.
5. Serve pie at room temperature,
   or slightly warmed. Top with
   whipped cream, if desired.

Temperature: 350°
Time: 45 minutes or until set

Nancy F. Reale

sweet potato pie

Yield: 1 pie

A heavenly dessert steeped in Southern tradition.

2 sweet potatoes
½ cup sugar
½ cup brown sugar
1 stick butter, softened
½ teaspoon cinnamon
½ teaspoon nutmeg
½ teaspoon vanilla
1 egg, slightly beaten
enough light cream to
   make pouring
   consistency (about ½
   cup)
1 9-inch unbaked pie shell

1. Boil potatoes in skins until tender (about 45 minutes). Drain. Remove potato skins.
2. In a bowl, beat the potatoes, removing any strings which may stick to the beater.
3. Add sugars, butter, and spices. Beat well.
4. Add vanilla and egg.
5. Add enough cream to make pouring consistency.
6. Pour mixture into an unbaked pie shell. Bake in preheated oven. Cool.

Temperature: 400°
Time: 1 hour

Hint: Bake pies in lower third of oven, but pie shells in middle of oven.

Ida Riley

chiffon pumpkin pie

Yield: 1 9-inch pie

Even after a huge holiday meal they want seconds of this.

1 16-ounce can pumpkin
1 cup light brown sugar
1 teaspoon cinnamon
½ teaspoon mace or
   allspice
⅓ teaspoon ground cloves
¼ teaspoon salt
¾ cup milk
3 eggs, separated
1 9-inch unbaked pie
   crust

1. Mix pumpkin, sugar, spices, and salt together.
2. Add milk and egg yolks. Mix well.
3. In another bowl, beat egg whites until firm; fold into pumpkin mixture.
4. Pour pumpkin into pie crust. Bake.

Temperature: 450°
Time: 5 minutes then

Temperature: 350°
Time: 45 minutes

Hint: Grease all pie plates with solid vegetable shortening before lining with pastry.

Linda W. Davey

flaming pecan pumpkin pie

Yield: 1 9-inch pie

For extra élan at your Halloween bash.

1 9-inch unbaked pie
   crust, chilled

Filling
1 pound can pumpkin
3 tablespoons bourbon
2 eggs, slightly beaten
¾ cup brown sugar
1½ cups light cream
1 teaspoon cinnamon
½ teaspoon ginger
½ teaspoon salt

Filling
1. Mix together all ingredients and pour into pie crust.
2. Bake.
3. Cool completely.

Topping
2 tablespoons butter
¼ cup brown sugar
4 tablespoons bourbon
1 cup pecan halves

Topping
1. Combine butter and sugar in a saucepan. Heat and stir until sugar dissolves.
2. Add 2 tablespoons of the bourbon and pecans. Stir until nuts are covered completely with glaze.
3. Spoon nuts around edge of cooled pie.
4. At serving time, warm remaining 2 tablespoons bourbon, ignite, and pour quickly onto pie.

Temperature: 425°
Time: 10 minutes then

Temperature: 350°
Time: 50 to 60 minutes

Hint: Best made one day ahead.

Lucia H. Shaw

baklava

Yield: 35 pieces

Wonderful Greek pastry recipe, rich with honey, from a beekeeper's wife.

Syrup
¾ cup sugar
¾ cup water
1⅔ cups honey
2-inch stick cinnamon
4 lemon slices
4 orange slices

Syrup
1. Combine sugar and water in medium saucepan. Bring to boil, stirring to dissolve sugar.
2. Add honey, cinnamon, lemon slices, and orange slices. Simmer, uncovered, 10 minutes.
3. Strain. Cool.

Base

2 cups finely chopped
   walnuts
1 cup finely chopped
   blanched almonds
¾ cup sugar
½ teaspoon cinnamon
¼ teaspoon nutmeg
1 one-pound package
   phyllo or strudel pastry
   leaves
1½ cups butter, melted

Base

1. Mix walnuts, almonds, sugar, and spices.
2. Place 2 pastry leaves in 15½ x 10½ x 1-inch jelly roll pan. Brush top leaf with butter.
3. Continue, stacking 12 more leaves, buttering every other leaf. Sprinkle with a third of the nut mixture. (Keep other dough covered with damp cloth.)
4. Add 6 more leaves, brushing every other one with butter. Sprinkle with another third of the nut mixture.
5. Repeat step # 4.
6. Stack any remaining pastry leaves on top, brushing every other one with remaining butter, and buttering top leaf.
7. Trim edges, if necessary.
8. With sharp knife, cut through top layer on long side: make eight diagonal cuts at 1½-inch intervals. Then make nine cuts the other direction at 1½-inch intervals, to form diamonds. (Cut top layer only, do not cut through layers.)
9. Bake until golden and puffy; turn off heat. Leave in oven 60 minutes more. Remove.
10. Pour cooled syrup over hot baklava. Following diamond pattern, cut all the way through baklava. To absorb syrup, cool in pan on wire rack.

Must do ahead.

Temperature: 325°
Time: 60 minutes

Priscilla L. Minster

ick's bees make the best honey in Fairport, New York. He told us what to do should our honey crystallize Simply place the jar of honey in a pan of warm water and heat gently on the stove until it liquefies.

almond puff pastry delight

Yield: 12 servings

Surprisingly easy - a Danish gourmet treat.

1 cup flour
2 tablespoons sugar
¼ teaspoon salt
½ cup butter, softened
2 tablespoons cold water

1. Stir together flour, sugar, and salt.
2. Cut in butter until mixture has the texture of cornmeal.
3. Add cold water. Mix until pastry holds together in a ball.
4. Press pastry into bottom of a 9 x 13-inch pan.

Filling

1 cup water
½ cup butter
1 cup sifted flour
4 eggs

Filling

1. In a heavy saucepan, combine water and butter. Heat until butter is melted, then bring to a full, rolling boil over high heat.
2. Add the flour all at once. Remove from the heat, and stir vigorously until the mixture becomes a very thick paste that clings together and comes away from the sides of the pan.
3. Stir in eggs, one at a time, and beat with a spoon until the paste is smooth and shiny.
4. Spread the paste over pastry base. Bake.

Glaze

2 cups confectioners sugar
2 tablespoons milk
1 teaspoon almond extract
1 cup slivered almonds

Glaze

1. Combine sugar, milk, and almond extract. Beat until smooth.
2. While pastry is warm, drizzle with glaze and sprinkle with almonds.
3. (Can reheat at 350° for 5 to 10 minutes, uncovered.)

Temperature: 425°
Time: 35 minutes

Susan T. Nystrom

cakes

cakes

after-school applesauce cake

Yield: 9 servings

A family favorite for 20 years.

Cake

½ cup butter or
   margarine
1 cup brown sugar
1¾ cups flour
2½ teaspoons baking
   powder
1 cup applesauce
½ teaspoon orange
   extract
½ teaspoon ground cloves
1 teaspoon cinnamon
1 tablespoon aromatic
   bitters
1 cup raisins mixed with 1
   tablespoon flour

Caramel Frosting

¼ cup butter or
   margarine
½ cup brown sugar
2 tablespoons milk
1½ cups sifted
   confectioners sugar

Cake

1. Cream butter and brown sugar.
   Set aside.
2. Sift together flour and baking
   powder.
3. Mix applesauce with orange
   extract, cloves, cinnamon, and
   bitters.
4. Gradually and alternately add
   flour and applesauce mixtures
   to creamed butter and sugar
   mixture. Mix well after each
   addition. Fold in floured raisins.
5. Pour batter into an 8-inch
   square greased pan. Bake. Cool
   before frosting.

Caramel Frosting

1. Melt butter, and add brown
   sugar. Boil and stir for 1 minute
   or until slightly thick. Cool
   briefly.
2. Add milk. Beat until smooth.
3. Add sugar. Beat until mixture
   has a spreadable consistency.
4. Spread on cooled cake.

Temperature: 350°
Time: 45 minutes

Nancy M. Giles

*D*ick *had seven great aunts and all were wonderful cooks. They spent years trying to outdo each other, each developing a specialty for which she became well known. Part of the mystique was their consistent refusal to reveal recipes. Aunt Sarah's apple pie was the family's ultimate delight, and Dick's mom was bent on uncovering the secret. One day she hid in the barn and, peeking out, observed Aunt Sarah choosing apples for the pie. As she watched her Aunt picking apples, she could see the truth emerge: Aunt Sarah used apples from three different varieties of apple trees and no one else in the family had that same combination of trees!*

new york nobby apple cake

Yield: 8 to 9 servings

Loaded with apples, great after-school.

3 tablespoons butter or
  margarine
1 cup sugar
1 egg, beaten
1 cup flour, sifted
1 teaspoon baking soda
½ teaspoon cinnamon
½ teaspoon nutmeg
½ teaspoon salt
3 cups diced, pared
  apples
¼ cup chopped nuts
1 teaspoon vanilla
whipped cream or ice
  cream, optional

1. Cream butter and sugar. Add egg, and mix well. Set aside.
2. Sift together flour, baking soda, cinnamon, nutmeg, and salt. Add to butter and sugar, and mix well.
3. Stir in apples, nuts, and vanilla. Pour into a greased 8-inch square pan. Bake.
4. Serve warm or cool with whipped cream or ice cream.

Temperature: 350°
Time: 40 to 45 minutes

Nancy R. Murphy

chocolate zucchini cake

Yield: 10 to 12 servings

From the garden into an earthly delight.

2 cups sugar
¾ cup oil
3 eggs
2 teaspoons vanilla
2 cups coarsely shredded
  zucchini
2½ cups flour
½ cup cocoa
2½ teaspoons baking
  powder
1½ teaspoons baking
  soda
1 teaspoon salt
1 teaspoon cinnamon
½ cup milk

1. In large bowl beat sugar, oil, and eggs. Add vanilla and zucchini.
2. Mix dry ingredients together. Add alternately with milk to zucchini mixture. Blend well.
3. Pour into a 10-inch tube or Bundt pan. Bake. Allow to stand 10 minutes, then remove from pan.

Temperature: 350°
Time: 50 to 60 minutes

Susan S. Yesawich

deluxe carrot cake

Yield: 3-layer cake

There are many carrot cakes—this one is extra moist and chock-full of carrots.

Carrot Cake
2 cups flour
2 cups sugar
2 teaspoons baking soda
1 teaspoon salt
2 teaspoons cinnamon
4 eggs
1 cup cooking oil
4 cups grated raw carrots
(about 1 pound)
¾ cup chopped nuts

Carrot Cake
1. Mix flour, sugar, baking soda, salt, and cinnamon together. Set aside.
2. In a large bowl, beat eggs until foamy. Slowly beat in oil.
3. Add flour mixture slowly, beating until smooth.
4. Mix in carrots and nuts.
5. Pour into 3 greased and floured 9-inch round cake pans. Bake. Test for doneness. Allow to cool for 10 minutes before removing from pans. Then cool completely on racks.

Coconut Cream Cheese Frosting
4 tablespoons butter or margarine
2 cups coconut
8 ounces cream cheese
2 teaspoons milk
3½ cups confectioners sugar, sifted
½ teaspoon vanilla

Coconut Cream Cheese Frosting
1. Melt 2 tablespoons of the butter in a skillet. Add coconut, stirring constantly over low heat until golden brown. Spread on absorbent paper to cool.
2. Cream remaining butter with the cream cheese. Add milk and sugar alternately, beating well.
3. Add vanilla, and stir in 1¾ cups of the coconut. (Remaining coconut will be used as a garnish.)
4. Frost between cooled cake layers and on top. Sprinkle with reserved coconut.

Temperature: 350°
Time: 25 minutes

Sally S. Moore

If you don't want your kids to eat the yummy batch of brownies all at once, try this ploy: Freeze half and label it "liver."

bradford chocolate cake

Yield: 9-inch, 2-layer cake

Heaven for a chocolate lover.

Cake
½ cup butter or
  margarine
2¼ cups sugar
2 eggs
4 ounces semi-sweet
  chocolate, melted
1¼ teaspoon vanilla
2¼ cups sifted cake flour
½ teaspoon salt
1¼ teaspoons baking
  soda
½ cup buttermilk
1 cup hot coffee

Cake
1. Cream butter. Beat in sugar gradually. Add eggs one at a time, mixing well after each addition.
2. Blend in chocolate and vanilla. Set aside.
3. Sift together flour, salt, and baking soda. Add alternately with the buttermilk and coffee to the chocolate mixture. Blend well after each addition.
4. Pour into 2 greased and floured 9-inch round pans. Bake. Cool completely.

Mocha Frosting
1½ tablespoons butter
2½ tablespoons cocoa
2 cups confectioners
  sugar
strong black coffee

Mocha Frosting
1. Mix together butter, cocoa, and sugar. Add enough coffee to make frosting spreadable.
2. Spread between cake layers.

Boiled Frosting
2 egg whites
1½ cups sugar
5 tablespoons cold water
¼ teaspoon cream of
  tartar
1 teaspoon vanilla

Boiled Frosting
1. Combine all ingredients, except vanilla, in the top of a double boiler over rapidly boiling water. Beat constantly with a whisk or electric mixer for 7 minutes.
2. Remove from heat. Add vanilla. Continue beating until frosting has a spreadable consistency.
3. Frost sides and top of cake.

Chocolate Glaze
2 ounces unsweetened
  chocolate
2 teaspoons butter

Chocolate Glaze
1. Melt chocolate and butter together.
2. Pour over top of cake, allowing to drip randomly down the sides.

Temperature: 350°
Time: 25 to 30 minutes

Linda H. Butwid

pineapple dream cake Yield: 8 to 10 servings

Perfect for a dessert party . . . very rich.

3 eggs
1½ cups sugar
1¼ cups flour
1 teaspoon baking powder
½ teaspoon baking soda
¼ teaspoon salt
1½ cups crushed
  pineapple, drained
1 cup chopped walnuts
2 cups heavy cream,
  whipped
pineapple rings or chunks
  and maraschino
  cherries for garnish

1. Beat eggs and sugar together thoroughly. Set aside.
2. Sift together flour, baking powder, baking soda, and salt.
3. Add dry ingredients, pineapple, and walnuts to egg and sugar mixture.
4. Pour into 2 greased 8-inch round pans. Bake. Cool completely.
5. Frost with whipped cream. Garnish with pineapple rings or chunks and maraschino cherries. Refrigerate.

Temperature: 350°
Time: 30 minutes

Veronica A. Doty

 peach kuchen Yield: 8 servings

More than special, a family jewel.

2 cups sifted flour
2 tablespoons sugar
¼ teaspoon baking
  powder
½ teaspoon salt
½ cup butter or
  margarine
12 peach halves
1 cup light brown sugar
1 teaspoon cinnamon
2 egg yolks
1 cup heavy cream

1. Mix together flour, sugar, baking powder, and salt. With a pastry blender, cut in the butter until the mixture resembles coarse cornmeal.
2. Press the flour mixture over the bottom and up the sides of a buttered 10-inch round pan.
3. Place the peaches, cut side up, over the pastry.
4. Combine the brown sugar and cinnamon, and sprinkle over the peach halves. Bake for 15 minutes.
5. Mix the egg yolks and cream. Pour over the peaches, and continue to bake for 30 minutes or until brown.
6. Serve warm or cool.

Temperature: 400°
Time: 45 minutes

Ann Merley

mandel kaka

Yield: 8 to 10 servings

A distinctively flavored Swedish family recipe.

3 eggs, separated
1 cup sugar
1 cup flour, sifted
1 teaspoon almond
  flavoring
½ cup butter, melted
½ cup sliced almonds

1. Beat egg whites until stiff. Add egg yolks, and beat until fluffy.
2. Gradually add sugar, blending thoroughly.
3. Fold in flour. Stir in flavoring and melted butter.
4. Pour into a buttered and floured 1½-quart square casserole. Sprinkle with almonds. Bake.
5. This is best served warm and topped with whipped cream.

Temperature: 350°
Time: 35 to 40 minutes

Sue M. Hanson

mc apple spice cake

Yield: 8 to 10 servings

Destined to be the hit of the day.

1½ cups sifted flour
½ cup plain wheat germ
2 teaspoons baking soda
2 teaspoons cinnamon
1 teaspoon salt
2 to 3 large apples
2 tablespoons lemon juice
2 cups sugar
1¼ cups oil
4 eggs
1 teaspoon vanilla
¾ cup chopped nuts

1. Combine flour, wheat germ, baking soda, cinnamon, and salt. Set aside.
2. Pare and shred enough apples to equal 3½ cups. Combine with lemon juice in a large bowl of cold water.
3. Blend sugar, oil, eggs, and vanilla thoroughly.
4. Mix in well-drained apples, nuts, and dry ingredients.
5. Pour into a greased bundt or 9 x 13-inch pan.
6. Bake. Cool. (Cake can be frozen before frosting.)

Frosting
4 ounces cream cheese
1 teaspoon vanilla
2 cups confectioners
  sugar
2 teaspoons apple juice

Frosting
1. Blend cream cheese, vanilla, sugar, and apple juice until of spreading consistency.
2. Frost cooled cake.

Temperature: 350°
Time: 50 to 60 minutes

Sherrie Zebrasky
McCurdy's Home Economist

284

lemon-apple filling

Yield: enough filling for a 3-layer cake

Serve as a spread with gingerbread for an old-fashioned touch.

3 large apples, cored, peeled, and grated
1 lemon (juice and grated rind)
1 heaping cup sugar
¼ cup flour
1 teaspoon butter
1 egg yolk

1. Mix all ingredients together well and cook in a saucepan until thick, stirring constantly.
2. Let cool. Spread between layers of a white or yellow cake. Frost with a boiled fluffy frosting*.

Time: 15 minutes

*Hint: There is a recipe for this type of frosting in our Bradford Chocolate Cake (see index).

Lucia H. Shaw

orange slice cake

Yield: 10-inch cake

A wonderful holiday cake; better than traditional fruit cake.

1 cup butter, softened
2 cups sugar
4 eggs
½ cup buttermilk
1 teaspoon baking soda
3½ cups sifted flour
½ pound diced dates
1 one-pound bag orange slice candy, chopped
1 3½-ounce can coconut
2 cups chopped walnuts
1 cup orange juice
2 cups sifted confectioners sugar

1. Cream butter and sugar until fluffy. Add eggs, one at a time, beating well after each addition.
2. Combine buttermilk and baking soda in another bowl. Then add alternately with flour to butter mixture, setting aside a bit of flour for dredging.
3. Dredge diced dates, chopped candy orange slices, and coconut in reserved flour. Add to cake batter along with chopped walnuts.
4. Pour into 10-inch greased tube pan, and bake.
5. While cake is baking, mix orange juice and confectioners sugar. When cake is done, pour this glaze over cake immediately.
6. Let cake cool in pan overnight, then remove.

Must do one day ahead.

Temperature: 250°
Time: 2 to 2½ hours

Suzanne H. Barbee

strasenburgh torte

Yield: 12 servings

This gala chocolate torte was created for Robert Strasenburgh, an eminent, philanthropic Rochesterian, on his 60th birthday.

Filling

2 eggs, separated
1 teaspoon water
2⅔ ounces bittersweet
  chocolate*
vanilla to taste

Filling

1. Beat egg yolks until fluffy and lemon colored. Set aside.
2. Beat egg whites until stiff peaks form. Set aside.
3. Put the water in the top of a double boiler over hot, not boiling, water. Add chocolate and melt. Stir in vanilla.
4. Blend chocolate by spoonfuls into the egg yolks. Fold in the egg whites.
5. Chill overnight in a bowl, or shaped in a 9 x 4½-inch rectangle in a lined pan.

Cake

4 tablespoons cocoa, high
  quality
1½ tablespoons instant
  coffee granules
¾ cup plus 2½
  tablespoons sugar
2 tablespoons water
½ cup milk
2 eggs, separated
½ cup unsalted butter
2 teaspoons vanilla
¼ cup sugar
1 cup flour
½ teaspoon cream of
  tartar
½ teaspoon baking soda

Cake

1. Combine cocoa, coffee, 2½ tablespoons of the sugar, and water in the top of a double boiler over hot, *not boiling*, water. Cook until thickened.
2. Remove from heat. Stir in milk. Set aside.
3. Beat egg whites until stiff, gradually beating in ½ cup of the sugar. Set aside.
4. Cream together butter, vanilla, and remaining ¼ cup sugar, until light and fluffy.
5. Beat in the egg yolks one at a time. Blend in the cocoa mixture thoroughly.
6. In a separate bowl, sift together flour, cream of tartar, and baking soda. Beat into the batter.
7. Fold in the egg whites. Pour into a 9-inch square pan which has been buttered and lined with waxed paper.

strasenburgh torte *continued*

8. Bake. Cool completely. Then cut the cake in half vertically, and split each half horizontally. This will create 4 layers, 9 x 4½ inches each.

Glaze
¾ cup raspberry
   preserves, strained
2 tablespoons sugar
1 tablespoon Kirsch

Glaze
1. Combine all ingredients. Cook over moderate heat for 2 to 3 minutes, or until mixture forms a soft ball when a drop of it is placed in cold water.
2. While glaze is still warm, spread it between the first and second layers of cake and between the third and fourth layers. Join the second and third layers with the chilled filling.

Frosting
2 ounces unsweetened
   chocolate* (or 6
   tablespoons cocoa)
1 cup sugar
7 tablespoons milk
¼ cup butter
1 tablespoon corn syrup
1 teaspoon vanilla
candied violets for
   garnish, optional
*It is extremely important to use only high quality chocolate for this recipe.

Frosting
1. Mix together chocolate, sugar, milk, butter, and corn syrup in a saucepan. Bring to a rolling boil, stirring constantly. Boil for 1 minute.
2. Remove from heat and cool for 20 minutes. Add vanilla. Beat until thick and spreadable, about 10 minutes.
3. Frost top and sides of glazed and filled torte. Garnish with candied violets.
4. Chill. Serve in thin slices.

Filling must be made one day ahead.

Temperature: 350°
Time: 40 minutes

Jane, a weight watcher, hid food from herself all over the house. A favorite spot was the clothes dryer, until one day, neglecting to remove the caloric booty, she found herself with a whole dryer load of cake crumbed clothes!

chocolate fudge cake

Yield: 9-inch 2-layer cake

Moist, delicious, and perfect for kids.

Cake
- 4 ounces unsweetened chocolate
- 2¼ cups sifted cake flour
- 2 teaspoons baking soda
- ½ teaspoon salt
- ½ cup butter or margarine
- 2¼ cups brown sugar
- 3 large eggs
- 1½ teaspoons vanilla
- 1 cup sour cream
- 1 cup boiling water

Cake
1. Grease and flour cake pans. (Can use cocoa in place of flour).
2. Melt chocolate in a small bowl over hot water. Set aside to cool.
3. Sift flour, baking soda, and salt into a large bowl.
4. Cream butter in another large bowl. Add brown sugar and eggs. Beat at high speed until light and fluffy, for 5 minutes.
5. Beat in vanilla and chocolate.
6. Stir in dry ingredients alternately with sour cream. Beat well with a wooden spoon, after each addition, until batter is smooth.
7. Stir in boiling water. Batter will be thin.
8. Pour at once into prepared pans. Bake.
9. Remove from pans. Cool completely. Frost with Chocolate Fudge Frosting.

Chocolate Fudge Frosting
- 4 ounces unsweetened chocolate
- ½ cup butter or margarine
- 1 one-pound box confectioners sugar
- ½ cup milk
- 1 teaspoon vanilla

Chocolate Fudge Frosting
1. Melt chocolate and butter in a small, heavy saucepan, over low heat.
2. Combine sugar and milk in a medium-size bowl. Add chocolate mixture.
3. Set bowl in ice water, and beat with a wooden spoon until thickened. Stir in vanilla.
4. Spread on cooled cake.

Temperature: 350°
Time: 35 minutes

A. Kimberly Yunker

strawberry rhubarb icebox cake

A springtime treat, light and fruity.

Cake

6 cups rhubarb, cut into ½-inch pieces
½ cup sugar
1 cup water
2 3-ounce packages strawberry gelatin
2 cups heavy cream, whipped
1 teaspoon vanilla
2 4-ounce packages unfilled ladyfingers, split

Cake

1. Combine rhubarb, sugar, and water in a saucepan. Bring to a boil, and simmer 6 to 8 minutes until tender. Remove 1 cup of the cooking liquid, and reserve for glaze.
2. Purée the rhubarb in a blender or food processor. Return the purée to the saucepan, and bring to a boil.
3. Pour the rhubarb purée over the gelatin, and stir until dissolved. Chill until thickened slightly.
4. Fold in the whipped cream and vanilla.
5. Line the sides and bottom of a 9-inch springform pan with the ladyfingers.
6. Layer rhubarb mixture and remaining ladyfingers alternately in the pan, ending with the rhubarb mixture. Chill overnight.

Glaze

¼ cup sugar
1½ teaspoons cornstarch blended with small amount of cold water
whole fresh unhulled strawberries and/or fresh mint leaves for garnish

Glaze

1. In a saucepan, mix the cup of reserved cooking liquid and sugar. Bring to a boil, stirring often.
2. Add the cornstarch and water. Stir and cook until thick and clear. Cool.
3. Spread the glaze over the top of the rhubarb icebox cake. Garnish.

Must be done ahead.

Terryl S. Butwid

chocolate pumpernickel torte

Yield: 10 to 12 servings

Rich, creamy, and intoxicating.

2½ cups fresh
   pumpernickel crumbs
   (do not use crust)
⅓ cup light rum
6 eggs, separated
⅛ teaspoon salt
1 cup sugar
1 teaspoon vanilla
4 ounces semi-sweet
   chocolate, finely grated

1. Put crumbs in a bowl, and sprinkle with rum. Set aside.
2. Beat egg whites with salt until soft peaks form. Gradually add sugar, beating until stiff peaks form.
3. In another large bowl, stir vanilla into egg yolks, blending lightly.
4. Fold about ¼ of egg white mixture into egg yolks. Pour this mixture over remaining egg white mixture.
5. Sprinkle combined egg mixtures with bread crumbs and chocolate, a few tablespoons at a time. Fold gently after each addition.
6. Divide batter evenly between three 8-inch greased, floured, and waxpaper-lined cake pans. Bake.

Filling
2 cups heavy cream,
   whipped
3 tablespoons sugar
2 tablespoons light rum
chocolate curls

Filling
1. Combine whipped cream, sugar, and light rum.
2. To assemble, spread ⅓ of the cream between each layer, and frost with final ⅓. Decorate with chocolate curls.
3. Chill at least 2 hours.

Must do ahead.

Temperature: 350°
Time: 30 minutes

Kristine W. Williams

spicy raisin cake

Yield: 8 to 10 servings

Moist old-fashioned cake for the family.

1 cup raisins
3 cups boiling water
½ cup butter or
   margarine
1 cup brown sugar
1 egg

1. Boil raisins and water together for approximately 15 minutes until 1 cup of liquid is left. Reserve raisin liquid.
2. Cream butter and brown sugar thoroughly. Add egg. Set aside.

spicy raisin cake *continued*

1¾ cups flour
1 teaspoon baking soda
1 teaspoon cinnamon
1 teaspoon ground cloves
½ teaspoon nutmeg

3. Combine flour, soda, cinnamon, cloves, and nutmeg. Add alternately with raisin liquid to butter and sugar mixture.
4. Stir in raisins. Pour into greased and floured 8-inch square pan. Bake.
5. Frost with a butter cream icing flavored with vanilla or almond.

Temperature: 350°
Time: 35 to 40 minutes

Linda L. Clark

old fashioned fruit cake

Yield: 4 8½ x 4½-inch loaves

This recipe was passed down with measurements such as "25¢ worth pecans" and "5¢ worth dates."

1 pound butter, at room temperature
1 pound confectioners' sugar
1 dozen eggs
1 lemon (juice and rind)
¾ cup whiskey or brandy
1 pound flour
1 tablespoon cinnamon
1 tablespoon allspice
1 tablespoon ground cloves
1½ teaspoons nutmeg
2 teaspoons baking powder
2 teaspoons salt
3 pounds raisins, 1 pound chopped
1 pound citron, chopped
1½ pounds figs or dates, chopped
5 cups pecans, chopped
additional whiskey for soaking cloth

1. Cream butter and sugar. Add eggs, and mix well.
2. Blend in lemon juice, rind, and whiskey thoroughly.
3. Sift together flour, spices, baking powder, and salt.
4. Blend flour mixture into butter mixture. Stir in fruits and nuts.
5. Fill greased and floured loaf pans ¾ full. Bake.
6. When cool, remove cakes from pans, and wrap in whiskey-soaked cloth.
7. Store for at least 5 days, or up to 4 months, in a covered container. Add more whiskey if cloth gets dry.

Must be made 5 days ahead. **Temperature: 325°**
Time: 1 hour, 15 minutes

Susan K. Lepkowski

291

coffee cloud cake

Yield: 8 to 10 servings

A lovely light cake topped with a superb sauce.

Cake
1 tablespoon instant coffee
1 cup boiling water
2 cups flour
3 teaspoons baking powder
½ teaspoon salt
6 eggs, separated
½ teaspoon cream of tartar
2 cups sugar
1 teaspoon vanilla
1 cup chopped pecans

Cake
1. Dissolve coffee in boiling water. Allow to cool.
2. Sift together flour, baking powder, and salt. Set aside.
3. Beat egg whites and cream of tartar until soft mounds form. Begin adding ½ cup of the sugar, 2 tablespoons at a time, beating until stiff peaks form. Set aside.
4. Beat the egg yolks. Gradually add remaining sugar and vanilla. Beat at high speed for 4 or 5 minutes until eggs are lemon colored. Stir in flour mixture alternately with coffee.
5. Fold the egg yolk mixture and pecans into the egg whites.
6. Pour into a greased 9 x 13-inch pan. Bake. Cool 1 hour. Serve with Chocolate Sauce.

Chocolate Sauce
4 ounces unsweetened chocolate
1½ cups sugar
⅓ cup unsweetened cocoa
½ cup butter
1 cup heavy cream
1 teaspoon vanilla

Chocolate Sauce
1. Melt chocolate squares in a double boiler. Add sugar, cocoa, and butter. Cook for 45 minutes.
2. Add heavy cream, and stir for 3 minutes.
3. Cool for 10 minutes. Add vanilla.

Temperature: 350°
Time: 60 to 70 minutes

Hint: This sauce is delicious served over ice cream or with other cakes.

Margy M. Richardson

*M*argy received the recipe for this wonderful cake at her bridal shower. She insists that its sweet, delicate taste has kept her marriage together. Whenever her husband returns home from a business trip, she welcomes him with his favorite cake.

old fashioned gingerbread

Yield: 9-inch cake

Be a child again.

½ cup butter
½ cup sugar
1 egg, beaten
1 cup molasses
2½ cups sifted flour
1½ teaspoons baking
  soda
1 teaspoon cinnamon
1 teaspoon ground ginger
½ teaspoon ground cloves
½ teaspoon salt
1 cup hot water
whipped cream, optional

1. Cream butter and sugar. Add egg and molasses. Set aside.
2. Sift together flour, baking soda, cinnamon, ginger, cloves, and salt. Add to the butter mixture. Blend well.
3. Add hot water. Beat mixture until smooth. The batter will be soft.
4. Bake in a 9-inch square pan. Serve with our Lemon Apple Filling (see index) or whipped cream.

Temperature: 350°
Time: 35 minutes

Linda Wells Davey

apple rum cake

Yield: 9-inch cake

Good and nutty with a fantastic sauce.

Cake
¼ cup shortening
1 cup sugar
1 egg
¼ teaspoon salt
1 teaspoon cinnamon
1 teaspoon nutmeg
1 teaspoon baking soda
1 cup flour
2 tablespoons hot water
1 teaspoon vanilla
½ cup chopped nuts
2½ cups pared, cubed
  apples

Cake
1. Cream together shortening and sugar.
2. Add remaining ingredients in order listed. Mix well.
3. Pour into greased, 9-inch round, cake pan or pie plate. Bake. (Can be frozen. Thaw well before adding sauce.)
4. Serve with warm rum sauce.

Rum Sauce
½ cup butter
¾ cup brown sugar
¼ cup cream
½ teaspoon rum-flavored
  extract or
1 to 2 tablespoons rum

Rum Sauce
1. Melt butter. Add brown sugar, and boil 1 minute.
2. Add cream, and boil a few more seconds.
3. Remove from heat. Stir in rum extract or rum.

Temperature: 350°
Time: 45 to 60 minutes

Emily D. Henderson

white chocolate cake

Yield: 3-layer cake

A rich, heavy cake for special occasions.

Cake
¼ pound white chocolate
   (plain or with almonds)
½ cup boiling water
1 cup butter
1¾ cups sugar
2½ cups sifted flour
1 teaspoon baking soda
4 eggs, well beaten
1 cup buttermilk
1 cup coconut
1 cup pecans, floured
   lightly
1 teaspoon vanilla

Cake
1. Melt chocolate in boiling water. Cool.
2. Cream butter and sugar. Add to chocolate mixture.
3. Mix flour and baking soda. Add alternately with eggs and buttermilk to the chocolate mixture. Beat well after each addition.
4. Add coconut, pecans, and vanilla. Blend thoroughly.
5. Pour batter into 3 greased and floured 8- or 9-inch round cake pans.
6. Bake. Cool, remove from pans, and frost.

Frosting
½ cup butter
8 ounces cream cheese,
   softened
3 cups confectioners
   sugar
1 teaspoon vanilla
½ cup coconut
pecan halves

Frosting
1. Cream butter and cream cheese. Add sugar and vanilla.
2. Frost and sprinkle with coconut between layers and on top. Decorate top with pecan halves.

Must do one day ahead.

Temperature: 350°
Time: 30 minutes

Suzanne H. Barbee

italian cream cake

Yield: 9-inch 3-layer cake

Knocks the competition out of the ring.

Cake
2 cups sugar
½ cup butter
½ cup solid vegetable
   shortening
5 eggs, separated
1 teaspoon baking soda
1 cup buttermilk
2 cups flour

Cake
1. Cream sugar, butter, and shortening together. Add egg yolks one at a time, beating well after each addition.
2. Stir soda into buttermilk, and let sit 10 minutes.
3. Meanwhile, beat egg whites until stiff. Set aside.

294

½ teaspoon salt
1 tablespoon vanilla
1 cup coconut
1 cup chopped pecans

4. Sift together flour and salt. Add alternately with buttermilk to sugar and butter mixture.
5. Add vanilla, coconut, and pecans.
6. Fold in egg whites.
7. Pour batter into 3 greased and floured 9-inch cake pans. Bake.

Icing
8 ounces cream cheese
½ cup butter
1 one-pound box confectioners sugar
1 teaspoon vanilla

Icing
1. Combine all ingredients.
2. Spread between layers and on outside of cooled cake.

Temperature: 325°
Time: 35 minutes

Suzanne H. Barbee

chocolate cheesecake

Yield: 9-inch

Richest chocolate taste ever!

Crust
1 8½-ounce package chocolate wafers
⅓ cup butter, melted
2 tablespoons sugar
¼ teaspoon nutmeg

Crust
1. Crush chocolate wafers into fine crumbs. Combine with butter, sugar, and nutmeg.
2. Press evenly over bottom and sides, to ½ inch from the top, of a 9-inch spring form pan. Refrigerate.

Filling
3 eggs
1 cup sugar
3 8-ounce packages cream cheese, softened
12 ounces semi-sweet chocolate pieces, melted
1 teaspoon vanilla
⅛ teaspoon salt
1 cup sour cream
whipped cream, optional

Filling
1. Beat eggs and sugar until light. Add cream cheese, and beat until smooth.
2. Blend in melted chocolate, vanilla, salt, and sour cream thoroughly. Pour batter into crumb crust.
3. Bake until cheesecake is just firm when pan is jiggled slightly.
4. Cool in pan on wire rack. Refrigerate, covered, overnight.
5. Top with whipped cream when served.

Must do ahead.

Temperature: 350°
Time: 1 hour

Caroll A. Meyers

toasted coconut cake

Yield: 6 to 8 servings

Delicious, attractive, and easily made.

Cake
½ cup milk
1 tablespoon butter
2 eggs
1 cup granulated sugar
1 cup flour
1 teaspoon baking powder
¼ teaspoon salt
1 teaspoon vanilla

Cake
1. Bring milk and butter to a boil. Remove from heat, and set aside.
2. Beat eggs until foamy. Gradually beat in sugar.
3. In a separate bowl, sift together flour, baking powder, and salt. Add to the beaten egg mixture.
4. Blend the hot milk and vanilla with the flour and egg mixture. Pour into an 8-inch square baking pan, and bake.

Topping
3 tablespoons butter
8 tablespoons brown sugar
3 tablespoons cream or milk
1 cup moist coconut

Topping
1. Combine all topping ingredients. When cake is done, spread it with topping.
2. Put the cake under a broiler for about 5 minutes or until coconut is golden brown.

Temperature: 350°
Time: 30 to 35 minutes

Celia G. Riley

praline cheesecake

Yield: 10 to 12 servings

Brought cheers of joy at the Junior League board meeting.

1 cup graham cracker crumbs
3 tablespoons sugar
3 tablespoons melted butter or margarine
3 8-ounce packages cream cheese, softened
1¼ cups dark brown sugar
2 tablespoons flour
3 eggs
1½ teaspoons vanilla
½ cup finely chopped pecans
maple syrup
pecan halves for garnish

1. Combine crumbs, sugar, and butter. Press into the bottom of a 9-inch spring form pan. Bake at 350° for 10 minutes. Set aside to cool.
2. Combine cream cheese, sugar, and flour. Mix well.
3. Add eggs, one at a time, beating well after each addition.
4. Blend in vanilla and chopped pecans.
5. Pour into crust, and bake. Cool before removing from pan.
6. Chill. Brush with maple syrup. Garnish with pecan halves before serving.

Temperature: 350°
Time: 50 to 55 minutes

Marge H. Nelson

🍎 wine country cheese cake

Yield: 10 to 12 servings

The dessert for company—elegant in appearance and taste.

Crust
1½ cups vanilla wafer
   crumbs (34 wafers)
3 tablespoons sugar
⅓ cup butter, melted

Crust
1. Combine vanilla wafers, sugar, and butter.
2. Press onto bottom, and part way up the sides, of an ungreased 9-inch spring form pan.
3. Bake at 350° for 10 minutes. Cool.

Filling
3 8-ounce packages
   cream cheese, softened
¼ cup semi-dry Rosé or
   white wine
½ teaspoon salt
1 cup sugar
4 eggs

Filling
1. Combine cream cheese, wine, and salt. Gradually mix in the sugar.
2. Add eggs, one at a time, beating well after each addition. Pour into baked crust.
3. Bake. Cool completely.
4. Run knife around sides of cake, and remove pan.

Glaze
1 one-pound can apricot
   halves
½ cup sugar
4 teaspoons cornstarch
½ cup semi-dry Rosé or
   white wine
3 or 4 drops red food
   coloring
¼ cup seedless grapes

Glaze
1. Drain apricots, reserving ½ cup of syrup.
2. Combine sugar and cornstarch in a small saucepan. Gradually add syrup and wine, stirring constantly. Cook over medium heat, stirring until mixture comes to a boil and thickens. Add food coloring.
3. Cool glaze to room temperature.
4. Arrange apricots and grapes on top of cheese cake.
5. Spoon glaze over fruit, letting it drip down sides of cake. Chill.

Temperature: 300°
Time: 1 hour to 1 hour, 20 minutes

Karin N. McNamara

cheesecake
à l'orange

Yield: 10 to 12 servings

Satiates the most voracious sweet tooth.

Crust
1 cup sifted flour
¼ cup sugar
1 tablespoon grated
    orange rind
½ cup butter
1 egg yolk
½ teaspoon vanilla

Crust
1. Combine flour, sugar, and
   orange rind. Cut in the butter
   with a pastry blender until the
   mixture resembles coarse meal.
2. Blend in the egg yolk and vanilla
   thoroughly.
3. Pat ⅓ of the dough evenly over
   the bottom of a 10-inch
   spring form pan. Bake at 400°
   for 5 minutes, then cool.
4. Pat remaining dough evenly
   around sides to ½ inch from the
   top. Set aside, and prepare
   filling.

Filling
5 8-ounce packages
    cream cheese, softened
1¾ cups sugar
3 tablespoons flour
1 tablespoon grated
    orange rind
¼ teaspoon salt
¼ teaspoon vanilla
5 eggs
2 egg yolks
¼ cup frozen orange juice
    concentrate, thawed
fresh orange sections and
    mint for garnish

Filling
1. Combine first six ingredients in
   large mixing bowl. Beat at a low
   speed, with an electric mixer,
   until smooth.
2. Add eggs and egg yolks one at a
   time, beating well after each
   addition.
3. Stir in orange juice. Pour filling
   into prepared crust.
4. Place filled spring form pan on a
   cookie sheet, and bake at 400°
   for 8 to 10 minutes. Reduce
   oven to 225°, and continue
   baking for 1 hour and 20
   minutes.
5. Cool to room temperature.
   Refrigerate until well chilled.
6. Garnish with fresh orange
   sections and mint.

Temperature: 400°
Time: 8 to 10 minutes then

Temperature: 225°
Time: 1 hour, 20 minutes

Carol Michna

298

chocolate crunch roll   Yield: 10 servings

A medley most likely to succeed.

Cake

4 eggs, separated
¾ cup sugar
2 tablespoons hot water
1 teaspoon vanilla
¾ cup flour
¼ cup cocoa
½ teaspoon baking soda
¼ teaspoon salt
confectioners sugar

Cake

1. Beat egg whites until foamy. Gradually add sugar, and continue beating until stiff peaks form.
2. Add egg yolks, water, and vanilla. Beat until well blended.
3. Combine dry ingredients, and stir gently into batter.
4. Gently pour batter into a 15 x 10-inch jelly roll pan which has been greased, floured, and lined with greased and floured wax paper. Spread batter to edges. Bake.
5. Remove from oven, loosen edges, and invert immediately onto a towel sprinkled with confectioners sugar.
6. Roll cake lengthwise inside towel while still warm. Cool, wrapped.

Filling

1½ cups heavy cream
1½ teaspoons instant coffee granules
1 cup crushed peanut brittle

Filling

1. Whip cream with instant coffee until stiff.
2. Fold in peanut brittle.
3. Unroll cake. Spread with filling, and reroll. Wrap well with plastic wrap, and refrigerate.

Glaze

2 ounces unsweetened chocolate
3 tablespoons butter
1 cup confectioners sugar
1 teaspoon vanilla
1½ to 2 tablespoons hot water

Glaze

1. In saucepan, melt chocolate and butter.
2. Remove from heat, and stir in confectioners sugar and vanilla.
3. Mix in water until glaze is of spreading consistency.
4. Spread glaze on cooled cake just before serving.

Must do ahead.

Temperature: 350°
Time: 18 to 22 minutes

Hint: For very special occasions, pipe on swirls of whipped cream with a pastry bag.

Kathyn P. Weider

pumpkin roll

Yield: 10 to 12 servings

This subtly flavored cake roll freezes beautifully.

Cake

3 eggs
1 cup sugar
¾ cup flour
1 teaspoon baking powder
2 teaspoons cinnamon
1 teaspoon ground ginger
½ teaspoon nutmeg
½ teaspoon salt
⅔ cup cooked or canned pumpkin
1 teaspoon lemon juice
1 cup walnuts, finely chopped
confectioners sugar

Cake

1. Beat eggs at high speed for 5 minutes. Gradually beat in sugar. Set aside.
2. Mix flour, baking powder, cinnamon, ginger, nutmeg, and salt together. Set aside.
3. Combine pumpkin and lemon juice. Add flour mixture, stirring gently.
4. Fold pumpkin mixture into beaten egg mixture. Pour into a greased and floured 10½ x 15½ x 1-inch jelly roll pan. Sprinkle with walnuts, and bake.
5. Sprinkle confectioners sugar on a clean towel. When cake is done, invert it on the towel. Gently roll the towel and cake lengthwise. Allow to cool completely while you prepare filling.

Filling

1 cup confectioners sugar
2 3-ounce packages cream cheese
4 tablespoons butter
½ teaspoon vanilla

Filling

1. Combine filling ingredients. Beat until smooth and spreadable.
2. Unroll cooled cake; spread with filling. Roll again. Place seam side down on a serving dish. Trim ends. Serve in 1-inch slices.

Temperature: 375°
Time: 15 minutes

Karen Pellett

When Annette's 5 children helped her bake pumpkin cake one of them left out the sugar which was needed to catalyze the baking soda so that the cake would rise. Without the sugar such a leaden cake resulted that her dinner guests, who had been looking forward to sampling their favorite cake, wound up initiating her new garbage disposal instead!

cookies

cookies

almond cookies

Yield: 4 dozen

A nice finish to a Chinese meal.

4 egg whites
2½ cups sifted
    confectioners sugar
juice of ½ lemon
grated rind of ½ lemon
2½ to 3 cups finely
    chopped almonds
5 teaspoons cinnamon

1. Whip egg whites until very stiff.
2. Slowly add sugar and lemon juice. Set aside 1 cup of this mixture.
3. To the remaining mixture, add lemon rind, almonds, and cinnamon.
4. Drop small amounts of mixture onto well-greased cookie sheet.
5. Top each cookie with a bit of reserved egg white mixture.
6. Bake until lightly browned. Store in airtight container.

Temperature: 350°
Time: 10 to 15 minutes

Ann Irwin

adirondack camp cookies

Yield: 100 4-inch cookies

These chocolate chip cookies are truly man-size.

3 cups granulated sugar
1 pound brown sugar
2 pounds all vegetable
    shortening
8 eggs
3 tablespoons vanilla
8½ cups flour
4 teaspoons baking soda
2 teaspoons salt
2 12-ounce packages
    semi-sweet chocolate
    chips
¾ cup coconut, optional

1. In a very large bowl, beat sugars, shortening, eggs, and vanilla until creamy.
2. Add flour, baking soda, and salt. Mix well.
3. Gently stir in chocolate chips and coconut.
4. Using a size 30 ice cream scoop or a rounded soup spoon, drop cookies 2 inches apart on an ungreased cookie sheet.
5. Bake.

Temperature: 350°
Time: 15 to 18 minutes

Terry S. Butwid

*M*any campers complain that the cookies so lovingly baked and mailed by mom arrive all broken. We found that packing them in popcorn keeps the cookies intact and allows an extra snack at the same time.

chokladveskvier cookies

Yield: 2 to 3 dozen

Impressive and delicious.

3 egg whites
1 cup sugar
6 Holland Rusks, ground
½ cup ground almonds

Icing #1
¾ cup unsalted butter
1 tablespoon cocoa
1 teaspoon vanilla
½ cup confectioners
  sugar

Icing #2
⅔ cup confectioners
  sugar
2 teaspoons water
4 tablespoons cocoa
1 cup roasted almonds

1. Beat the egg whites and sugar.
2. Mix in the ground Holland Rusks and ground almonds. Drop by teaspoon on well-greased cookie sheet.
3. Bake until brown.
4. Remove carefully, and cool on waxed paper.
5. Beat #1 icing ingredients until fluffy. Spread on underside of cookie. Chill.
6. Beat #2 icing ingredients. Spread on top of first icing.
7. Top with roasted almonds. Chill again.
8. Store in tightly closed container in the refrigerator, putting waxed paper between layers.

Temperature: 300°
Time: 20 to 30 minutes

Malinda B. Fisher

no-bake chocolate oatmeal cookies

Yield: 5 to 6 dozen

Children and Dads love them. A good recipe for the young cook.

½ cup butter
2 cups granulated sugar
3 tablespoons
  unsweetened cocoa
  powder
1 cup peeled and grated
  apple
pinch of salt
3 cups regular rolled oats
1 cup chopped pecans
1 teaspoon vanilla extract
½ cup coconut (optional)
confectioners sugar

1. Melt butter in a large saucepan. Add sugar, cocoa, apple, and salt. Combine thoroughly.
2. Bring mixture to a boil and boil 1 minute. Remove from heat.
3. Immediately add oats, nuts, vanilla, and optional coconut. Mix well.
4. Drop by teaspoons onto waxed paper.
5. When cool, roll in confectioners sugar.

Cynthia L. Bartlett

raisin nut drop cookies

Yield: 4½ dozen

Handed down from Grandmother with love.

1 cup raisins, packed
½ cup water
½ cup shortening
1 cup sugar
2 eggs, well-beaten
1 teaspoon vanilla
½ cup chopped nuts
2 cups plus 2 tablespoons
  flour
½ teaspoon baking soda
1 teaspoon baking powder
½ teaspoon salt
1 teaspoon cinnamon
½ teaspoon nutmeg

1. Boil raisins in water for 3 minutes. Let cool.
2. Mix together shortening, sugar, eggs, vanilla, and nuts. Add the cooled raisin-water mixture.
3. Sift together flour, baking soda, baking powder, salt, cinnamon, and nutmeg. Add to raisin mixture. Combine well.
4. Drop by rounded teaspoonfuls on greased cookie sheet. Bake.

Temperature: 375°
Time: 10 to 12 minutes

Ann E. Prince

 coconut corn nut cookies

Yield: 4 dozen

Delicious cookies with a little extra nutrition.

1 cup margarine
1 cup sugar
1 cup brown sugar
2 eggs, beaten
2 cups flour
1 teaspoon baking soda
½ teaspoon baking
  powder
½ teaspoon salt
2 cups corn flakes
2 cups coconut or
  chopped nutmeats
1 teaspoon vanilla

1. Cream margarine and sugars.
2. Add eggs.
3. Stir in remaining ingredients, and spoon onto greased cookie sheet.
4. Bake.

Temperature: 375°
Time: 12 minutes

Elizabeth B. Edgerton

cowboy cookies

Yield: 6 dozen

A lunchtime favorite from the Fairport Central Schools.

1½ cups butter
1⅔ cups sugar
1 cup plus 2 tablespoons
  brown sugar
3 eggs
2 teaspoons vanilla
2¾ cups unsifted flour
¾ teaspoon baking
  powder
1½ teaspoons baking
  soda
½ teaspoon salt
3 cups rolled oats
6 ounces chocolate chips

1. Cream butter and sugars.
2. Add eggs and vanilla. Beat until light and fluffy.
3. Sift together flour, baking powder, soda, and salt. Blend into creamed mixture.
4. Add rolled oats and chocolate chips.
5. Drop by teaspoonsful onto greased cookie sheet.
6. Bake.

Temperature: 375°
Time: 10 to 12 minutes

The Fairport Central Schools

diamond cream squares

Yield: 8 servings

No one can ever stop at one.

Crust
5 tablespoons butter,
  softened
⅓ cup brown sugar
1 cup flour
¼ cup chopped nuts

Crust
1. Cream butter and brown sugar.
2. Add flour and nuts to creamed mixture, and mix well. Set aside one cup of crust mixture to use as topping.
3. Press remaining crust in bottom of 8 x 8-inch pan. Bake for 12 to 15 minutes at 350°.

Filling
½ cup sugar
1 8-ounce package cream
  cheese, softened
1 egg
2 tablespoons milk
1 tablespoon lemon juice
½ teaspoon vanilla

Filling
1. Cream sugar and cheese.
2. Add egg, milk, lemon juice, and vanilla. Mix well.
3. Pour into baked crust and sprinkle with reserved topping. Bake another 25 minutes.
4. When cool, refrigerate. Cut into diamond shapes after completely chilled.

Temperature: 350°
Time: 37 to 40 minutes

Lynne G. Bishop

little chocolate cake cookies

Yield: 6 to 7 dozen

This soft cookie is a children's favorite.

Cookies
½ cup butter or
    margarine
1½ cups brown sugar
2 eggs
2 teaspoons vanilla
4 1-ounce squares
    unsweetened chocolate,
    melted
1½ cups sour cream
3 cups sifted flour
¼ teaspoon salt
1½ teaspoons baking
    soda

Cookies
1. Cream butter and sugar.
2. Add eggs and vanilla.
3. Stir in chocolate, then sour
   cream.
4. Add the dry ingredients, and
   mix thoroughly.
5. Drop by the rounded tablespoon
   on a lightly greased cookie
   sheet.
6. Bake until they spring back
   when touched lightly in center.
7. Remove to rack. Frost when
   cool.

Frosting
6 tablespoons butter
1 pound confectioners
    sugar
2 teaspoons vanilla
milk

Frosting
1. Cream butter, sugar, and vanilla.
2. Add just enough milk for
   spreading consistency.
3. Frost the cooled cookies.

Temperature: 375°
Time: 7 to 9 minutes

**Hint: Use these to provide chocolate cake crumbs for Cinnamon
Star cookies (see index).**

Susan P. Larson

peanut butter cup cookies

Yield: 3 to 4 dozen

A guaranteed success!

1 cup butter, softened
1⅔ cups graham
    cracker crumbs
1 cup peanut butter
1 pound confectioners
    sugar
1 6-ounce package
    semi-sweet chocolate
    bits

1. Mix butter, graham crackers,
   peanut butter, and sugar by
   hand.
2. Press mixture into a greased 9
   x 13-inch pan. Refrigerate at
   least one hour, preferably two
   hours.
3. Melt chocolate bits.
4. Frost peanut butter mixture
   with melted chocolate.
5. Immediately cut into small
   squares with a chopping (heavy)
   knife. They are very rich!

Linnea O. Donahower

scottish shortbread

Yield: 3 to 4 dozen

Cut pieces small; these are very rich.

1 pound butter (no
  substitutes)
1 cup sugar
5 cups sifted flour

1. Soften butter at room
   temperature for several hours.
   Add sugar and beat until light
   and fluffy.
2. Add flour. Blend with a pastry
   cutter until thoroughly mixed.
   Mixing with a spoon or electric
   mixer will make shortbread
   tough.
3. Press mixture into 2 greased,
   8-inch square pans. Prick the
   tops with tines of a fork.
4. Bake until golden and firm to
   the touch.
5. To avoid cracking, cut into
   squares while still warm. Allow
   to cool before removing from
   pans.

Temperature: 350°
Time: 35 to 40 minutes

Pat M. Gilges

mincemeat bars

Yield: 18 bars

Excellent during the holidays.

1½ cups brown sugar
½ cup butter
3 eggs
1 teaspoon baking soda
1 cup hot water
2 cups flour
1 teaspoon nutmeg
1 cup chopped pecans or
  walnuts
1 cup raisins
1 9-ounce package
  mincemeat
powdered sugar
confectioners sugar

1. Cream sugar and butter in a
   bowl or food processor.
2. Add eggs and mix thoroughly.
3. Dissolve baking soda in water
   and stir into mixture.
4. Mix together flour, nutmeg, nuts,
   raisins, and mincemeat. Add to
   other ingredients.
5. Pour batter into two 8-inch
   square pans. Bake.
6. Cool slightly, and dust with
   powdered sugar. When
   completely cool, cut into
   squares.

Temperature: 350°
Time: 30 minutes

**Hint: Bars may be topped with whipped cream, hard sauce, or
vanilla ice cream.**

Susan K. Lepkowski

paul's pumpkin bars

Yield: 2 dozen

Very moist; our best autumn goodie!

4 eggs
1⅔ cups sugar
1 cup cooking oil
1 16-ounce can pumpkin
2 cups flour
2 teaspoons baking
  powder
2 teaspoons cinnamon
1 teaspoon salt
1 teaspoon baking soda

Frosting
1 3-ounce package
  softened cream cheese
½ cup margarine,
  softened
1 teaspoon vanilla
2 cups sifted
  confectioners sugar

1. Beat eggs, sugar, oil, and pumpkin in bowl until light and fluffy.
2. Combine flour, baking powder, cinnamon, salt, and soda. Add to pumpkin mixture, and mix thoroughly.
3. Spread batter in an ungreased 15 x 10 x 1-inch jelly roll pan.
4. Bake, cool, and frost.

Frosting
1. Cream cheese and margarine.
2. Stir in vanilla.
3. Slowly add sugar, beating until mixture is smooth.
4. Frost cooled bars.

Temperature: 350°
Time: 25 to 30 minutes

Cecy R. Szuba

molasses crinkles

Yield: 5 dozen

Just like Grandmother's.

¾ cup shortening
1 cup brown sugar
1 egg
¼ cup molasses
2¼ cups flour
2 teaspoons baking soda
½ teaspoon salt
½ teaspoon ground cloves
1 teaspoon cinnamon
1 teaspoon ginger
granulated sugar

1. Cream shortening and sugar.
2. Add egg and molasses. Beat well.
3. Add dry ingredients. Mix until well blended.
4. Shape dough into 1-inch balls. Roll each in granulated sugar.
5. Place on lightly greased cookie sheet. Sprinkle with a few drops of water: just wet your hand and shake it over the cookies.
6. Bake.

Temperature: 375°
Time: 10 to 12 minutes

Margo C. Shaw

crispy date bars

Yield: 2 dozen bars

Perfect for a "coffee-and" party.

Crust
½ cup whole wheat flour
½ cup flour
½ cup brown sugar
½ cup butter, softened

Crust
1. Combine both flours, brown sugar, and butter. Mix well until crumbly. Press into ungreased 9 x 9-inch pan. Bake 10 to 12 minutes or until golden brown. Cool.

Filling
1 cup chopped dates
½ cup sugar
½ cup butter
1 egg, well-beaten
2 cups crispy rice cereal
¾ cup chopped nuts
1 teaspoon vanilla

Filling
1. In medium saucepan, combine dates, sugar, and butter. Cook over medium heat until mixture boils, stirring constantly. Simmer 3 minutes.
2. Blend ¼ cup of hot mixture into the egg, then return egg mixture to the saucepan. Cook until mixture bubbles, stirring constantly.
3. Remove from heat. Stir in cereal, nuts, and vanilla. Spread over baked crust, and cool completely.

Frosting
2 cups confectioners sugar
2 to 3 teaspoons milk, if desired
½ teaspoon vanilla
3-ounce package cream cheese, softened

Frosting
1. Combined confectioners sugar, milk, vanilla, and cream cheese in small mixer bowl. Beat at low speed until smooth.
2. Spread over cooled filling. Cut into bars.

Temperature: 375°
Time: 10 to 12 minutes

Hint: Refrigerate leftovers.

Emily M. Henderson

crispy rice bars

Yield: 24 bars

An all-time favorite for kids and kids at heart.

1 cup light corn syrup
1 cup sugar
1 cup peanut butter
6 cups crisp rice cereal

1. Melt corn syrup and sugar together in saucepan, over low heat, until bubbling. Remove from heat.

1 6-ounce package
    butterscotch chips
1 6-ounce package
    chocolate chips

2. Add peanut butter and rice
    cereal.
3. Spread into a greased 9 x
    13-inch pan.
4. Melt both packages of chips
    together in a pan over low heat.
    Spread this butterscotch-
    chocolate mixture on top of the
    first mixture.
5. When icing cools, cut into bars.

Carol Parker

mint frosted brownies
Yield: 16 brownies

Entrancing as a love potion!

2 squares unsweetened
    chocolate
½ cup butter or
    margarine
2 eggs
1 cup sugar
½ cup flour
½ cup chopped nuts

1. Melt chocolate and butter
    together in double boiler.
    Remove from heat. Cool slightly.
2. Add eggs, one at a time, beating
    well after each addition.
3. Add sugar, mix well.
4. Add flour, mix well.
5. Add nuts.
6. Spread into a greased 9-inch
    square pan. Bake, *no longer*
    than 25 minutes. Brownies will
    be fudge-like. Cool.

White Frosting

1½ cups confectioners
    sugar
3 tablespoons butter
2 tablespoons heavy
    cream or milk
⅛ teaspoon salt
¾ teaspoon mint extract

White Frosting

1. Combine sugar, butter, cream,
    salt, and extract, in mixer bowl.
    Beat until smooth.
2. Spread over brownie layer.
    Cover. Chill 1 hour.

Chocolate Glaze

4 ounces sweet or
    semi-sweet chocolate or
    ¾ cup chocolate chips
2 tablespoons butter
1 teaspoon vanilla

Chocolate Glaze

1. Melt chocolate and butter over
    low heat. When melted, add
    vanilla. Drizzle over mint
    frosting.
2. Chill until firm, about 1 hour.

Temperature: 350°
Time: 25 minutes

Hint: Best served cool rather than room temperature.

Nicole R. Doolittle

til mc cutcheon's ginger cookies

Yield: 5 dozen

My mother's aunt Til had a bake shop in Valois, New York in the mid 1800's. This is the ginger cookie recipe from her shop.

8 cups sifted flour
3 teaspoons ginger
1 heaping teaspoon cinnamon
1 teaspoon salt
1 cup sugar
2 cups molasses
1 cup shortening
3 teaspoons baking soda
⅔ cup hot water
1 egg

1. Combine flour, ginger, cinnamon, and salt. Make a well in center.
2. Stir in sugar and molasses.
3. Add shortening. Pour in hot water that has been combined with soda, and mix.
4. Add egg. Stir until completely blended. Dough will be soft and sticky.
5. Chill thoroughly.
6. Roll out on floured pastry cloth or board until ¼-inch thick. Cut with large round cookie cutter.
7. Sprinkle with sugar. For an added touch, place a dab of jam in center of each cookie. Bake on greased cookie sheet.

Temperature: 400°
Time: 10 minutes

Hint: These keep a long time in airtight containers.

Bernice Bridges

Over 150 years ago, Til McCutcheon created wonderful ginger cookies. They became her little shop's calling card and, through the years, her claim to cookie fame. We served them at a huge tasting luncheon where a local food editor loved them so much she brought a bunch back to the newsroom for her colleagues to share. They all agreed that you haven't really eaten a ginger cookie until you've had Til's!

cat tongues

Yield: 3 dozen

This is a wafer thin, buttery cookie. Very elegant!

½ cup butter
⅔ cup superfine sugar
¼ cup egg whites (about 2)
1 teaspoon vanilla
1 cup cake flour
cookie press: The cookie press is only used to dispense cookies in correct amount. Cookies will not maintain a star shape, but will be very thin and oval shaped.

1. Cream butter.
2. Beat in sugar, egg whites, and vanilla.
3. Add flour.
4. Place dough in cookie press. The dough will be very soft. With "star" end on cookie press, make a strip about 3 inches long on well greased cookie sheet. Leave plenty of space between cookies to allow them to spread very thin.
5. Bake. Watch closely. They are done as soon as they are just lightly browned at the edge.
6. Remove promptly to cooling rack.

Temperature: 350°
Time: 7 to 9 minutes

Priscilla L. Minster

cinnamon crisps

Yield: 6 to 7 dozen

A great 'side-kick' for homemade ice cream or sherbet.

2 cups flour
dash of salt
2½ teaspoons cinnamon
1 cup butter
1 cup sugar
1 egg, separated
⅓ cup finely chopped or ground pecans, optional

1. Sift flour, salt, and cinnamon together. Set aside.
2. Cream butter and sugar. Beat in egg yolk.
3. Gradually add the sifted dry ingredients. The dough will be quite stiff. Add optional pecans.
4. Form into small balls and flatten gently with hand. Criss-cross with a fork and brush with egg white.
5. Bake on an ungreased cookie sheet.

Temperature: 350°
Time: 6 to 8 minutes

Susan P. Larson

old fashioned sugar cookies

Yield: 3 dozen

Powdered sugar makes this dough no-stick!

1 cup butter, softened
1 cup confectioners sugar
2 teaspoons vanilla
dash of salt
2¼ cups flour

1. Cream butter, sugar, and vanilla.
2. Add flour and salt.
3. Chill dough, covered, for only 1 hour.
4. Roll out to ⅛-inch thickness; cut out into any shape. Bake on lightly greased cookie sheet. Frost, if desired, when cooled.

Temperature: 400°
Time: 8 to 10 minutes

Elizabeth T. Williams

toos's spice cookies

Yield: 3 to 4 dozen

My mom's Dutch friend made these for us each Christmas.

1 cup butter
½ cup sugar
3 teaspoons cinnamon
¼ heaping teaspoon cloves
sprinkle of mace and pepper
1 cup all-purpose flour
1 cup quick-mixing flour (if not available, use regular flour)
1 cup slivered almonds

1. Cream butter and sugar.
2. Add spices.
3. Add flours and almonds. Mix well. May knead with hands.
4. Make small balls about 1½-inches round. Place on ungreased cookie sheet.
5. Press down on each cookie with a glass dipped in sugar.
6. Bake. These should *not* brown.

Temperature: 350°
Time: 8 to 10 minutes

Priscilla L. Minster

unbeatable brownies

Yield: 3 dozen

You'll never use a mix again.

4 eggs
2 cups sugar
½ cup butter, melted
4 1-ounce squares unsweetened chocolate, melted

1. Beat together eggs, sugar, butter, and chocolate.
2. Add vanilla, flour, baking powder, and salt, mixing after each addition.
3. Stir in nuts, if desired.

312

unbeatable brownies *continued*

1 teaspoon vanilla
1 cup flour
½ teaspoon baking
   powder
½ teaspoon salt
1 cup chopped walnuts
   (optional)

4. Pour into a greased and floured 9 x 13-inch pan. Bake.
5. Let cool for 45 minutes before cutting.

Temperature: 350°
Time: 25 minutes

Pamela B. Mele

cinnamon stars

Yield: 3 dozen

Chewy texture, almond flavor. Sold by the dozens each Christmas.

1 pound almond paste
1 cup sugar
½ tablespoon cinnamon
1½ tablespoons cocoa
   powder
2½ to 3 cups chocolate
   cake crumbs
pinch of salt
pinch of ammonia
   powder*
1 whole egg
1 egg white

*ammonium carbonate, or
hartshorn, is available at drug
stores Baking soda can be
substituted but is not as good

1. Mix the almond paste, sugar, cinnamon, and cocoa powder.
2. Add chocolate crumbs, salt, ammonia powder, whole egg, and egg white.
3. Rest dough in refrigerator overnight.
4. Roll out dough ¼-inch thick on a floured board. Cut out stars. Place on greased cookie sheet and sprinkle with sugar.
5. Bake. Be careful not to overbake, otherwise they will become hard.

Temperature: 350 degrees
Time: 15 to 20 minutes

Hint: Can use Little Chocolate Cake cookies (see index) for the cake crumbs.

Sibley's Bakery Department

The most wonderful fat, chewy cookie in Rochester was baked every Christmas at Sibley's department store. Just before their bakery turned off its ovens for the last time we called them and they gave us their secret recipe. Cinnamon Star Cookies are so wickedly delicious that you will savor every mouthful. And once you taste them you won't regret for a moment the time it took to make them.

313

plantation cookies
Yield: 3 dozen small cookies

Light and tasty—possibly addictive!

1 egg
1 cup superfine sugar
½ teaspoon vanilla
4 tablespoons flour
¼ pound nutmeats, finely chopped (about 1 cup)

1. Beat egg thoroughly.
2. Add remaining ingredients in order given.
3. Drop by small teaspoons onto a buttered baking sheet.
4. Bake. Remove from sheet with a buttered spatula.

Temperature: 350°
Time: About 14 minutes

Hint: Do not be tempted to add any liquid or use any more flour.

Marie M. Hanson

pecan cookies
Yield: 2 dozen cookies

These resemble little snowballs.

½ cup butter, softened
2 tablespoons sugar
1 cup ground pecans
1 cup flour
1 teaspoon vanilla
1 cup confectioners sugar

1. Cream butter and sugar.
2. Add pecans, flour, and vanilla.
3. Cover, and refrigerate dough for ½ to 1 hour.
4. When chilled, roll small pieces of dough in hands to form little balls.
5. Bake on an ungreased cookie sheet until lightly browned on bottom.
6. While cookies are still hot from the oven, roll each in confectioners sugar. Let cool on racks.

Temperature: 325°
Time: 15 minutes

Ann B. Irwin

people seed

A no-cook, easy snack that is very habit-forming.

raisins
chocolate chips
popped popcorn
peanuts
Chinese noodles
sunflower seeds
chopped dates
small pretzels

1. Combine equal amounts of any of the listed ingredients to suit your taste.
2. Store in covered container.

Carolyn H. Saum

frosted pecans

Yield: 1 pound

If you love pecans and nibbling, this is for you!

½ cup butter
2 egg whites at room
  temperature
1 cup light brown sugar
1 pound large pecans

1. Melt butter in 9 x 13-inch pan in oven. Set aside.
2. Beat egg whites until very stiff. Gradually add sugar until mixture is thick and smooth. Take time doing this so the meringue has body.
3. Fold in pecans until they are thoroughly coated.
4. Drop mixture by spoonfuls into the pan with the melted butter.
5. Bake. Every ten minutes gently turn and separate the nuts using a small spatula so they are brown and evenly covered with butter.
6. Cool in the pan.

Temperature: 300°
Time: 1 hour

Sally Foster

glazed almonds

Yield: 2 cups

This would make a great hostess or holiday gift!

2 cups whole blanched
  almonds
1 cup sugar
¼ cup butter
½ teaspoon vanilla
salt

1. Heat almonds, sugar, and butter in a heavy skillet over medium heat, stirring constantly, until almonds are toasted and sugar is golden brown, about 15 minutes. The sugar should be syrupy.
2. Remove from heat. Stir in the vanilla.
3. Spread the mixture on foil or an ungreased cookie sheet. Sprinkle with salt and allow to harden.
4. When nuts are cool, break into clusters.

Arlene A. Wright

caramel popcorn

Yield: 6 quarts

My kids and my friends keep asking me to make it again and again.

1 cup butter
2 cups brown sugar
½ cup light corn syrup
1 teaspoon salt
½ teaspoon baking soda
1 teaspoon vanilla
6 quarts popped corn
peanuts, optional

1. Melt butter in saucepan.
2. Add sugar, corn syrup, and salt. Stir continuously until mixture comes to a boil. Let mixture boil *without* stirring for 5 minutes.
3. Remove from heat. Stir in baking soda and vanilla.
4. Slowly pour caramel over popped corn and optional peanuts. Mix well.
5. Spread on 2 large baking pans. Bake, stirring every 15 minutes.
6. Remove from oven and break apart. Store in covered container.

Temperature: 250°
Time: 1 hour

Linnea O. Donahower

butter toffee

Yield: 2 dozen pieces

Wonderfully toothsome!

1 cup sugar
½ teaspoon salt
¼ cup water
½ cup butter
candy thermometer
1 12-ounce package semi-sweet chocolate morsels
1½ cups chopped pecans

1. Mix sugar, salt, water, and butter in a medium-sized saucepan. Cook without stirring to the light-crack stage (285°).
2. Spread the toffee out on a well-greased cookie sheet. Cool.
3. Melt the chocolate in a double boiler. Spread half of the chocolate on top of the toffee, and sprinkle immediately with ¾ cup of the pecans. Cool, but *do not refrigerate*.
4. Turn the toffee over. Lift a corner carefully with a spatula; the entire piece will come off of the cookie sheet. Spread with the remaining chocolate. Sprinkle with the nuts.
5. Refrigerate until firm. Break into pieces.

Susan B. Finnegan

chocolate cream caramels

Yield: 4 dozen large pieces

A chocolate-lover's dream since 1919.

1 cup sugar
1 cup light corn syrup
2 1-ounce squares bitter
  chocolate, cut into
  small pieces
1 pint heavy cream
¼ teaspoon cream of
  tartar
⅛ teaspoon salt
1 teaspoon butter
2 tablespoons vanilla

1. In a large saucepan mix sugar, corn syrup, chocolate pieces, ½ pint of the cream, cream of tartar, salt, and butter.
2. Bring to a boil and boil for 10 minutes, stirring almost constantly.
3. Gradually add the remainder of the cream.
4. Cook until it forms a rather firm ball or until a candy thermometer reads 246°.
5. Remove from heat. Add vanilla.
6. Pour into an 8-inch square greased glass baking dish.
7. When cool, cut into squares. Wrap pieces in waxed paper. Caramels will be soft.

Jane R. Hanford

country caramels

Yield: 120 pieces

Yummy! Keep them around for an energy pick-up.

1½ pounds sugar
1 16-ounce bottle plus 2
  tablespoons light corn
  syrup
¼ teaspoon salt
1½ pints heavy cream
1 cup evaporated milk
6 tablespoons butter
1 teaspoon vanilla
chopped nuts (optional)
4 1-ounce squares
  chocolate, melted
  (optional)

1. Cook sugar, corn syrup, and salt in a 6-quart pan until candy thermometer reads 230°.
2. While boiling, slowly add cream and evaporated milk, stirring constantly until thermometer reads 240°.
3. Add butter, vanilla, and nuts.
4. (Optional: For chocolate caramels, add melted chocolate.)
5. Pour in a buttered 9 x 13-inch pan.
6. Cool. Cut into 1-inch squares. Wrap pieces in waxed paper.

Elizabeth T. Williams

🍎 chocolate fudge

Yield: 9-inch pan

Go ahead, try it! Your pleasure awaits.

2 cups sugar
⅔ cup evaporated milk
12 marshmallows
½ cup butter
dash of salt
6 ounces semi-sweet
  chocolate morsels
1 teaspoon vanilla
1 cup walnuts, chopped
  (optional)

1. Mix sugar, milk, marshmallows, butter, and salt in heavy saucepan.
2. Cook, stirring constantly, over medium heat until mixture comes to a boil. Boil 5 minutes, stirring constantly. Mixture will bubble on top.
3. Remove from heat. Stir in chocolate, vanilla, and walnuts.
4. Spread in a buttered 9-inch square pan.
5. Cool. Cut into desired size squares.

Sally B. Foster

canine cookies (for dogs)

Yield: 6 dozen

Dogs are delighted to receive these delicacies for good behavior.

3½ cups flour
2 cups whole wheat flour
1 cup rye flour
2 cups unprocessed
  wheat
1 cup corn meal
½ cup instant non-fat dry
  milk
3 tablespoons salt
1 envelope active dry
  yeast
1 teaspoon dry beef
  bouillon
¼ cup hot water
2 eggs, beaten with
2 tablespoons milk
few drops red food
  coloring
3½ cups chicken broth

1. In a large bowl, combine first 7 ingredients.
2. In a separate bowl mix yeast, bouillon, and hot water until yeast and bouillon dissolve. Add egg mixture and food coloring. Mix well.
3. Add 2 cups of the broth and yeast mixture to flour mixture.
4. Mix with hands until dough is quite stiff. If dough is too firm, add more broth.
5. On a well-floured surface, roll out dough to ⅓-inch thickness. Cut into shapes of bones, fire hydrants, slippers, or doughnut holes.
6. Place on greased cookie sheets. Bake until brown at edges.
7. Turn oven off and leave cookies in oven overnight.

Must do ahead.

Temperature: 300°
Time: 40 minutes

Kaci M. Peer

318

Apples and Cheese

For a different dessert or impromptu snack, serve apples with your favorite cheese. The tart crispness of the apple offsets the smooth, mellow quality of the cheese. Simply serve the apple whole with a knife nearby or cut it into slices, "matchsticks," or use a slicer-corer. Some cheese and apple combinations we like are below but go ahead and match up whatever duo delights you.

Apples	*Cheese*
Cortland	Danis Crema
Golden Delicious	Camembert
Jonathan	Gruyere
McIntosh	Brie
Northern Spy	Bel Paese
Red Delicious	Blue
Stayman	Roquefort

applehood

Apple Hints

1. A cake will stay fresh several days longer if an apple, cut in half, is stored with the cake.
2. One pound of apples (3 medium) yields 3 cups pared and sliced or diced.
3. Apples will not crack while they are baking if you peel a 1-inch band around the middle or top.
4. Glaze cooked fruits with contrasting fruit jellies, especially apple or quince.
5. Lemon juice is good to prevent discoloration of apples, pears, avocados, bananas, and mushrooms.
6. To ripen fruit, put it in a paper bag in a dark place for a few days.
7. For a different type of frozen treat, make a "cider cicle." Simply put a wooden stick in a small paper cup filled with cider, and freeze!
8. Add apple juice to your favorite stuffing, instead of the usual broth, for a delicious change—great for stuffing pork, turkey, or chicken.
9. Apple juice added to a ham or meat loaf will make a delicious difference and makes it more juicy.
10. Stir apple juice into a spicy red dip for shrimp—it will mellow its taste and make it richer.
11. Sprinkle crumbled English toffee or maple sugar over canned applesauce and garnish with a rosette of whipped cream.
12. Instead of baking apple turnovers, fry them in deep hot fat (375°) until a delicate brown. Drain. Sprinkle with powdered sugar, and serve hot or cold.
13. Old-fashioned bread pudding can be spruced up by adding apple slices and raisins, and topped with brown sugar. After baking, serve with lemon sauce or whipped cream to which crushed peanut brittle has been added. Delicious!
14. Try apple pancakes for a change. Simply mix apple slices into the batter, or top the stack of pancakes with a generous serving of warmed, drained apple slices with a little brown sugar and butter.
15. Melt apple jelly in a double boiler over hot water; mix butter or margarine with it; keep mixture slightly warm. Spoon over pancakes. Or mix half honey and half melted apple jelly with butter or margarine.
16. Mix apple juice half and half with orange juice, tomato juice or beef broth for new exciting flavor combinations.

American apples have become an institution as respected and delicious as motherhood and apple pie. They were introduced to this country by Governor John Endicott of Massachusetts nine years after the landing of the May-flower. Fifty years later when milk was scarce New England mothers were very grateful to John E. when they were able to feed diluted apple cider to their babies.

Apple nurseries were first established in the East in the 1730's. The early plantings of seedling and grafted trees on Long Island and in Rochester, New York were rapidly disseminated across the country. John Chapman started apple nurseries in Ohio and Indiana and singlehandedly distributed the seeds to pioneers moving westward. He became the real life legend, Johnny Appleseed.

Apple Brandy, a tempting concoction, was made in the late 1700's- and could be used to pay one's land taxes. Would that it were so today! Over a century later a popular social event known as the "Apple Bee" evolved. Iowa pioneers would gather around the kitchen hearth swapping stories as the apples were pared, cored, strung, and hung on a long pole in preparation for drying. The following spring ox teams and wagons were loaded with nursery stock and hauled to the Pacific Northwest. These early plantings became the basis for Washington State's apple crop.

Today, new strains of apples are created through cross-breeding at the N.Y. Agricultural Experiment Station in Geneva, New York. But *all* apples, regardless of their breeding, are healthy. They contain the A B C vitamins, average less than 100 calories apiece, are high in potassium, low in sodium and may very well be an effective deterrent to the common cold. In time, "an apple a day keeps the doctor away," may be scientifically proven. But for now, it's enough to know that something that tastes so good is good for you, too!

No matter where you live in this country you can obtain apples which are suitable for both cooking and eating out of hand. Some of the best recipes are created from mixing different varieties so don't be afraid to experiment as apples are truly a versatile fruit.

Apple Varieties

Apple	Origin	Best Use
Baldwin	Wilmington, Mass. (1740)	fresh, cooking
Cortland	New York (1915)	fresh, cooking
Duchess	Russia (before 1700)	cooking
Empire	New York (1966)	fresh
Golden Delicious	West Virginia (1914)	fresh, cooking
Gravenstein	Denmark (1669)	cooking
Grimes Golden	Brook County, W. Virginia (1804)	fresh, cooking
Idared	Idaho (1942)	fresh, cooking
Jonagold	New York (1968)	cooking
Jonathan	Woodstock, New York (1826)	fresh, cooking
McIntosh	Canada (1800)	fresh
Monroe	New York (1949)	fresh, cooking
Mutsu	Japan (1848)	fresh, cooking
Northern Spy	Western New York (1800)	cooking
Red Delicious	Iowa (1872)	fresh
Rhode Island Greening	Rhode Island (1700)	cooking
Rome Beauty	Ohio (1816)	cooking
Spigold	New York (1962)	cooking
Stayman Winesap	Leavenworth, Kansas (1866)	fresh
Twenty Ounce	New York (1844)	cooking
Wealthy	Excelsior, Minnesota (1860)	fresh, cooking
Winesap	New Jersey (1817)	fresh, cooking
Yellow Newtown	Long Island (before 1759)	cooking
Yellow Transparent	France (1869)	cooking
York Imperial	York, Pennsylvania (1830)	fresh, cooking

Apple Storing

Crisp, mouthwatering apples are excellent keepers which will maintain their fresh taste and firm texture for months if stored properly. Simply sort the fruit, selecting the ones with bruises, soft spots, or skin breaks for immediate use. Wash the remainder, pat dry, and store in a moisture-tight bag in the refrigerator or a cold, well ventilated place. Larger quantities may be stored in baskets in clean, cold (about 35°F.) well ventilated rooms in late fall or winter. Slightly moist air is needed to deter shriveling. Check the apples periodically, and remove any that have developed soft spots.

index

metric conversions

Weight Equivalents

1 ounce	=	30 grams	9 ounces =	250 grams
2 ounces =		55 grams	10 ounces =	285 grams
3 ounces =		85 grams	11 ounces =	310 grams
4 ounces =		115 grams	12 ounces =	340 grams
5 ounces =		140 grams	13 ounces =	370 grams
6 ounces =		170 grams	14 ounces =	400 grams
7 ounces =		200 grams	15 ounces =	425 grams
8 ounces =		225 grams	16 ounces =	450 grams

Granulated Sugar

1 teaspoon = 4 grams   ⅓ cup = 65 grams
1 tablespoon = 12 grams   ½ cup = 95 grams
         ¼ cup = 50 grams   1 cup = 190 grams

Flour (unsifted, leveled with knife)

1 tablespoon = 8.75 grams   1 cup = 140 grams
         ¼ cup = 35 grams   1½ cups = 210 grams
         ⅓ cup = 45 grams   2 cups = 280 grams
         ½ cup = 70 grams   3 cups = 420 grams

Volume Equivalents*

¼ teaspoon = 1.25 milliliters (ml)   ⅓ cup = 80 ml
½ teaspoon = 2.5 ml   ½ cup = 125 ml (1¼ dl)
1 teaspoon = 5 ml   1 cup = 250 ml = 2.5 dl = ¼ l
1 tablespoon = 15 ml   2 cups = 500 ml = ½ l
         ¼ cup = 60 ml   4 cups = 1 liter

*Abbreviations   l = liter
                dl = deciliter = 1/10 liter
                ml = milliliter = 1/1000 liter

equivalents

1 teaspoon = ⅓ tablespoon   2 cups = 1 pint
1 tablespoon = 3 teaspoons   4 cups = 1 quart
2 tablespoons = 1 fluid ounce   1 pint, liquid = 16 fluid ounces
4 tablespoons = ¼ cup   1 quart, liquid = 2 pints
5⅓ tablespoons = ⅓ cup   1 gallon, liquid = 4 quarts
8 tablespoons = ½ cup or 4 ounces   8 quarts, dry measure = 1 peck
16 tablespoons = 1 cup or 8 ounces   4 pecks, dry measure = 1 bushel
1 cup = ½ pint or 8 ounces

Fahrenheit to Centigrade: Subtract 32, muuply by 5, divide by 9.
Centigrade to Fahrenheit: Multiply by 9, divide by 5, add 32.

index

Notes

Notes

Notes

Applehood and Motherpie was inducted into the Walter S. McIlhenny Hall of Fame for Community Cookbooks in 1990. Additionally, it was nominated for the R.T. French Tastemaker Award and it has been featured in several national magazines.

Also Available…
   For Goodness Taste

For Goodness Taste is a unique collection of exciting recipes that reflect the rich flavor and cultural diversity of upstate New York life-styles, traditions, and geographic regions.

For Goodness Taste brings you more than 400 delicious recipes, with a tempting selection of ingredients ranging from garden fresh to processed fresh, accommodating today's contemporary trends and fast-paced schedules.

These wonderfully easy-to-prepare recipes are fresh and surprising, yet reliable and uncomplicated, following the tradition of this best-seller, **Applehood & Motherpie.**

JLR Publications
The Junior League of Rochester, Inc.
Rochester, New York